Laughing with God

Humor, Culture, and Transformation

Gerald A. Arbuckle, SM

Foreword by Jean Vanier

M
G

A Michael Glazier Book

LITURGICAL PRESS
Collegeville, Minnesota

www.litpress.org

A Michael Glazier Book published by Liturgical Press

Excerpts from documents of the Second Vatican Council are from *The Documents of Vatican II*, edited by Walter M. Abbott, SJ © 1966 (London: Geoffrey Chapman).

Scripture texts in this work are taken from the *New Revised Standard Version Bible* © 1989, Division of Christian Education of the National Council of the Churches of Christ in the United States of America. Used by permission. All rights reserved.

Cover design by David Manahan, OSB. Rembrandt etching: *Abraham Entertains the Three Angels*, 1656, Rijksprentenkabinet, Amsterdam.

1	2	3	4	5	6	7	8

Library of Congress Cataloging-in-Publication Data

Arbuckle, Gerald A.
    Laughing with God : humor, culture, and transformation / Gerald A.
  Arbuckle ; foreword by Jean Vanier.
       p.   cm.
    "A Michael Glazier book."
    Includes bibliographical references and index.
    ISBN 978-0-8146-5225-1
    1. Wit and humor—Religious aspects—Christianity.   I. Title.

BR115.H84A73 2008
261.5—dc22   2007044973

Dedicated to my mother and father and people of L'Arche—
examples of how to laugh with God.

By the same author

Strategies for Growth in Religious Life
(Alba House / St Pauls Publications, 1987)

Out of Chaos: Refounding Religious Congregations
(Paulist Press / Geoffrey Chapman, 1988) (Catholic Press Award)

Earthing the Gospel: An Inculturation Handbook for Pastoral Workers
(Geoffrey Chapman / Orbis Books / St Pauls Publications, 1990) (Catholic Press Award)

Grieving for Change: A Spirituality for Refounding Gospel Communities
(Geoffrey Chapman / St Pauls Publications, 1991)

Refounding the Church: Dissent for Leadership
(Geoffrey Chapman / Orbis Books / St Pauls Publications, 1993) (Catholic Press Award)

From Chaos to Mission: Refounding Religious Life Formation
(Geoffrey Chapman / Liturgical Press, 1996)

Healthcare Ministry: Refounding the Mission in Tumultuous Times
(Liturgical Press, 2000) (Catholic Press Award)

Dealing with Bullies: A Gospel Response to the Social Disease of Adult Bullying
(St Pauls Publications, 2003)

Confronting the Demon: A Gospel Response to Adult Bullying
(Liturgical Press, 2003)

Violence, Society and the Church: A Cultural Approach
(Liturgical Press, 2004)

Crafting Catholic Identity in Postmodern Australia
(Catholic Health Australia, 2007)

A 'Preferential Option for the Poor': Application to Catholic Health and Aged Care Ministries of Australia
(Catholic Health Australia, 2008)

Acknowledgments

My particular thanks to the community of Campion Hall, Oxford University, for providing me with a congenial research atmosphere to prepare this book; to Margaret Zucker for her patient and detailed reading and commenting on the text; to Kevin Waldie, SM, for assistance with scriptural references; and to Peter Dwyer, director of Liturgical Press, and Mary Stommes, editor at Liturgical Press, for their advice, encouragement, and willingness to publish the book.

Contents

Foreword

Isn't it fun! At last a book about humor and laughter. But let's be serious: laughter is important!

When we know we are right, or when we want to control situations, we can become stiff and taut. Our voices become aggressive. When we are with friends, we relax, smile, and laugh together. We have fun. Our hearts are open.

Maybe for some time now we've got things upside down, as if God was terribly serious and wanted to control us into doing good! But God is Love. God is Communion. When the Word became flesh and was born of Mary, they must have looked into each other's eyes and smiled. A moment of delicious communion, trust, openness, and love flowing from one to another. Maybe a few weeks later the baby Jesus giggled, and their smile turned into laughter as they played together. What a joy to be welcomed onto this earth by Mary and Joseph. There was also pain, of course, horrible pain, children killed by Herod's soldiers. But the love that brought Jesus, Mary, and Joseph together was joyful, ecstatic.

The Word became flesh so that all of us can live this communion that flows from the heart of the Trinity. We, in the communities of L'Arche and of Faith and Light, love to celebrate together, to have fun singing, dancing, and laughing. We are called to celebrate life together. Jesus, after choosing the first disciples, brought them to a wedding feast. What fun! A time of rejoicing and drinking. That, of course, was the problem: they ran out of wine. Thank God Mary realized the problem and Jesus did something about it. Jesus tells us that the Kingdom of God is like a wonderful wedding feast (Matt 22). And the Kingdom of God is already present on this earth, so let's celebrate.

Yes, we must work hard to put things right. But we have to remember that "right" is when we are living in unity and peace, celebrating life together, giving thanks for all creation and for all that Jesus is giving us: his immense love for us all. Let's stop fighting and learn to drink from the source of all life and give thanks. Let's become little and humble, little children born of love and for love and laughter. Thank you, Gerry, for this marvelous book.

Jean Vanier
L'Arche
60350 Trosly-Breuil
France

Introduction

[T]he holy book we call the Bible revels in a profound laughter, a divine and human laughter that is endemic to the whole narrative of creation, fall and salvation, and finally a laughter that results in a wondrous, all-encompassing comic vision. . . . The comic vision can embrace the tragic side of existence without eliminating or negating it.
    J. Cheryl Exum and J. William Whedbee[1]

For everything there is a season . . . a time to weep, and a time to laugh; a time to mourn, and a time to dance.
    Ecclesiastes 3:1, 4

That the Bible revels in laughter might come as a surprise to many. Yet in the divine humor of Scripture, God calls us to be personally and culturally transformed by the inexhaustible and energizing love that inspires it. Divine humor is found in our attempts as humans to judge the actions of God according to our expectations and then to discover that our conclusions are dramatically wrong.

We surely should expect to find humor in Scripture because this is one of the most effective ways to communicate and to convey profound truths in an appealing and respectful manner. In fact comic incongruities are abundant in Scripture. One fundamental truth in Scripture concerns God's relationship with each of us. We may expect God to be a distant person, demanding punishment for our waywardness. Yet God's vulnerable side is love, not condemnation. We are pursued by God's love in ways that from our human perspective are wildly illogical and nonsensical. God has an overwhelming and abiding love for each one of us, despite our frailties and sinfulness. Even though we "may forget" this love, says God our Parent, "yet I will not forget you. See, I have inscribed you on the palms of my hands" (Isa 49:15-16). Can anything be more incongruous, more humanly surprising, more worthy of celebration! God comes to us as a vulnerable baby born to a socially lowly mother, is accepted by only a few followers, and redeems the world by crucifixion—as a politically and religiously dangerous person—and subsequent resurrection. Rejecting worldly wisdom and signs, God chooses to save those who believe through the foolishness of the preaching of Jesus Christ (1 Cor 1:21). We call these incongruities expressions of divine humor.

Pope Benedict XVI structures his first encyclical, *Deus Caritas Est,* around the theme of this divine incongruity. He writes of God's "unpredictable and in some sense unprecedented activity." So great is God's forgiving love in the Old Testament that "it turns God against himself, his love against his justice." It turns the culturally normal upside down, for God refuses to act in ways we think God should (Isa 55:8). The most marginalized in society, those without economic and political power, are especially loved by God. In the New Testament divine humor takes on a "dramatic form when, in Jesus Christ, it is God himself who goes in search of the 'stray sheep,' a suffering and lost humanity." Mary proclaims that the Messiah would place the powerless at the heart of the Kingdom (Luke 1:48-53). What is thought to be humanly and culturally impossible becomes a reality. God in Jesus Christ becomes a "disabled God." In the mystery of the cross God's love is so forgiving that "he follows [humankind] even into death, and so reconciles justice and love."[2]

In addition to discovering the comic incongruities in Scripture, the second purpose of this book is to show that as evangelizers we must use humor as a teaching method but in ways that are adapted to, and transformative of, our cultures. The God of the Israelites and God's spokesmen, the prophets, frequently used humor in teaching, adapting themselves to the comic styles of the culture of the times. God repeatedly does humanly surprising and extraordinary things through impossible people. And, in order to prepare himself to be an accomplished teacher of the wonders of God, Jesus Christ spent years observing people and their cultures. He wanted to capture their imagination, to reach into their hearts, to change their lives. For this reason he told humorous stories, used comical expressions, and acted at times in quite amusing ways. Little wonder that people "were astounded at his teaching" (Luke 4:32).

Observers may rightly conclude that many of our homilies and our rituals of Christian worship are obliged to be gloomy or joyless. Liturgies should surely reflect the celebratory qualities of divine humor, but how infrequent this is. Again, although God is shown in the Scriptures to have the gift of humor, how rare it is to see this quality in contemporary works of Scripture scholars, theologians, writers on spirituality, and in the pronouncements of ecclesiastics. In fact over the centuries these groups have grudgingly tolerated, ignored, or condemned humor. [3] Saint John Chrysostom, bishop of Constantinople in the fifth century, held that the devil is the source of jests and jokes; in this vale of tears God expects us always to be serious.[4] Certainly any toleration of humor ceased at the Reformation, although there has been some marginal revival of interest in recent times. Yet Cardinal Walter Kasper correctly comments: "One of the main elements of Christian faith is . . . humour, and the lack of humour and irritability into which we in the contemporary Church and contemporary theology have so often slipped is perhaps one of the most serious objections which can be brought against present-day Christianity."[5]

Our reluctance to accept the importance of humor in the Scriptures can be due to our failure to read them correctly. Consider Mel Gibson's film, *The Passion of the Christ*.[6] It was an immense media success, but the film dismally failed to express the divine humor of the paschal mystery. It is a film of relentless physical suffering and violence, without the balancing emphasis on the liberating, nonviolent power of the resurrection. Because of this gloomy concentration on violence the film reinforces the incorrect view that joy is somehow foreign to our redemption. Liturgies must be joyless to conform to the sadness of the crucifixion. To be truly holy we must look sad. Yet at the heart of our redemption by Christ there is the resurrection. From a human perspective this is the mysteriously surprising expression of God's divine humor in which God is laughing at death: "Death has been swallowed up in victory" (1 Cor 15:54). The resurrection gives us hope that violence is not the way to freedom and healing. For ourselves there will be a time when "[d]eath will be no more; mourning and crying and pain will be no more, for the first things have passed away" (Rev 21:4).

But to say that humor is evident in Scripture and sorely needed in the church today is not to say that humor means just anything funny or hilarious. This is too simplistic. In fact, humor evades an easy description. I like Gerard Bessiere's comment: "Humour has never allowed itself to be confined within a definition. It has always treated itself with 'humour.'"[7] Although there is no scholarly consensus about how to define it, most would agree on one thing: a sense of humor is a reaction to something incongruous. Humor emerges from the contradiction or "double meanings" evoked by two differing definitions of the same reality. Woody Allen joked: "I am not afraid to die; I just don't want to be there when it happens." The first phrase states the predictable notion, but the second introduces the unpredictable meaning that is inconsistent with what we would expect. In the words of seventeenth-century philosopher Blaise Pascal, "Nothing produces laughter more than a surprising disproportion between that which one expects and that which one sees."[8] It is not necessary, however, that a person actually laughs or smiles at something funny. On the contrary, an inner feeling of joy, peace, and renewed energy may at times be a more important indicator of a sense of humor than is physical laughter.

Contemporary Relevance

> A cheerful heart is a good medicine, but a downcast spirit dries up the bones. (Prov 17:22)

A book on the importance of humor is always relevant. The fundamental function of humor is its ability to liberate us from the many inhibitions and restrictions in our daily lives that rob us of spontaneous and flexible behavior. Thus companies now encourage humor because it stimulates creativity in the workplace.[9] Laughter can also help to counteract physical pain and evoke pain-free sleep because the emotional and psychological act of laughing produces endorphins in the body, which causes the sense of well-being. Many cardiac units encourage professionally-led humor sessions for precisely this purpose.

More important, the gift of positive humor stops us from taking ourselves too seriously and forgetting our human finitude. As Soren Kierkegaard, a Lutheran theologian of humor, writes: "Comic perception frees me to transcend my tragic seriousness by beholding it as finite, hence not absolute."[10] Benedict XVI, in a lighter tone, says: "I think it's very important to be able to see the funny side of life and its joyful dimension and not to take everything too tragically. I'd say it's necessary for my ministry."[11] I fully endorse the pope's comment. I am so grateful to my mother and father for gently reminding me during my early years as a priest not to worry so much. "Don't forget, Gerald," my father would quietly say whenever I thought the salvation of the world depended on me, "God is in charge, not you!" I could not have survived the darker times of my ministry over the last four decades if my mother and father had not taught me the wisdom of humor.

This book is especially relevant in today's world of escalating fear and violence. The world at all levels—secular and religious—is threatened by the over-seriousness of fundamentalists. They may be economic rationalists who unquestioningly support neo-capitalism with its underlying belief in the dollar as the measure of all success. They may be Christians, Muslims, Hindus, or Israelis who believe they alone have the fullness of divine truth and that their task is to impose this on others in whatever way possible, including emotional and physical violence. If only fundamentalists could laugh at themselves, at their own rigidities and arrogance, the world would be a better place. Humor is the best cure for fundamentalism or any form of intolerance. It deflates pomposity and inflated egos. It is the beginning of humility. A society or religion that is at peace with itself will not only allow but foster a public humor that is self-critical.

Christians must remember, though, that a natural sense of humor is not enough to keep us balanced in this postmodern world. Many people suffer despair, confusion, and spiritual disintegration. Relationships can splinter quickly, friends and relatives die unexpectedly, devastating loneliness leaves us to drift, without a clear sense of how to move forward. In these chaotic situations we can identify with the "disabled God" of Gethsemane, be comforted as Jesus was by the Father. It is this mystery of divine humor that keeps us grounded in hope. When we find it difficult to forgive ourselves for our foolishness and others for the hurts they have caused us, we turn to God and discover God has forgiven us time and time again. That is divine foolishness. We can do the same. Then "the peace of God, which surpasses all understanding" (Phil 4:7) will enter the depths of our hearts, healing them of all pain.

Some readers may fear that too much inquiry into the nature and complexities of humor could destroy our ability to fully appreciate it. They might reason thus: "The moment humor is placed in the hands of scholars they will kill even this spontaneous and energy-evoking escape to normality. So, please, not another book on humor!" Fear not. This book will not destroy humor. In fact, it aims to foster the use of good humor as a way of discovering more of God's goodness. In this we will do nothing more than attempt to walk in the footsteps of Jesus who used humor so effectively for this purpose.

Structure of the Book

This book is written for readers who have no specialized knowledge of Scripture or cultural anthropology: college students, pastors, teachers, and caregivers of the sick. But it will also benefit theologians and Scripture scholars who have little or no acquaintance with cultural anthropology and its contribution to biblical studies. Cultural anthropology explores how people feel and communicate with one another within and across cultures. It is also a comic subversive discipline because it offers us surprisingly new ways of uncovering the rigidities of culture. Because of the confusion about the nature of humor, the first chapter ("Defining Humor, Its Expressions and Uses") concentrates on theory and builds a solid foundation on which to approach humor as a divine invitation into relationship with God and others; chapter 2 ("Humor in the Scriptures") gives examples of how humor is used in Scripture, particularly concentrating on expressions of divine humor and the ways in which Jesus uses humor as a method of teaching. This chapter is a rich resource for teachers and pastors.

Chapter 3 ("Joking and Life's Transitions") demonstrates that initiation rituals in which people move from one status and phase in life to another possess an inherent joking dynamic. This chapter provides theoretical foundations for the next two chapters, drawing particularly on contemporary anthropological research into initiation rituals. Chapter 4 ("Joking Transitions and Laughter of the Heart in the Old Testament") and chapter 5 ("Transformative Joking in the New Testament") describe through examples the joking pattern of many initiation rituals in the Scriptures. I have published in the past material on rituals of grieving in the Scriptures,[12] but I now view them from the perspective of the dynamic of joking in cultures. Since this is a unique approach readers will find in these chapters new and refreshing ways of presenting scriptural truths.

Chapter 6 ("Understanding Humor in Cultures") summarizes four culture models,[13] specifically, the types of humor that characterize these models and their potential to facilitate evangelization. Humor is a quality of all cultures. When we understand how and why people are humorous we can begin to grasp what may deeply concern them. Chapter 7 ("The Churches and Humor: Reflections") is a historical summary of the attitudes of Christians toward the use of humor in spirituality and theology. Chapter 8 ("Laughing with God: Transformation through Humor") concentrates on some insights of humor in contemporary culture and how evangelizers are able to enrich these insights with the power of the Gospel.

Genesis of the Book

I have wanted to write this book for over fifty years. It all started when my good philosophy professor declared that Jesus could never have laughed because as God he knew everything, so nothing would have been incongruous to him. I did not believe, and still do not, that Jesus, the human face of God, never laughed or smiled. Without the gift of humor he would have been unable to relate to people.

Then several years after this happened I was present as a young man lay dying of cancer. He taught me a profound lesson that I have longed to share with others. A brilliant academic and athletic future had been open to him, but no more. His coming death made no sense. Why was God allowing this to happen? The young man wordlessly answered the question for me. In the midst of his suffering, though often unable to speak, his face would radiate an inner peace and joy. I kept asking myself—could this be laughter? Yes, a profound laughter, not physical, but of the heart. This man had developed a humorous attitude to the things the world thought important. He had come to see things as God does, inwardly rejoicing in the knowledge that God in Christ loved him beyond all human understanding. He had come to laugh with God at the things he had mistakenly once thought so important in his life.

Much later, people in L'Arche have helped me to understand how human comedy finds its roots in divine humor and the importance of celebration as a way of relaxation and teaching Christ's message. L'Arche is a movement founded by Jean Vanier for people with learning disabilities (called core members). In mid-2005, while attending a large international gathering of delegates, including representative core members, I was puzzled by the fact that at any moment, even in sessions dealing with serious issues, participants would break into joyful song, with playful clapping, balloons, and dancing. During my keynote address, at what I thought was a particularly solemn moment in my analysis, one core member stood up in the midst of the auditorium and smilingly waved his arms around. It was time to sing. We did. People stood up and musicians led us in song. At first I was unnerved by this intervention. My brilliant insights were being ignored! Then, to my astonishment, I found myself clapping in time with the music and doing a mini-jig on the stage. It was a wonderful, joyful, relaxing experience, something I would never have initiated myself as an academic. When I finally returned to the podium I was able to interact with participants in a far more positive way than before. My over-seriousness and rigid commitment to the formal rules of lecturing had blocked my contact with the audience, my creativity, and the learning of participants.

Celebration in L'Arche is an integral quality of its culture. Why is this so? The answer, which is simple yet profound, lies at the heart of this book. When core members of L'Arche celebrate for what seems trivial reasons, they are saying to themselves and to the world: "Join us in living Christ's especial love of those the world thinks unimportant, even useless, for we are your teachers, reminding you who appear strong that you are also in your hearts vulnerable and disabled, ever needing God's healing love." Their celebration is a sacrament in which Christ's divine humor breaks repeatedly into our world of human predictability and feeling of superiority. I hope the example of L'Arche members may help readers as it has helped me.

Chapter 1

Defining Humor, Its Expressions and Uses

The office of drama is to exercise . . . human emotions. The purpose of comedy is to tickle those emotions into an expression of light relief; of tragedy, to wound them and bring the relief of tears.
   Laurence Olivier[1]

If humor without faith is in danger of dissolving into cynicism and despair, faith without humor is in danger of turning into arrogance and intolerance.
   Conrad Hyers[2]

This chapter explains:

- the meaning of humor and the pattern in joking;
- some expressions of humor with secular and biblical illustrations;
- some personal and social uses of humor.

   In this introductory chapter we try to define humor and some of its expressions and uses. These theoretical considerations are necessary in order to appreciate how humor in the Scriptures is presented in subsequent chapters. But we immediately strike a problem because understanding the dynamics of humor, even of a simple joke, is a particularly complex task. And the challenge is made more difficult because there are no universally accepted definitions or views on the topic.[3] W. C. Fields

1

(1880–1946), the great American comedian, succinctly summarizes the problem: "The funniest thing about comedy is that you never know why people laugh. I know *what* makes them laugh, but trying to get your hands on *why* is like trying to pick an eel out of a tub of water."[4] People can identify when others have a good or weak sense of humor, but they find it difficult to come up with a precise definition. When the comedic movie actor Stan Laurel (1890–1965) was asked on his deathbed for the definition of comedy, he said he had no idea. All he knew was what made him laugh.[5]

Despite these rather discouraging warnings we offer a working definition of humor, followed by explanatory notes. Later, some expressions and uses of humor are presented, but because there is no common agreement on its nature, we must expect different views on these issues.

Meaning of Humor

- Humor or "the comic" is a form of culturally-based drama that helps us to cope with the vicissitudes of life. The situation or event can be something formally staged such as a play, a structured joke, or something that happens spontaneously or unrehearsed.

- A sense of humor is the aptitude within us that sets up the dynamic process of contemplating the incongruities of life. This process may be expressed in actions, speech, literature, or other art forms, resulting in surprisingly new resolutions of these incongruities. Humor is positive when it respects the dignity of people; it is negative, or unkindly, when it degrades or mocks people.

- Positive humor may evoke two types of laughter by way of response: formal or audible laughter, although this is never an infallible sign of a sense of humor; and "laughter of the heart," which is an interior peace or joy. This book focuses primarily on the latter.

Form of Culturally-based Drama

The word "drama" is used for many types of entertainment: tragedy, comedy, suspense, and mystery. Drama creates a series of events that involve a powerful conflict of forces. Through conflict and its resolution people who are watching or listening to what is happening are invited to experience a whole range of human emotions (as Laurence Olivier's quote at the beginning of this chapter aptly states). In the conflicts of a tragic drama, for example, good people suffer and audiences are encouraged to identify with their sufferings; but in the comic form of drama, conflicts are resolved in ways that stimulate joy in spectators. The contrast is spectacular: sadness and joy.[6]

The words "culturally-based" mean that unless the cultural context is understood by listeners they do not know what social norms are being broken in the humorous experience. For example, travelers commonly complain that foreigners have no sense of humor—a traveler might do his or her best to explain a joke but often receive the response, "I don't get it." This response, however, does not mean the listener has no sense of humor. Though humor is a universal characteristic there is no universal language or universally understood cultural frame of reference. Consider the following joke:

> Why did Mary go with haste into the hill country of Judah?
> Because she had given her Fiat to the angel.

To appreciate this joke it is necessary to know the biblical reference to Mary, who went with haste to see her cousin Elizabeth (Luke 1:39); at the same time the word "fiat" has a double meaning. It is the Latin word to describe Mary's agreement to become the mother of Jesus, but it also is the word for an Italian car! Hence, an understanding of Scripture as well as of contemporary automobile brands is necessary just to appreciate this simple joke. The fact is that most humor goes beyond language; for the comic to be understood people need to be familiar with the culture, of which formal language is only one part.[7]

Cultural Differences and Humor: Examples

The popular practice in Australian humor is that of the hooligan "having a go" at authority, or one who keeps struggling against adversity. The early settlers had to confront the harsh rigors of climate and geography; they had to learn to coexist with this environment, knowing that at any time it could overwhelm them. This has led to a type of sardonic humor that is "edged with bitterness, a cynical detachment, and a mockery of the self or others."[8] At the same time, there is an inner resilience in the face of adversity and a deep respect for those who keep "battling on."[9]

continued on next page

The French education tradition, with its strong Cartesian roots, emphasizes logical thinking. This ill-prepares French people to appreciate Anglo-Saxon humor. A French Cartesian mind would be unable to grasp the following, which lacks logical structure: "The governor of the Bank of England began an address to an assembly of bankers with these words: 'There are three kinds of economists, those who can count and those who can't.'"[10] On the other hand, French people readily appreciate farce. Hence, in addition to their own farces French audiences appreciate people like Jerry Lewis, the American whom they label *le roi du crazy*.

Process of Contemplating the Incongruities of Life

While humor may be focused on the incongruities or peculiarities or foibles of people, their dignity as human persons must be respected. Therefore we need to distinguish negative and positive humor so that it can be viewed in terms of a continuum. At one pole of the continuum there is negative humor marked by bitterness, hostility, humiliation, for example, as in ethnic jokes that ridicule or disparage people. At the other pole there is positive humor characterized by pleasantness, joy, happiness, and other qualities that energize the mind and heart. Negative humor is directed against others. Positive humor is about "laughing with" others, that is, the humorists explicitly or implicitly acknowledge that they themselves have comic-evoking weaknesses in common with others.[11] Unless otherwise indicated, humor in this book refers to positive humor.

Incongruity, or paradox, is the quality at the heart of humor. Peter Berger says that from "its simplest to its most sophisticated expressions, the comic is experienced incongruence"[12] and in "principle, *any incongruence* may be perceived as comical."[13] To find something humorous is to be amused with some incongruity or paradox. For example, in jokes we are thinking along Trail A, but then suddenly we find ourselves moving on Route B. Our way of thinking is unexpectedly overturned, and if we enjoy the mental jolt, we are amused. The nonsense that follows from the perception of incongruity is understandable when we see the unexpected meaning or "get the point."[14] Consider this joke:

Doctor: Did that medicine I gave your uncle straighten him out?
Patient: It certainly did. They buried him yesterday!

Here we find an incongruous interaction of disparate elements and then coherence. The story line of the joke (the medicine straightened out the uncle?) crumples, but we immediately discover that the anomaly can be explained by another previously hidden story line ("straighten him out" can also mean death for the patient). A sense of humor requires the gift of detachment—one meaning must be abandoned to allow a new one to take its place.

Incongruity by itself may not always be sufficient for something to be humorous. It is the surprising nature of the incongruity and its resolution that evokes humor, as is evident in the above example. When applied to divine humor, the contraries of God as creator and judge relating to sinful humankind and their resolution through God's infinite mercy and love are startlingly incongruous. They are beyond simple reason to comprehend (see chap. 2). This is summarized eloquently in the words of the psalmist: "For though the LORD is high, he regards the lowly" (Ps 138:6) and "If you, O LORD, should mark iniquities, Lord, who could stand? But there is forgiveness with you . . ." (Ps 130:3-4).

There are levels of incongruity in humor. There is humor that involves just the incongruities of words, in puns, for example. The foundation of humor here is the embarrassment of language itself. Then there is the coming together of the incongruities of a situation and of personalities, as happens in Charlie Chaplin films, John Cleese (of *Monty Python*), or Peter Sellers. At the highest level of humor there is the incongruity of life itself: the stupidities of its vanities, the inevitability of its ending contrasted with its hopes and dreams. In Psalm 37 the psalmist expresses this level of humor: "The wicked plot against the righteous, and gnash their teeth at them; but the LORD laughs at the wicked, for he sees that their day is coming" (vv. 12-13).

The quality of incongruity is shared by both comedy and tragedy. A positive humorist finds incongruous flaws in human nature, but in ways that do not hurt people. Tragedy, however, highlights the gaps between the exalted dignity that people strive for but fail to achieve, resulting in sadness and pain for those involved. Peter Berger describes the relationship of the tragic and the comic in this way: "The tragic is the suffering contradiction, the comical, the painless contradiction."[15] For Northrop Frye, a Scripture scholar and literary critic, the comic follows a U-shaped approach, but a tragedy has an inverted U-shaped process. Tragedy may allow its actors a brief experience of glory, but they then fall into a period of destructiveness and remain there. Comedy, however, has a happy resolution, even after a period where the actors have tragic-like experiences.[16] Thus, according to Frye, Saul's life is a tragedy but the description of Job is comic, a point that will be further explained in a later chapter.

Evoking Laughter

Laughter as a sign of humor has grave limitations. Laughter is a physiological reaction that may or may not point to a sense of humor. For example, laughter can be evoked by tickling, or anxiety may cause people to laugh.[17] People may also feel socially pressured to laugh in order to save face and maintain peaceful interpersonal relationships.[18] On the other hand, people may react to the comic simply by an interior sense of joy, feeling an inner newness or energy of their spirit or heart. Some comedies, in fact, may not evoke laughter in audiences, and some tragedies can induce hysterical laughter. Hence, we can distinguish two kinds of laughter: "formal laughter," which is visible or audible, and "laughter of the heart," which may or may not manifest itself in visible form.

Joking Pattern

The word "joke" is used broadly to cover all expressions of humor, that is, anything that is said or done to excite formal laughter or laughter of the heart. Joking is a dynamic process of recounting or acting out something that is comic or humorous. There are three stages in joking: separation, liminality, and reaggregation (see figure 1.1).[19] In the separation stage listeners are alerted to the fact that something different from ordinary life is about to occur; next, liminality is the stage when people are confronted with the incongruity and its resolution. This is sometimes referred to as the chaos stage, since the incongruity is a breakdown of predictable meanings. In the third stage, reaggregation, there is the experience of renewed joy and return to the world of reality.

Separation

Definite, lighthearted cues are given to audiences to indicate that a joke is about to take place. The ordinary pattern of living is about to be interrupted. It might be done in a formal way, for example, by comments such as, "Have you heard this one?" "Have you heard the one about the politician?" Or it might be by a sudden change in the voice or facial expression of the joke teller, even a pause in the flow of speech. In the case of joke telling it is reasonably easy to identify the cues, but in observing other comic situations the separation stage may not be readily recognized. People could have a sudden hunch or an intuition that something funny is to about to occur. For example, I once observed a rather pompous politician presenting a very animated and exaggerated list of his achievements to his constituents. Swept along by his own eloquence he failed to see that he was walking closer and closer to the unprotected end of the stage. I sensed that if he continued his unguarded walk he would go over the edge into a flower bed. He did!

Liminality

This is the stage in which the incongruity is presented and a resolution called for. In the case of the politician in the flower bed I find he is uninjured and the incongruous situation suddenly hits me. A pompous politician who had up to that moment been trying to bully an audience into believing what was not really true had fallen into a flower bed! I, along with the others in the crowd, could not muffle our chuckles. The clash between an embarrassed, pompous politician in a flower bed and his common humanity is resolved because he is now seen to be like the rest of us, prone to accidents. When the incident is looked at from a symbolic perspective, there is an incongruous clash between two contraries: pomposity and common humanity. The latter wins through.

Reaggregation

This is the stage in which the invigorating experience of the joke or comic incident is to be carried through into daily life. I left the political campaign meeting with little memory of what the politician had said but with the decision never again to be bullied by politicians who misuse their power. This theoretical analysis of joking will be applied to the Scriptures in chapters 4 and 5.

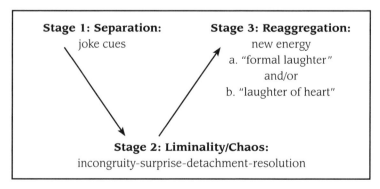

Figure 1.1: Dynamics of Joking

Expressions of Humor

Once we attempt to clarify various expressions and uses of humor we are again up against the problem mentioned at the opening of this chapter and so well stated by Bergson: [Humor], "this little problem . . . has the knack of baffling every effort, of slipping away only to bob up again, a pert challenge."[20] While humor can be expressed theoretically in many diverse ways—irony, caricature, satire, parody, or wit—in practice it is not always easy to identify how these terms differ. For example, caricature can contain irony and wit at the same time. While bearing this caution in mind readers may be helped by the following clarifications. Although subsequent chapters directly focus on the role of humor in Scripture, several examples, some already contained in existing scriptural commentaries, will be presented here to illustrate the theory.

Irony

Irony is to say one thing and mean another, commonly the opposite. For example, Australian humor is frequently characterized by ironic statements. An Australian farmer whose property was plagued with catastrophic drought was asked how he was coping. He replied, "Mate, it has been a bloody good month. I have lost hundreds of sheep and had to sell several thousand more to survive. It's really been an encouraging month!" Irony in comedy can expose as folly the stupid or dangerous pretensions of an imposter, such as Charlie Chaplin's mimicry of Hitler. Ironic humor is an effective way to critique an oppressive situation in a nonconfrontational style. On the negative side, however, irony can so mock every certainty that there is nothing left to trust or believe in. For example, irony so dominates postmodernity in Western culture that commonly there is skepticism of every ideal and a suspicion of any ultimate religious claim (see chap. 6).

Irony: The Parables of Jesus

Jesus used parables as humorous critiques of the oppressive culture in which he lived. Parables mock those who foolishly believe they can avoid their obligations to others. For example, the parable of the Unjust Steward (Luke 16:1-13) is an ironical criticism of those who claim that they obtain eternal blessings with the help of religious and moral exploitation. Jesus appears to be agreeing with this immoral approach until we see his real view in verse 10: "Whoever is faithful in a very little is faithful also in much; and whoever is dishonest in a very little is dishonest also in much." The parable of the Laborers in the Vineyard (Matt 20:1-16) is an ironical censure of people who, like the Unjust Steward, assume that they can enter the kingdom through some kind of neat mechanical calculation. There is similar irony in the parables of the Rich Fool (Luke 12:13-21) and the Rich Man and Lazarus (Luke 16:19-31). Both men are so blindly ignorant of the true values of life that they do not change when they have the opportunity to do so. Jesus' aim is to remind his listeners of the need to look at life from the perspective of the kingdom and not in worldly terms.[21]

Caricature

Caricature consists of the graphic distortion of body or behavior in the salient points of a person's appearance so as to excite amusement; any unusual feature is deliberately exaggerated. A cartoon, for example, can be used to critique a political group by exposing or lampooning their fraud, hypocrisy, and injustice because cartoonists are often able to portray a theme far more powerfully and emotively than the written word.

Verbal or drawn caricature of religious or political leaders is always an extremely risky affair. For example, the publication in Denmark of cartoons against the prophet Muhammad in September 2006 resulted in riots of protest among Islamic peoples in many parts of the world. Not uncommonly, the less democratic the government, the less developed the sense of humor of its leaders. They feel that humor directed at their behavior jeopardizes their self-worth and the power they exercise. In North Korea any caricaturing of political leaders is forbidden since everything is assumed to be perfect in the people's paradise! Hence, there is no reason for caricature. Totalitarian governments, however, do use negative humor to bolster their power base by using cartoonists and comedians; Hitler, for example, encouraged the mass media to ridicule Jews as part of his genocidal campaign against them.

Caricature: The Pharisees

The Pharisees were a Jewish sect at the time of Christ. Historically, while many Pharisees were violently opposed to the teachings and the person of Jesus, some in the Christian community in Jerusalem saw in Christ the one who would fulfill their Jewish faith (Acts 15:5) and some of them explicitly defended Jesus (John 7:50; 9:16) and early believers (Acts 5:34; 23:9). Saint Paul himself had been one of their most famous representatives (Acts 26:5; Phil 3:5), so also Nicodemus and Gamaliel.

On the other hand, the gospels record some harsh condemnations, which might be construed as caricatures, by John the Baptist and Jesus against the Pharisees. John the Baptist spoke of them as a "brood of vipers" (Matt 3:7) and Jesus castigated them as blind guides, hypocrites, and murderers (e.g., Matt 12:34; 23:13-32). These strong denunciations must be read within the cultural context of the evangelist's time. They were typical of how prophets caricatured the weaknesses of their listeners. Audiences would have understood that Jesus and the evangelists were using this culturally-based teaching method. Jesus dramatically aimed to draw attention to the excesses of the sect, their legalistic emphasis on externals in religion (Matt 15:1-20), and their limitations on love marked by excluding people such as sinners and publicans. Raymond E. Brown, when explaining Matthew's inclusion of the Pharisees in the plot to arrest Jesus (Matt 26:4-5), notes that the evangelist is reflecting the anti-Jewish attitude of many ordinary converts at that time. Since the parallel verses in Mark and Luke make no mention of this, Brown concludes Matthew's version is but a caricature that reflected contemporary prejudices.[22]

Satire

A satirist reveals, criticizes, mocks, and deflates pretentiousness, hypocrisy, and dishonesty. A satirist has the ability to mix the harsh realities of life and humor in a way that need not be destructive of society and people, but the ultimate aim is to ridicule the world in order to change it. Here is an example of a satirist challenging unjust values in the corporate world: "Corporate employees wishing to succeed in life must be experts in their field, diplomatic, utterly committed to the financial goals of the organization, but be without a family." A satirist has to be fearless—even foolish—and careless of the personal consequences. Of course there is a real danger that a satirist will slip into the use of negative humor and be destructive of human dignity. Sarcasm is a particularly harsh form of satire. It expresses itself in ridicule, aggression, and vindictiveness; unlike irony, sarcasm aims to destroy its victims. Ironic humorists will tend to muffle or even hide their feelings; this is not so for those who use sarcasm.

Sarcasm and Satire: The Prophets and Jesus

The prophets were given to both sarcasm and satire. [23] They mocked the belief in idols (Isa 44:9-20; Hos 13:2) and the ostentatious display of feminine jewelry (Isa 3:16-23). The Old Testament story of Joseph and his brothers gives yet another example of sarcasm in Scripture. Joseph's brothers denigrate his talents and sarcastically say of him, "Here comes this dreamer" (Gen 37:19). And, since sarcasm aims to destroy its victims, the brothers finally throw Joseph into the pit and sell him to foreign merchants (Gen 37:26-28).

In the New Testament account of Jesus healing the man born blind there is a mixture of irony, wit, and sarcasm. The Pharisees try to manipulate the healed man to agree that Jesus is a sinner, but he will not cooperate: "I do not know whether he is a sinner. One thing I do know, that though I was blind, now I see" (John 9:25). When his interrogators try again he replies sarcastically, "Do you also want to become his disciples?" (John 9:27). The incident concludes with an ironic comment, touched with a playful sarcasm, that those who could see have decided to be blind, but a person born without sight receives the ability to see and the gift of faith.[24]

Parody

Parody, like caricature, can be a type of satire in which the humorist impersonates people in an exaggerated way in order to ridicule them. The humorist aims to draw attention to the foibles or weaknesses of others in an effort to make them change their ways. Some authors interpret the fictional prophet Jonah's sometimes selfish values to be a parody because they are the inverse of those of authentic prophets.[25] Jonah resists the divine call, and when he does respond he carries out his task with vengeance, demanding that the repentant Ninevites be punished even though he has himself received unwarranted compassion.

As in sarcasm there is always a victim, so that parody can become a cruel way of relating to people who, if they are in a group, generally find it difficult to respond adequately. On the other hand, it may be a legitimate way for people who have little political power to draw attention to the faults of public figures. For example, the depiction of the priest and Levite in the parable of the Good Samaritan (Luke 10:29-37) is a deliberate parody by Jesus, who wanted to critique the religious hypocrisy of many leaders of his day.

In many cultures rituals of status reversal or rebellion are a type of parody. In traditional societies, for example, among Pueblo Indians and Zinacantecan communities of Highland Chiapas, Mexico,[26] parody, burlesque, and ridicule are important elements in ritual humor. Individuals in ritual humor are given significant freedom to dispense with normal behavior and to parody activities that are vigorously disapproved of or even forbidden in normal everyday life. Either the rituals directly attempt to change the existing authority system, for example, from a dictatorship to a democracy, or to reinforce the moral norms of the society by shaming deviates who do not live up to socially accepted standards.[27]

Parody: New Testament Examples

Many of Jesus' actions and parables could be considered rituals of reversal (a point to be further developed in chap. 5). Thus, Jesus dined with socially marginalized people such as tax collectors and sinners, reminding his critics of the fundamental Jewish imperative to welcome all peoples no matter what their social status. Contrary to cultural norms, he publicly conversed with women in order to draw attention to the fact that God created men and women equal. Jesus preached that the kingdom of God was actually present in his own ministry, as testified to by his exorcisms (Luke 11:20), yet he did not act as a worldly king. He was born in a stable and even rode on a lowly donkey into Jerusalem before his passion (John 12:13-14) to illustrate that authentic authority must be exercised by serving, not dominance.

Wit

A witty person has "the talent or quality of using unexpected associations between contrasting or disparate words or ideas to make a clever humorous effect."[28] Because wit is commonly expressed in the subtle play on words, it is difficult to detect examples in languages of which the observer has a limited grasp. For this reason it is hard for a non-scriptural scholar with no intimate knowledge of biblical languages to identify witty expressions in the texts of both Testaments.[29] It is possible, however, to detect witty language in the translated conversation of Jesus with three would-be followers (Luke 9:57-61). To one Jesus says: "Foxes have holes . . . but the Son of Man has nowhere to lay his head" (v. 58); to the second: "Let the dead bury their own dead . . ." (v. 60); to the third: "No one who puts a hand to the plow and looks back is fit for the kingdom of God" (v. 62).

Particular Uses of Humor

The above examples depicting the various expressions of humor show that it is essential in human communication and survival. The following section takes the analysis of humor further by concentrating on some of its particular uses.

As a Subversive Force

The most important function of positive humor is its subversive quality. It deflates pomposity and undermines the rigidity of the status quo. When humor pokes fun at the oppressive stringencies and conventions of society people have the chance to reimagine alternative ways of behaving. Mikhail M. Bakhtin (1895–1975), Russian linguist and critic, wrote, "Laughter demolishes fear . . . before a world, making of it an object of familiar contact and thus clearing the ground for an absolutely free investigation of it."[30]

Subversive humor is of two kinds: "relaxing" and "prophetic." The former has the general aim of recreation. When we are in a festive spirit and laughing we can escape from our usually worried, introverted selves into a calming state of being, and the humorous mood melts the rigidity of our imagination and narrow horizons. In consequence it disposes us to be open to all kinds of unforeseen creative dreams. In Freudian psychoanalytical terminology humor unleashes the energy of the subconscious against the control of the conscious. Or from a cultural anthropological perspective, humor breaks the controlling power of the predictable, resulting in a brief experience of chaos or loss of meaning, which disposes people to imagine new ways of being and doing.

Play is a type of relaxing humor.[31] Play, which is open to people of all ages, is any activity that is voluntary, gives pleasure, and has no goal other than the enjoyment of all involved. Winning at play is not its primary purpose. In play we flee from the seriousness of everyday affairs, and the relaxing experience disposes us to creative questioning of our structured lives. However, the more play is commercialized, the more it loses its emphasis on enjoyment and noncompetitiveness. For example, war terminology is often used to describe competitive football games, in which defeat of the rival team is the overriding purpose.

Play in Scripture

In the Old Testament children seem to be God's privileged ones, not only because of their native weakness, but also because of their potential for playful, spontaneous enjoyment, their willingness to give and receive, and their lack of concern for the competitive status that characterizes the cultures of adults. God prepares for himself praise from the mouths of children and very young ones (Ps 8:2). A psalmist, to express his confident abandonment to God, finds no better image than that of a young child who sleeps on the mother's bosom (Ps 131:2). The high point of messianic prophecy is the birth of Emmanuel, the sign of deliverance (Isa 7:14-16).

With the birth of the Christ child the new covenant is inaugurated (Luke 2:11-12), a symbol of what his followers must be—trusting, playful with one another, contrary to the plotting ways of the powerful. As an adult Jesus adopts the same attitude toward children as God has exemplified in the Old Testament. He blesses the children (Mark 10:16), thus showing that they have equal dignity when it comes to being part of the kingdom of God. In a culture where children had barely any rights this blessing would have been an incongruous affair for those who witnessed what Jesus said and did. Jesus presented children as the symbols of genuine disciples (Matt 19:13-15) and said we are to accept the kingdom as a little child would, with loving gratitude (Mark 10:15). Indeed the secret of authentic greatness is making oneself humble like a child (Matt 18:4).[32]

Prophetic humor has a deliberate focus, namely, to break the mold of thinking and provide a designated radically new alternative behavior pattern for the good of humankind. Jesus used prophetic humor throughout his ministry (see chap. 6), for example, when he washed the feet of his disciples (John 13:1-16). This incongruous action ran contrary to the belief that people in powerful positions had the right to dominate others in oppressive ways. Jesus explained unmistakably the purpose of his action: "servants are not greater than their master" (John 13:16).

As a Confirmatory Force

Humor can be confirmatory, that is, the aim of humor is to reaffirm the social or political status quo. For example, humor directed at the follies of politicians can be confirmatory while at the same time being a caricature. Here, the primary aim of the humorist is to shame the wayward politicians into behaving according to the accepted norms of behavior. Much personal caricature in England in the eighteenth century served to critique the greed and lechery often embodied in the corruption of the army, the church, law, and medicine, and to shame culprits into changing their ways.[33]

As Self-directed

The more one knows oneself, the more one sees oneself as a joke, when measured by the love and mercy of God. As Soren Kierkegaard says, "the more thoroughly and substantially a human being exists, the more he will discover the comical."[34] This joke, this comical being who is myself, can remain the sustained object of my humor only through faith and conversion that is nurtured by prayer. Humanly speaking the last thing I want to know well is myself. I would prefer to escape this knowledge and its consequences by being amused at the expense of others. Self-directed humor demands honesty, a willingness to recognize personal failings and attempts to hide them from others. Any endeavor to cover our faults and stupidities is an example of incongruity and therefore a reason to laugh at ourselves. Fundamentalists cannot laugh at themselves; if they do so they risk having to question their rigid assumptions about reality.

As a Coping Technique

Cynical, resigned, and often heartrending humor make deprivation and despair to some degree bearable. Humor helps people detach themselves from potentially depressing situations. Lament psalms in their own way are humorous coping mechanisms (see chap. 5). The grim portrayal of personal and national lament is softened by the trust people have in God's paradoxical loving and supportive mercy.

On a more mundane level, police or others involved in frontline emergency situations crack jokes among themselves that to outsiders may sound callous or unfeeling. In fact, the jokes are a positive method of releasing tension and frustration.[35] Victor Frankl, a concentration camp inmate, considered that the ability to crack jokes was a crucial way to maintain normality in the midst of the horrific atmosphere: "Humor was another of the soul's weapons in the fight for self-preservation . . . [H]umor, more than anything else in the human make-up, can afford an aloofness and an ability to rise above any situation, even if only for a few seconds."[36] Even today among Australian Aboriginal peoples, who have been forced for generations to be second-class citizens in a country where they were the first owners, humor is a way to cope with their feeling of marginalization.

As a Vehicle for Learning

Humor can be a "lubricant" for social interaction. Many a successful speaker begins a serious topic with a joke. This is the relaxing function of humor described above. Good humor touches the hearts of people, encouraging them to relax from the burdens of daily life, and in this stress-free mode they become open to listen and learn. Others, however, use humor throughout their lectures or conversations as a deliberate teaching and learning technique. The hugely successful American television program *Sesame Street* teaches millions of children to learn at least the rudiments of knowledge—how to count and spell. They are able to do this while falling about with laughter at the antics of characters such as Oscar the Grouch or Big Bird.

Matthew's Gospel: Learning through Humor

Scripture scholar F. Scott Spencer has proposed a fascinating thesis about the comic qualities of the genealogy of Jesus in chapter 1 of Matthew's gospel. In the midst of great heroes such as Abraham and David, four women are listed: Tamar, Rahab, Ruth, and the wife of Uriah.[37] These women have been involved in some of the most outlandish and weird—even verging on bizarre—incidents described in Scripture.

Spencer argues that the incongruous positioning of these women at the beginning of the gospel is not merely to tell a joke in order to relax his readers, as writers and speakers commonly do. Rather, it is part of the overall divine comic theme of the gospel. Matthew wishes to relax his readers, and the comic beginning sets the stage for more profound humor in the text that follows. Matthew is saying that God's plan of salvation involves incidents and people who are considered of least importance in cultural terms—those without power, such as widows, prostitutes, foreigners, and adulteresses. The genealogy concludes, as we know, with an unsuspecting and unknown Jewish woman who is to be the mother of Jesus. Then the comic story continues with references to marginalized people who are especially loved by Jesus. In other words, Matthew is being deliberately comic. He wants his readers to learn through humor, beginning rather dramatically in the first chapter, and ending with the most incongruous of all events—the death and resurrection of Christ.

As a Control of Deviance[38]

Fear of ridicule or of being publicly shamed can make people conform; it is a particularly common form of maintaining control in traditional culture. People listening to some of the parables in Matthew's gospel would have chuckled at the stupidity of those who failed to behave appropriately, for example, the man who did not have a wedding garment (Matt 22:11-14) and the foolish virgins who were not prepared for the bridegroom (Matt 25:1-13). The fear of being publicly shamed should have made the people in the parables behave correctly, but they did not. Jesus is telling his listeners, and is telling us, to either obey his commands or suffer justified shame and ridicule before God (Matt 25:31-46).[39] The fear of ridicule, however, can be a negative force in any society, for example, when envy and jealousy of an innovative person are behind the ridicule. Any form of humor that results from envious or jealous reactions does not fulfill a requirement of positive humor: namely, that it be a kindly contemplation of the incongruities of life.

As a Reaffirmation of Identity

Jokes can be ways of setting boundaries for a group. People who understand the cultural elements of a joke can feel a sense of bonding with one another, but there can be a negative side to this as well. Those who cannot grasp the joke feel a sense of hurtful exclusion. Ethnic, sub-group, and sexist jokes also exclude people; the out-group becomes the butt of the jokes and, in the process, the in-group's superiority is reaffirmed. The identity function of negative humor is evident in the way the chief priests and scribes behave toward Jesus on the cross (Mark 15:31-32). Their scoffing reinforces their own sense of identity and superiority, as did the mockery of those who scoffed at the early Christians because of their belief in the resurrection of the dead (Acts 17:32).

Summary

- Humor is a complex form of culturally-based drama. It brings together opposites, emphasizes contradictions, and reveals the ridiculousness of what is irreconcilable. It is the absurdity that makes us smile, laugh, or experience an inner joy. Humor is positive or kindly when it refreshes the human spirit, but it is negative when it degrades people. Laughter is not an automatic sign of humor. People may react to the comic simply by an interior sense of joy, a feeling of inner newness, called laughter of the heart. Positive humor can be a way of countering arrogance and oppression at the personal and social levels. As C.S. Lewis writes, self-humor "involves a sense of proportion and a power of seeing yourself from the outside."[40]

- Humor can be an effective method of communication simply because it helps people to forget their worries and the pressures of life. For this reason humor can have a subversive role in society. It is subversively relaxing when it has no particular purpose other than to help people unwind. Stress-free individuals are open to imaginative and alternative ways of being and doing. Prophetic humor aims deliberately to dispose people to act in a particular way that is subversive of the cultural or personal status quo.

- Throughout this foundation-setting chapter we have seen briefly how Scripture is rife with humor. The following chapters will turn to this in more detail.

Chapter 2

Humor in the Scriptures

[The one] without humour, even if he's the pope, doesn't know God.
    Gerard Bessiere[1]

[We need] an Unsolemn approach to an Unsolemn God . . . Our insistence upon being serious with God heavily limits our experience of the Godhead.
    Wanda Nash[2]

This chapter explains:

- that divine humor is a fundamental theme in both Testaments;
- that many psalms describe the meaning of laughter of the heart;
- the different ways in which Jesus Christ uses humor in teaching and action.

Humor is expressed in both Testaments in various ways. There are explicit examples of individuals, including God, laughing. There are incidents that would have been laughter evoking for bystanders; others focus on the laughter of mockers. When the humor is positive it ends in an uplifting experience.

More important, however, divine humor pervades the Scriptures. We call the actions of God toward us divine humor because they so dramatically

19

diverge from our human expectations of how God should relate to us. People expected the Messiah as a king to be born in princely splendor, but Mary gave birth to him in a stable. We expect God to distance himself from sinful creatures but, incongruously, God does not. Through Christ, God becomes one with us. Saint John struggles to put into words the fundamental incongruity of divine humor: "In this is love, not that we loved God but that he loved us and sent his Son to be the atoning sacrifice for our sins" (1 John 4:10). We are called to contemplate such a divine paradox through the eyes of faith and come to experience even in this vale of tears "an indescribable and glorious joy" (1 Pet 1:8), that is, the hope-filled laughter of the heart. This chapter further reflects on some of the many ways in which the mystery of divine humor concretely manifests itself and some various human responses to this mystery. We then seek to unravel some of the ways in which humor is used in both Testaments.

Divine Humor

By the use of the term "divine humor" we try to describe in inadequate human terms the totally unexpected, surprising ways that God as creator and redeemer relates to humankind (figure 2.1). To our astonishment we repeatedly discover the truth of Yahweh's admonition: "For my thoughts are not your thoughts, nor are your ways my ways" (Isa 55:8). The Scriptures emphasize the awesome gap between God as creator of the universe and humankind. Yet despite this incredible chasm, God loves what has been created. In one of the most dramatic scenes of the Old Testament we see God proclaiming to Moses that God is neither vengeful nor inconstant and does not prize justice over mercy: "The Lord . . . [is] a God merciful and gracious, slow to anger, and abounding in steadfast love and faithfulness, keeping steadfast love for the thousandth generation, forgiving iniquity and transgression and sin" (Exod 34:6-7). When the Israelites thought of God they instinctively had in mind God's "steadfast love," an expression used over fifty times in the Psalms alone. That is divine humor; for, humanly speaking, God would be expected to demand justice rather than show mercy and love for wayward humankind.

Divine humor is especially evident in Yahweh's covenant relationships with the Israelites. The covenants between God and the Israelites are initiated through God's kindness; they articulate God's gracious assurance and faithfulness toward the chosen people. Judged from a purely human perspective this is surely a humorously incongruous situation: God freely entering into a contractual relationship with people he has created! The most important of the covenants—the Mosaic covenant given at Sinai—sets out obligations for both parties involved (Deut 30:15-20). If the Israelites fail to obey the requirements of the covenant, then they must suffer the consequences. God could even revoke the covenant (Hos 1:9), and its renewal would depend entirely on God's mercy (Exod 34:6-9; Jer 31:31-33).[3] There is the constant tension between justice, which requires that the Israelites be punished for breaking the covenant, and Yahweh's forgiving mercy toward them.

What wins—punishment for sins or mercy? Everything human points to the former, but that is not how God will act. In Jeremiah, Yahweh vividly describes the sinful state of Israel because it has broken the covenant: "Your hurt is incurable, your wound is grievous. . . . for I have dealt you the blow of an enemy, the punishment of a merciless foe, because your guilt is great, because your sins are so numerous" (Jer 30:12, 14). But here is the comedic irony. Despite this well-deserved condemnation, Yahweh will forgive people for their sinful ways. The impossible gives way to the possible. Mercy overshadows justice. The last word is clemency: "For I will restore health to you, and your wounds I will heal. . . . And you shall be my people, and I will be your God" (Jer 30:17, 22). The prophet Hosea describes Yahweh's pursuing love of Israel despite its repeated infidelities: "Therefore, I will now allure her . . . and speak tenderly to her" (Hos 2:14). This is divine illogicality! The psalmist, when reflecting on his own sins and the justice of God, nonetheless trusts in God's abiding forgiveness: "If you, O LORD, should mark iniquities, Lord, who could stand? But there is forgiveness with you, so that you may be revered" (Ps 130:3-4).

In the New Testament the contrast between human expectations of how the creator should act and what actually happens is dramatic. God's love for humankind is so overwhelming that God gives his Son even unto death (John 3:16; 15:12-13). Further, "the Son of Man came not to be served but to serve, and to give his life a ransom for many" (Matt 20:28). In fact God's love for us is frequently described in terms of forgiveness (Mark 11:25; Matt 6:12, 14-15), a fact that is also portrayed in parables: the good shepherd searches for the stray sheep (Matt 18:12-14); the father welcomes back the prodigal son who had acted with selfishness and brashness (Luke 15:11-32). In seeking to describe Christ's love for us, Paul speaks of Jesus "taking the form of a slave" (Phil 2:7) in order to save humankind.

Divine Humor: God's incongruous forgiving / healing love:
pursuing fickle humankind (Hos 2:14-15; Ps 145:8)

Human Face of God: Christ
(1 Cor 1:18-21)
expresses divine incongruity by:
1. teaching, e.g., parables
2. actions:
   –servant leadership
   –associating with marginalized
   –promoting gender equality
   –dying on cross
   (John 15:13)

We reveal divine humor as the
human face of Christ to the world
(Gal 2:20)
when:
   –we act in love and justice
   (John 13:35; Phil 2:5)

Figure 2.1: Divine Humor in Action

Divine and Human Humor: Views

Father Karl Rahner, SJ, connected divine and human humor in this way: "A good laugh is a sign of love; it may be said to give us a glimpse of, or a first lesson in, the love that God bears for every one of us. . . . God laughs, says the Bible. When the last piece of human folly makes the last burst of human laughter ring out crisp and clear in a doomed world, is it too much to imagine that this last laugh will resemble that of God . . . and seem to convey that, in spite of everything, all's well?"[4]

Peter Berger, a sociologist of religion, accepts Freud's and Bergson's view that the comic is a fundamental incongruity.[5] He argues that there is a primary incongruity between God and creation that is ultimately reflected in all positive expressions of humor. The human spirit is held captive by the created world of order, but through humor this spirit is able to briefly break through the imprisonment to make contact with God's joy.[6] Humor is thus a "signal of transcendence," a sign that God exists, and a subtle, but powerful, cry of the human spirit for redemption. Hence a person's positive humor is "an ultimately religious vindication of joy."[7]

Earlier Soren Kierkegaard proposed a somewhat similar view. Humor cannot be confined within this-worldly premises and humanistic assumptions. On the contrary, it points implicitly but constantly toward the incarnational premise that humanity is being enabled by grace to share in the divine nature and has the image of God stamped precisely upon its very creaturely existence. Some facet of comedy always alludes to the Incarnation, the most paradoxical of all events, the "offence" of God entering time.[8]

Formal Laughter

Incidents of formal laughter are extremely rare in the Scriptures. When it does occur it is of two types: the negative laughter of the fool who does not recognize truth, even refusing to believe; and the positive laughter of the believer.[9] There are, however, many incidents that must have evoked laughter in bystanders as well.

Negative Laughter

The mocker is not like a wise person (Prov 9:12; 29:8), because the scoffer responds to the Word of God with ridicule (Jer 20:7-8). People laugh at the defeat of their enemies; men laugh at the misfortunes of Job (Job 30:1), the enemies of Jerusalem laugh at its collapse (Lam 1:7), Tobit's neighbors mock his good deeds (Tob 2:8), and the father-in-law of Lot laughs with incredulity at the possibility of Sodom being destroyed (Gen 19:14).

Only three times in the New Testament are people noted for laughing, and in all instances it is the negative laughter of mockery. The mourners in the house of Jairus laugh in disbelief at Jesus' promise to revive the girl (Matt 9:24; Mark 5:40; Luke 8:53), soldiers mock Jesus as a king after crowning him with thorns (Matt 27:29), and bystanders at the crucifixion also ridicule Jesus (Matt 27:39).

Positive Laughter

When Abraham and Sarah learn from God that Sarah is to bear a child they burst into mocking laughter (Gen 17:17; 18:12-15). Given their advanced age, their laughter of disbelief is understandable from a human perspective. Abraham and Sarah fail initially, through lack of faith, to see things from the perspective of divine humor. So it is ironic that they name their son "Isaac," which means "he laughed." The initial mocking laughter turns into a laughter of faith-filled joy as Sarah so well describes: "Now Sarah said: 'God has brought laughter for me; everyone who hears will laugh with me.' And she said, 'Who would ever have said to Abraham that Sarah would nurse children? Yet I have borne him a son in his old age.'" (Gen 21:6-7).

God laughs with good reason at the actions of the people who plot against the anointed king (Ps 2:2-4). At that time, could such arrogance of the plotters be more ridiculous! In another psalm God is again described as laughing at the behavior of the enemies of the virtuous, knowing "that their day is coming" and "their sword shall enter their own heart" (Ps 37:13, 15). This is prophetic humor because the psalmist wants future generations to recognize the foolishness of those who forget there is a God, the Creator of the universe "who sits in the heavens" (Ps 2:4) and sees all things. The believing person's laugh can express the joy of one who is blessed by God (Ps 126:2; Job 8:21). One of the Beatitudes of Luke (6:21) promises laughter of gladness to those who mourn, and one of the woes promises mourning to those who now laugh (6:25), where laughter is a sign of frivolity.[10]

Laughter-evoking Incidents

There are many examples of laughter-evoking incidents in the Old Testament, at times in the midst of very serious situations, involving people and even their relationships with Yahweh.[11] Moses, who "is slow of speech and slow of tongue"(Exod 4:10), is chosen to lead the Israelites out of slavery in Egypt. Noah is told to build a large boat a long distance from any water (Gen 6:11–9:29). Balaam, a non-Israelite prophet who is believed to have wide knowledge of many things, finally discovers the most memorable lesson in his life from, of all things, an ass (Num 22:22-35). When Gideon goes into battle against the Midianites he has no weapons and his soldiers have only clay pots, horns, and burning torches, but he succeeds by placing trust in God (Judg 7:1-23). The impious Ninevites are so anxious to repent that they adorn their cattle in mourning clothes and demand that they also fast (Jonah 3:6-9). David, physically ill equipped to fight Goliath, destroys the giant (1 Sam 17).

In the lives of the prophets we often see rather comic actions, and bystanders must have been amused by what they saw. Jonah conceals himself under shrubbery (Jonah 4:6-8). Isaiah strolls about naked for three years (Isa 20:2-3). Jeremiah breaks pots (Jer 19:1-13) and places a yoke around his neck (Jer 28:10-16). Ezekiel prepares his food at a fire fueled by human manure (Ezek 4:12) and even consumes God's word, which was written on a scroll, for a meal (Ezek 3:1-3).[12]

Isaac: His Humorous Actions

There are several comical incidents in the life of Isaac, for example, his blessing of Jacob rather than Esau and his manipulation by Rebekah.[13] Isaac favors Esau over Jacob; Esau pampers Isaac in his propensity for too much food, particularly game (Gen 25:28). In this and other scenes Isaac is portrayed as being a little foolish or abstracted from reality. He claims he is about to die and needs his last meal (though he does not die for another twenty years according to Gen 31:38 and 35:29); this is an excuse to get Esau to prepare more game for him. Then Rebekah enters the scene and plans to deceive Isaac by dressing Jacob, her favorite son, to feel like Esau to fulfill the prophecy of Genesis 25:23. Esau is hairy (Gen 25:25), unlike Jacob, so Rebekah covers Jacob's hands and neck with goat skins so that Isaac will think it is the hairy Esau he is blessing (Gen 27:15-16). The fact that Isaac has poor eyesight certainly aids the deception. But Isaac comes across as gullible, for he ignores the fact that the voice is that of Jacob (Gen 27:22-23). Isaac does not pursue his doubts, for he is more interested in his food than the importance of his role in Israelite history.

There follows a further deception of Isaac by Rebekah. She is concerned that Jacob will be killed by the angry Esau. So Jacob must leave, but Rebekah cannot tell Isaac this for fear that he will refuse permission. So she manipulates Isaac by convincing him of the shame to herself and Isaac if Jacob marries a Hittite woman (Gen 27:46). Isaac falls for this, and he blesses Jacob again and sends him on his way. This is a humorous situation for onlookers who see men who think they are in control in a patriarchal culture, but in reality are being unknowingly manipulated by women. Other similar examples are Abigail (1 Sam 25), Bathsheba (1 Kgs 1), Jezebel (1 Kgs 21), and Esther (Esth 3–4, 7).

Some incidents in the life of Jesus also display a comic quality. The wedding feast of Cana (John 2:1-11) contains several humorous plots. It is ironic that the first miracle recorded in John's gospel is the changing of water into wine (John 2:11). One might humanly have expected that Jesus would reveal his divine power in something more dramatic and directly concerned with the salvation of souls; yet divine humor is not confined by human hopes. Moreover, the new wine not only was of superior quality but was so abundant that the couple could have set up a wine shop with the surplus!

Then there is the incident when Jesus must pay the temple tax. He tells Peter to go fishing, and in the mouth of the first fish caught he will find the necessary coin (Matt 17:27). The spontaneous, over-confident behavior of Peter would surely at times have given rise to many a chuckle among the other disciples and onlookers, including Jesus himself. Consider Peter's energetic attempt to walk on the water, his sudden loss of faith in Jesus, and his sinking, but with a happy ending (Matt 14:28-31).

The miraculous feeding of the four thousand is incongruous enough, but even more so because there are seven baskets of leftovers (Matt 15:37).

In the midst of the terrible pain of the crucifixion it is possible to interpret the words of Jesus to the repentant criminal as humorous: "Truly I tell you, today you will be with me in Paradise" (Luke 23:43). One who steals on earth now "steals" a place in heaven before death.[14] Then there is the appearance of the risen Jesus to women and not to his male followers, an astonishing action in a patriarchal culture (John 20:11-18). There is a humorous side to the Emmaus story (Luke 24:13-35). The two disciples, on leaving Jerusalem after Christ's ignominious death, are thoroughly dejected because their vision of Christ as a powerful and triumphant Messianic leader had been destroyed. When Jesus appears at their side asking them why they are so sad, the pain in their response is obvious and deep (Luke 24:19-24). Despite the depressing nature of the scene for the disciples, one can imagine Jesus himself keeping a straight face, knowing all the time that he is the one they are talking about. In feigned innocent tones he simply asks, "What are you discussing with each other while you walk along?" (Luke 24:17). And the disciples pour out their sorrows. (The incident will be further explained in chapter 5.)

In the Acts of the Apostles there are several comical incidents.[15] Herod is persecuting the early believers, and Peter is one of those arrested (Acts 12:1-19). The storyteller describes in detail how impossible it is for Peter to escape as he is heavily chained and made to sleep between two guards.

Suddenly an angel of the Lord appears to release Peter's chains and lead him past the guards to freedom. But the comical situation does not end here. He seeks refuge in the house of a friend and is joyfully received by the maid of the house (Acts 12:12-14). When the maid tries to tell the family that Peter is outside, she is met with an abusive response: "You are out of your mind!" (Acts 12:15). The reader can only chuckle at the incongruous scene. Family members are so startled by her persistent responses to their disbelief that they claim the vision could only be an angel. Meanwhile, Peter continues knocking on the door until they finally acknowledge and joyously receive him.

A little later in Acts there is another hilarious scene where Paul and Barnabas are acclaimed as gods after Paul heals a crippled man (Acts 14:10). The crowds are so sure that Paul is the god Hermes and Barnabas Zeus that they immediately want to offer sacrifice in their honor. Poor Paul and Barnabas! Overwhelmed by the mistaken enthusiasm of the people they desperately try to convince them that they are not gods. They are shocked that the healing is attributed, not to God, but to them. They publicly tear their clothes in an effort to stop the adulation of the crowds. They proclaim in dignified language that God is the real source of the healing, the same God who created the world and sustains it in being. The scene is an amusing one—the desperate efforts of Paul and Barnabas to restrain the crowd but with limited effect: "Even with these words, they scarcely restrained the crowds from offering sacrifice to them" (Acts 14:18).

Laughter of the Heart

Recall that a positive sense of humor is the gift whereby we kindly contemplate the incongruities of life and express this meditative reflection in laughter, smiling, or simply an inner joy or peace. In the Scriptures, as already noted, audible laughter is exceptional. We find in Scripture, however, people who contemplate the many acts of divine humor and seek to mirror this humor in their own lives. This evokes inner joy, or "laughter of the heart," coming from their faith in God's paradoxical love for them and humankind.

Psalms: Laughter of the Heart

Since the psalms so poetically describe what the Scriptures mean by laughter of the heart, we need to give significant space to their analysis. Permeating all the psalms is the belief and trust in divine humor that evokes heart laughter in those who are praying. Especially in the lament psalms, the petitioners, while intensely suffering, experience a surprising inner energy, a newness or joy, a gift from a loving God.

Psalm 8 displays the vivid paradoxical contrast: God as creator, humankind as the created. Then the incongruous contrast is further intensified when humankind is called to collaborate with God in additionally enhancing creation. All the while God still cares for human beings as they work together in developing a world founded on love and justice. In beautiful and poetic language the psalm portrays the stunning nature of God's act of humor: "When I look at your heavens, the work of your fingers . . . what are human beings that you are mindful of them, mortals that you care for them? . . . You have given them dominion over the works of your hands; you have put all things under their feet" (Ps 8:3, 4, 6). There is a polar interaction between an awe that trembles at the very thought of God's majesty, so evident in the universe, and the amazement and joy that comes from discovering that God calls us to labor with him in continuing the creation of this world. God's act of humor toward humankind evokes a contemplative, humorous response from the poet. Humankind to collaborate with our creator! Is anything more incongruous than this? Only faith makes sense of this paradox, leaving the poet with an inner peace and joy that words alone cannot fully express.[16] Of course, God's humor is of the prophetic type. It is focused on evoking a response from us that is collaborative and founded on justice and love.

In the lament psalms the writers speak of chaos gravely affecting their lives as individuals or as the nation Israel. The former sense of order and serenity is shattered and this is articulated in powerfully emotive expressions: anger, self-pity, the sense of utter loneliness and abandonment, hatred. At first sight there is no room for humor or comedy; yet profound faith-based humor pervades these psalms. Psalm 88 is one of the most heartrending of the lament psalms in Scripture.[17] Unlike other lament psalms it contains no explicit statement of trust in Yahweh or promise of praise. Instead there are several desperation-filled petitions for help from Yahweh: "I cry out in your presence" (v. 1); "I, O Lord, cry out to you; in the morning my prayer comes before you" (v. 13). Yet Yahweh does not answer. The psalmist has a deep and abiding faith in Yahweh's presence, but there is no sign whatsoever that God is listening to, or even concerned with, the complete breakdown of the psalmist's life of peace and order. Yahweh's failure to respond, however, does not deter the psalmist because he only intensifies the anguish of his words: "I am counted among those who go down to the Pit" (v. 4); "like those forsaken among the dead, like the slain that lie in the grave" (v. 5); "You have put me in the depths of the Pit" (v. 6). If the psalmist is left like this, deprived of all contact with the community of worship, then how can he praise Yahweh? The words "Pit" and "Sheol" are synonyms for "chaos"[18] (a point to be explained further in chap. 4), that is, the formless mass that existed before the creation of the world. They describe the victim's desperate sense of desolation, a feeling of utter powerlessness when there can no longer be any communication with kinsfolk and friends.[19]

The psalmist eloquently describes the depth of his abandonment and loneliness: "You have caused friend and neighbor to shun me; my companions are in darkness" (v. 18). He feels so totally betrayed by them, for they reject him in his time of greatest need. Why is he shunned by his friends and family? The Israelites, like many peoples in premodern cultures, divide sickness into two types: disease and illness.[20] The former is the visible affliction itself, such as leprosy, blindness, and physical injury. The illness, however, is that which is hidden beneath the disease, such as the fear of death, the loss of self-esteem, feeling abandoned by friends. The sadness is exacerbated by the belief that the disease is the result of sin by the sufferer. Moreover, certain diseases automatically marginalized the sufferer from society, even from one's family and closest friends. To communicate with the diseased person meant risking ritual defilement. The illness, therefore, could be even worse than the disease. So, it is quite possible in Psalm 88 that the sick man has a disease that automatically isolates him from all social intercourse.

One senses the despairing cry—could he ever again become a dynamic member of his community of relations and friends? Not only is he cut off from the consoling presence of his friends and family, which is bad enough, but, worse still, he cannot find communion with God that he so earnestly seeks. Not only does he fear that he will be separated from God forever, but he directly blames Yahweh for causing it: "You have put me in the depths. . . . Your wrath lies heavy upon me, and you overwhelm me with all your waves. You have caused my companions to shun me; you have made me a thing of horror to them" (vv. 6-8). The psalmist hopes that the strength of his condemnation will elicit some compassionate acknowledgement from Yahweh. But there is no obvious response.

At first sight there appears to be no comic quality to this psalm of such despair, for it seems that the man has given up all hope. Yet three types of humor are identifiable: negative humor, laughter of the heart, and divine humor. His former friends can be expected to be mocking him on the sidelines because God is punishing him for his sins and will not hear his cries. The fact that the psalmist continues to pray, however, despite the fact that all the signs are pointing toward a devastating end, is an indication that the sufferer has hope and is experiencing, however faintly, the inner peace that accompanies laughter of the heart. He believes in the divine humor, that even in death Yahweh's majesty will be honored. The humanly incongruous situation—the tension between the pleas of the afflicted person and the silent God—is resolved through the psalmist's ongoing act of hope. The physical and mental pain remains with overwhelming intensity, but hope triumphs to the end. God and the psalmist are laughing together at the failure of the bystanders to see things from the divine perspective.

Psalm 88 has special personal significance for me. Years ago, when I was still young, I was told by a surgeon that I had a potentially fatal disease. When alone, I accidentally noticed this psalm. Every line described my feelings of desolation and abandonment by God. In the weeks that followed friends would visit me, but few could touch my interior pain. Yet, the more I read this psalm, the more I surprisingly discovered its underlying expression of hope in a God of inexhaustible love and compassion. God became my friend, my source of consolation, inner peace and joy. No words could adequately describe what I now call "laughter of the heart," the gift of divine humor. It is my favorite psalm.

New Testament: Laughter of the Heart

John the Baptist, while still in his mother's womb, "leaped for joy" (Luke 1:44) when meeting Jesus, who was, of course, still in his mother's womb. The shepherds receive the joyful news of Jesus' birth (Luke 2:10). Earlier, Mary, having accepted God's call to be the mother of Jesus, is so moved with joy at this divine act of humor that she travels many miles through rough territory to share her pleasure with her cousin Elizabeth (Luke 1:39-40). Elizabeth acknowledges this joy and Mary then replies in praise of God. Mary's laughter of the heart inspires her to recite one of the most subversive statements in all literature. In her Magnificat, the bridge between the Old and the New Testaments, she cheerfully states without ambiguity that Jesus has come especially for the healing of *anawim*, that is, for those who are powerless in society—not through their own fault but, rather, because structures of oppression condemn them to poverty.[21] For the faithful trapped in oppression it expresses a deep and dangerous hope of a better world.[22] Contrary to the human way of thinking, Christ is to be firmly on the side of the poor. The song proclaims three revolutions: a moral revolution ("He has shown strength with his arm; he has scattered the proud in the thoughts of their hearts" [Luke 1:51]); a social revolution ("He has brought down the powerful from their thrones, and lifted up the lowly" [Luke 1:52]); and an economic revolution ("He has filled the hungry with good things, and sent the rich away empty" [Luke 1:53]).[23]

For the believer the joy that comes even from suffering is founded on the hope of salvation, which consists in a willingness to suffer with Christ (1 Pet 4:13) but is the expression of the ultimate union with Christ in love. Hence, St. Paul is depicted as full of joy, experiencing an intense laughter of the heart, even though he feels especially oppressed (2 Cor 6:10), because it is no longer he who lives but Christ lives in him through his suffering with Christ (Gal 2:20). The paradox of human suffering is resolved through union in love with Christ. From humankind's perspective is there anything spiritually more incongruous! Edwin Good describes the interconnection of faith-based humor and divine humor in this way:

> We can talk . . . of a human comedy, or, [even] of a divine comedy. Faith can laugh both because God's world is splendid and because it is ridiculous. But its splendor . . . moves us to the laughter of joy. . . . [F]aith can laugh the laughter of mocking irony at the pretensions of those who consider themselves only splendid and the laughter of joyful irony with those who consider themselves only ridiculous.[24]

In the journeys of Peter there are some examples of divine and faith-based humor in action. Simon Peter, who is referred to in the New Testament far more frequently than any other disciple, is the focus of Jesus' attention at critical points. Yet Peter is a most unlikely character to be singled out for leadership. Coming from a poor socioeconomic background, he comes across before the resurrection as a blustery kind of person given to outbursts of dramatic enthusiasm and spontaneous proclamations of loyalty to Christ. Yet his enthusiasm at times fails to translate into action. Although Peter willingly "left everything and followed" Christ (Luke 5:11), he is slow to understand what Jesus is saying and loses heart when particularly tested. For example, he is slow to comprehend the lesson of Jesus wanting to wash his feet (John 13:6-11), and his faith gives way when he is invited to walk on the water toward Jesus (Matt 14:28-31). On one occasion Peter is even vigorously rebuked by Jesus, who refers to him as Satan (Mark 8:33). Finally, Peter denies being a friend of Jesus after Jesus' arrest (Mark 14:66-72). Through all this Jesus exercises his divine humor, trusting and waiting for Peter's conversion to become more deeply rooted in his heart and actions. Finally, that trust is rewarded: "The Lord turned and looked at Peter. Then Peter remembered the word of the Lord, how he had said to him, 'Before the cock crows today, you will deny me three times.' And he went out and wept bitterly" (Luke 22:61-62). Peter becomes a true and faithful leader in imitation of Jesus the Good Shepherd. What a humanly paradoxical odd ending for one whose behavior has been so unpredictable!

Paul's journey of conversion has its own entertainingly human aspects. During the ten years after his initial conversion, and prior to Paul's first really successful mission to Cyprus and Asia Minor, people find him a disturbing influence and are rather pleased to see him leave them because his over-fiery preaching has been attracting the murderous intentions of the authorities (see Acts 9:23-24). So his friends, in desperation, "took him by night and let him down through an opening in the wall, lowering him in a basket" (Acts 9:25). And "meanwhile the church throughout Judea, Galilee, and Samaria had peace and was built up" (Acts 9:31). Paul had been converted to Christ, but he still retained his overzealous, dogmatic pre-conversion style of preaching that caused only unnecessary conflict. The humorous point is that Paul is preaching the need to build a peaceful community, but acting in ways that prevent this happening.[25]

New Testament: Humor as a Teaching Method

An underlying incongruity permeates the entire New Testament. God is born to a peasant girl, not in a palace but in the rough atmosphere of a primitive stable, is accepted by only a few, and redeems the world by dying an ignominious death on the cross. We now examine some ways that humor is expressed and used in this part of the Bible.

Verbal Comments

Jesus is never described as laughing, but in his teaching he uses many images that would have been comical to himself and his listeners. There are also many incongruous incidents that would have evoked physical or spiritual laughter. For example, when Jesus described how difficult it is for rich people who are attached to their wealth and the power it gives them to enter the kingdom of God, he used the image of a camel trying to squeeze through the eye of a needle (Mark 10:25). The poor among his listeners would have chuckled at this metaphor, with its satirical description of the selfish wealthy people. Some further examples of how Jesus intentionally uses prophetic humor as a teaching method:

- "Why do you see the speck in your neighbor's eye, but do not notice the log in your own eye? Or how can you say to your neighbor, 'Friend, let me take out the speck in your eye,' when you yourself do not see the log in your own eye?" (Luke 6:41-42).

- To the scribes and Pharisees, he says: "You blind guides! You strain out a gnat but swallow a camel!" (Matt 23:24). He complains that their hypocritical behavior is like cleaning the outside of a cup while leaving the inside dirty (Matt 23:25).

- People would have smiled at the very idea of lighting a lamp and then putting it under a bushel basket instead of on a lampstand (Matt 5:15). That would have been a ridiculous thing to do.

- His listeners would also have considered it absurd for any parent to give their children stones instead of bread, or snakes rather than fish to eat (Matt 7:9-10).

- The discerning listener would have chuckled over the stupidity of anyone who tries to build their house on sand rather than on rock (Matt 7:26).

- The thought of a slave eating before the master of the household (Luke 17:7-10) or being considered socially equal would have caused smiles in an audience (Matt 10:24-25).

- Many would have mocked Jesus for what they considered foolish in his message: "If any want to become followers, let them deny themselves and take up their cross and follow me. For those who want to save their life will lose it, and those who lose their life for my sake will find it" (Matt 16:24-25). Here is the paradoxical condition for his followers: give up the desire for security and self-centered pleasure-seeking and be of service instead to others, especially those most in need of help. He promises a life of deep joy and tranquillity to those who accept this.

- Jesus at times draws his listeners' attention to people who act in absurd ways.[26] He describes a builder who has to stop building a house because he ran out of money (Luke 14:28-30). James and John, with the help of their mother, rashly tried to receive the places of honor beside Jesus in his kingdom (Mark 10:35-45). The behavior of those who think that the more words used at prayer, the more God will listen, is described in a humorous manner (Matt 6:7).

Jesus also makes ironic statements that would have been contrary to the social standards of his listeners and therefore seen as laughable. Children had no rights, but Jesus asserts that those who would follow him must become humble like children. Only then would they become "the greatest in the kingdom of heaven" (Matt 18:4). There is the culturally absurd point that a poor widow's small gift to the temple's treasury is considered greater than that of rich people (Mark 12:41-44).

Biblically, beatitudes are declarations of holiness because of some virtue. The bizarre nature of the Beatitudes of Jesus as viewed by his contemporaries, however, can be appreciated only when seen in the context of the prevailing culture. It was a culture that exalted authoritarian or bullying behavior. Hence, Jesus' praise of mercy would have been perceived as culturally absurd, as would a person who gave his wealth to the poor. Jesus is promising blessedness, not to people who act greedily and arrogantly, but to those who practice the opposite: "Blessed are the meek, for they will inherit the earth. . . . Blessed are the merciful, for they will receive mercy. . . ." (Matt 5:5, 7).

The pastoral epistles of St. Paul are sombre, but he uses ironical language to contrast the gaps between Christ's teachings and those of worldly people. In the First Letter to the Corinthians Paul responds to a community that is divided by various interpersonal strains and loyalties to different religious teachers. There are leaders who arrogantly forget that they are called to proclaim, not their own eloquence, but the love of God in Christ for all, especially for those without human status and power. Some wrongly believe that the body has no moral relevance at all, so they can indulge their sexual appetites and eat what they wish (1 Cor 5:1-8; 8:10, 12-13). The tensions are starkly stated. In condemning these people, Paul's style is that of cruel, sarcastic laughter (1 Cor 1:18).[27] Judged in human terms God is even considered foolish, a joke that surely God enjoys! God, the creator of the world, who "chose what is foolish in the world to shame the wise . . . [who] chose what is low and despised in the world . . . to reduce to nothing things that are, so that no one might boast in the presence of God" (1 Cor 1:27-29). Paul continues to use a humorous, yet stinging and mocking, style to highlight the differences between authentic followers of Christ and those whose loyalty is questionable. He does this by naming himself as foolish while his opponents are "wise" and "strong," held in "honor" but he is in "disrepute" (1 Cor 4:10).

The same wry humor is evident in Paul's self-assessment of his apostolic zeal in the face of personal suffering, as recorded in his Second Letter to the Corinthians. He likens himself to a fragile clay pot (2 Cor 4:7) because he is "afflicted in every way . . . persecuted . . . struck down" (2 Cor 4:8, 9); yet, paradoxically, he is not crushed or destroyed. Why? Because he is the recipient of God's "extraordinary power . . . so that the life of Jesus may also be visible" in his body (2 Cor 4:7, 10).

Comic Side of Parables

The parables are fictitious stories that Jesus tells in order to explain his teachings. In fact, about one-third of the documented sayings of Jesus in the Synoptic Gospels are in the form of parables.[28] The stories are of varying lengths, containing a meaning or message over and above the straightforward and literal, with an element of metaphor. Jesus follows the custom of his day by using richly figurative speech that is concrete, pictorial, and challenging in expressing religious ideas for which there are no corresponding abstract concepts. It is a common way of gaining people's attention. At the time of Christ, Jewish rabbis also use parables as a teaching method, but those of Jesus are extraordinary for their wit, terseness, pointed grasp of human behavior, and ability to convey profound truths in an ironic manner.[29]

The humor Jesus uses in parables is both relaxing and prophetic. Jesus' parables are relaxing in the way they disarm his listeners, who would at times be violently resisting his teachings had they not been "dressed-up" in story form. In listening to parables, hearers gradually discover that in passing judgment on what is happening they are in fact condemning their own behavior. Of course prophetic humor is the primary aim of Jesus' parables, for he intentionally aims to teach fundamental truths. In the parable of the two sons Jesus describes a situation in which both are separately asked by their father to work in his vineyard. One agrees but does not go; the other refuses, but later changes "his mind and went" (Matt 21:29). Jesus' listeners, when asked who "did the will of the father?" (Matt 21:31) rightly choose the first son. Jesus then applies their conclusion to his own teachings. Tax collectors and prostitutes are like the second son, for they are obeying Jesus' instructions and entering his kingdom ahead of the listeners (Matt 21:31-32)—a brilliantly worded expression of divine humor.

Other parables also have a humorous twist. Consider, for example, when Jesus describes the nature of the kingdom of God by likening it to a tiny mustard seed that, when planted, "became a tree, and the birds of the air made nests in its branches" (Luke 13:19). Again, the complacent, self-righteous Pharisee believes that he is superior to the tax collector, but Jesus condemns him for his arrogance and applauds the humility and honesty of the publican (Luke 18:10-14).

In the Prodigal Son story (Luke 15:11-32) the delinquent son, having lived in luxury, finds himself in an incongruous place—with the pigs, which are despised in Jewish culture. The incongruity is resolved through his conversion and decision to seek pardon from his father. Of course the ultimate meaning is even more paradoxical: God's love and mercy for the repentant and outcast in society. The tension between the demands of justice and mercy is resolved beyond human imagining in favor of compassion and mercy. Finally, there is a small aspect of the parable that would certainly have been seen as funny by Jesus' listeners: the father running toward his son (Luke 15:20). Wealthy and powerful men never ran. Indeed, it would have been a culturally shameful thing to have done, something beneath their dignity. Jesus' listeners, especially those who were poor, would have chuckled to themselves at the thought of such a topsy-turvy happening.

The humorous irony in the Good Samaritan story (Luke 10:29-37) is that the priest and the Levite, professionally committed to maintaining Jewish religious traditions, fail in their duties of care for the severely injured victim of a robbery. The Samaritan, a non-Jew, spontaneously goes to the aid of the wounded person. Again, the deeper meaning of the story is one of divine humor. Jesus exemplifies the qualities of the Good Samaritan. He reveals God's preferential love for those considered socially or physically powerless. But to return to the Samaritan, the immediate hero of the parable. Samaritans were considered by Jewish people to be racially inferior. For this reason those who listened to Jesus telling the story would have been not just surprised but shocked to hear that such a person—one marginalized by Jewish culture—becomes the caregiver. But the hero is also marginalized by his own Samaritan people. Traders in oil and wine were considered by both Jewish and Samaritans to be shady, thieving characters who commonly frequented inns, which were well-known as dirty and dangerous places.[30] In short, the Samaritan is a religious and social outcast, but he is the one who spontaneously helps the victim. There is a humorous aspect to the involvement of the fifth character in the story, the innkeeper. Since inns were dens of thieves the listeners to the parable would expect the innkeeper to be a thief himself, yet he is the one who is prepared to help the victim, for a price. The Samaritan seeks to build relationships with this shady character, but the caregiver is no dreamer, out of touch with the weaknesses of human nature. Knowing what to expect from the innkeeper, the Samaritan simply bribes him in order to guarantee that the patient will be looked after and kept alive: "Take care of him; and when I come back, I will repay you whatever more you spend" (Luke 10:35). So the humorous surprise in the story is the fact that one considered a religious and social outcast is the hero. He also turns his knowledge of how thieves operate to good advantage by so shrewdly negotiating with the innkeeper. It takes a thief to know the ways of a thief!

Comic Actions

Actions are for Jesus the most powerful form of preaching his mission. Since so many of these actions ran against the cultural norms of the time, they would have evoked mocking laughter in those who resisted conversion and the laughter of the heart or inner joy in people open to transformation (see figure 1.1). Once again, we need to be aware of the local culture to see the full relevance of Jesus' humorous actions.

Associating with Samaritans

As noted above, Jews looked on Samaritans in a racist manner, believing them to be innately stupid, lazy, and heretical. And the Samaritans had similar views of their Jewish neighbors. "There was no deeper breach of human relations in the contemporary world," comments John McKenzie, "than the feud of Jews and Samaritans, and the breadth and depth of Jesus' doctrine of love could demand no greater act of a Jew than to accept a Samaritan as a brother."[31] But Jesus goes out of his way to converse with Samaritans, as he did with the Samaritan woman at the well (John 4:9). The woman is startled to receive a request for water from a man who is a Jew, and further surprised that Jesus is willing to carry on a lengthy discussion with her. The disciples can see the culturally incompatible nature of the incident and are shocked and embarrassed to see Jesus conversing with the woman (John 4:27). The Good Samaritan is proposed as an example of love of one's neighbor (Luke 10:33-37). And this conversation has surprising results. The Samaritan woman comes to believe Jesus is the Messiah and, through her testimony, many other Samaritans believe in Jesus (John 4:39-42). Jesus not only associated with Samaritans, he healed them as well. Recall that only one of the ten lepers whom Jesus healed came back to thank him (Luke 17:16).[32] Who was this man filled with gratitude? A Samaritan!

Befriending People who are Marginalized

Contrary to the behavior of the Pharisees, Jesus associates with "tax collectors and sinners," that is, those who are publicly known to be violators of the Jewish moral and ritual code (Luke 15:1-2). The incident where Jesus meets Zacchaeus, the chief tax collector of Jericho, is humorously told in Luke (19:1-10). This local dignitary, small of stature, climbs a tree in order to see Jesus. Jesus calls Zacchaeus down from the tree and invites himself to Zacchaeus's house for a meal. This was shocking enough for observers, but when they heard of Zacchaeus's radical conversion to Christ they must have thought it outrageous. Surely there would have been a smile on the face of Jesus as he overheard the hypocritical comments of these spectators.

Conversing with the Oppressive Elite

While disagreeing theologically with the scribes and Pharisees, Jesus nonetheless remains friendly, open to them, or unprejudiced toward them. We even see him dining with a Pharisee, overlooking the fact at first that his host has given him no socially required welcome. But then a woman, who is a sinner, on hearing that Jesus is in the house, enters and begins to wash his feet, causing immense displeasure to the host. If Jesus was a true prophet, argues the Pharisee, he would not associate with such a public sinner (Luke 7:39). Jesus uses the occasion to point out gently what true conversion means; he reflects on the deep repentance and love of the woman who bathed "his feet with her tears and dried them with her hair" (Luke 7:44).

Acknowledging Gender Equality

According to Jewish culture, women were considered inferior to men and conversing with them in public was socially forbidden. Jesus, however, often expresses concern for the welfare of women, but in ways that are not condescending or prejudiced; he heals sick women (e.g., Mark 1:29-31; Matt 9:18-26) and forgives sinners among them. And he appears to Mary Magdalene before he reveals himself to the apostles; she is charged to carry the news of his resurrection to the disciples (John 20:11-18).[33] These episodes show a total lack of misogyny in Jesus, in dramatic contrast to the prevailing patriarchal attitudes that affected even his disciples.

Dying on a Cross

In this chapter we have highlighted various expressions and uses of humor in the Scriptures, but it ends with this ultimate paradox—the foolishness of the cross (1 Cor 1:18). In Jesus' time execution by crucifixion was considered the cruelest and most dishonorable form of capital punishment. Jesus, Son of God, was sentenced to this brutal form of death. The convicted person's name and crime were written on a placard for display. In the case of Jesus this was nailed above his head, but by Pilate's irony there was no criminal charge but the title "King of the Jews" (Matt 27:37). The added ignominy was to be crucified between two thieves who mocked him (Mark 15:32). Others also mocked him—the legionnaires (Mark 15:16-19), the general public (Mark 15:29-30), and "the chief priests, along with the scribes" (Mark 15:31-32).

The Foolishness of the Cross: An Example

In 1971 I spent a memorable Easter in a very remote village in the jungle of the highlands of Papua New Guinea. People had tramped for several days to participate in the Holy Week rituals. After the Good Friday ritual I noticed an illiterate member of the congregation looking intently but smilingly at the uncovered cross. I asked him why he appeared so joyful on such a day. His unforgettable reply in broken English startled me. "I smile because I am all happy all inside. Jesus died painfully, yes. But he came alive again three days later, all because he loves me. I am a poor man. I am a sinner. But Jesus loves me because he dies for me. That gives me peace right inside me! One day I will be with him. Then no more worries, no more big sufferings."

This is true laughter of the heart, the inner joy and peace that God alone can give through his death and resurrection: "By his great mercy he has given us a new birth into a living hope through the resurrection of Jesus Christ from the dead, and into an inheritance that is imperishable, undefiled, and unfading, kept in heaven for you" (1 Pet 1:3-4). We cannot speak of the divine humor of the cross if we deny the resurrection (1 Cor 15:12-14). My uneducated respondent in Papua New Guinea believed in the cross *and* the resurrection. And it was this belief that caused his inner joy of the heart, "the peace of God, which surpasses all understanding" (Phil 4:7), and the smile on his face. In the resurrection God is laughing at death and my respondent joined in that laugh with the apostle Paul: "Death has been swallowed up in victory. Where, O death, is your victory? Where, O death, is your sting?" (1 Cor 15:54-55).

How Paul would have loved listening to this simple man's wisdom! Paul at one point ponders how the face of the risen Christ reflects the glory of the creator God: "For it is the God who said, 'Let light shine out of the darkness,' who has shown in our hearts to give the light of the knowledge of the glory of God in the face of Jesus Christ" (2 Cor 4:6). Paul's heart was so transformed by this same light that he could exclaim: "I have been crucified with Christ; and it is no longer I who live, but it is Christ who lives in me" (Gal 2:19-20). The message of my respondent in all its simplicity was the same as Paul's, and it showed in his face. For myself, the event will always inspire me with faith and a deeper understanding of what true laughter of the heart means. An illiterate person teaching me theology! Is that not a sign also of divine humor itself?

Summary

- The holy book is filled with humor. It is the story of divine incongruity—God's pursuing and forgiving love of fickle humankind, to the point of dying that we might become "a new creation" (2 Cor 5:17). God keeps relating to us in humanly illogical ways that we describe as divine humor. We expect God to be a distant creator, one who is revengeful because we are so wayward, but the opposite is the case (Isa 58:9). And there are humorous incidents aplenty in the Scriptures, though little recording of visible laughter. But laughter of the heart, that is, the inner joyous spirit of those who are transformed by God's love, is manifestly present throughout. Hence, "in many important ways the Bible has sided with comedy, and, in turn, comedy has sided with the Bible."[34]

- In the psalms we find in a concentrated way the meaning of laughter of the heart. In times of praise, sorrow, and thanksgiving the psalmists discover what it means to be an intimate companion of God. This evokes an interior joy and trust, an energizing newness that even the most distressing suffering does not hide. Jesus Christ, the master teacher, uses humor in its various forms as his main method of teaching, especially in his parables. Human pride, pomposity, selfishness, and avarice are all the objects of the deflating power of humor. Yet Christ is more than the master teacher. He became divine humor incarnate in our midst. Moved by an overwhelming love for us, on the day of his resurrection he triumphed over death. This is the ultimate source of authentic laughter of the heart: "This is the day that the Lᴏʀᴅ has made; let us rejoice and be glad in it" (Ps 118:24).

• The next chapter explains how initiation rituals follow a joking pattern, which is essential for understanding the comic quality of the many rites of passage in both Testaments in the chapters that follow.

Chapter 3

Joking and Life's Transitions

> *A joke is a play upon form that affords an opportunity for realising that accepted pattern has no necessity. . . . All jokes have this subversive effect on the dominant structure of ideas. . . . In classing the joke as a symbol of social, physical and mental experience, we are already treating it as a rite.*
>
> Mary Douglas[1]

This chapter explains:

- the meaning of culture: symbols, myths, and rituals;
- that initiation rituals follow a joking pattern;
- that initiation rituals articulate the transition of people from one cultural status to another;
- that comedians call people to acknowledge the paradoxes within themselves and their cultures.

All cultures have rituals of initiation, often termed "rites of passage," or "rites of life's transitions." They refer to particular rituals that mark the progress of an individual or group between relatively stable, generally recognized states of rank, status, office, calling, or profession. These rituals are also called "joking rituals" because they follow the joking pattern as we briefly described in chapter 1. Since there are many such rituals in Scripture, we will now explain in some depth what they mean and why the use of the word "joking" is appropriate.

This explanation owes much to cultural anthropologists Mary Douglas[2] and Victor Turner. Douglas, in her groundbreaking anthropological analysis of joking, concludes that in rites of transition there is, as in joking, a letting go of one meaning and the acquisition of a totally different one—a transforming journey of detachment from once acceptable behavior and the embrace of new ways of thinking and acting. At the heart of the ritual there is the incongruous situation in which two contrary meaning systems are in conflict. One must give way to the other. Speaking of this kind of transition St. Paul writes, "When I was a child, I spoke like a child. . . . when I became an adult, I put an end to childish ways" (1 Cor 13:11).

Since initiation or joking rituals occur within a cultural context it is first important to understand the power and dynamics of culture.

Culture

A culture is not simply "what people do around here" but, more important, it is an ongoing, evolving pattern of meanings encased in symbols, myths, and rituals. This network of meanings provides people with a sense of identity, teaching them how to feel, think, and behave toward themselves and others.[3] A culture's primary purpose is to provide us with a feeling of predictable order, identity, and security; culture is about maintaining the comforting status quo. People often think that organizational change is simple, but they overlook the power of culture in their lives. In workshops on culture change I ask participants who think this way: "Are you open to change?" Of course, they reply, otherwise they would not have come to the workshop. Then I ask them: "Where did you sit before this morning's coffee break?" They generally respond with a blank look because the question seems irrelevant to them. Eventually they reply: "In the same seats we sat in after the break!" I ask them for their reasons and they admit that they just do not like to change since it means having to adjust to anxiety-creating and unfamiliar situations. Then they see the point of my original question. Culture, in brief, protects us from the disturbing experience of dislocation and ultimately chaos, which is the radical breakdown of security.[4]

Culture is mostly an unconscious process that shapes a people's emotional reactions to the whole world of people, events, and things. It permeates the deepest recesses of the human group and individuals, particularly their feelings. Culture is something that "tugs at one's heart." The following case study of a dissatisfied migrant illustrates the powerful emotional pull of his culture of origin.

The Power of Culture

A young British migrant who had lived in Australia for several years decided to return to Liverpool; the reasons given illustrate the power of culture to "tug at the heart." A newspaper records his comments:

> Everything is wonderful, but we don't like it. When we wake up in the morning, I'm sick of looking at the blue sky. I want the grey, misery, drizzle, rain. . . . We just have a yearning to be among our ilk. . . . Australian birds cannot sing like British birds. . . . I just want to go out and throw a stone just to get rid of the birds. . . . Hidden behind every bush you've got a snake or a poisonous spider. . . . [White ants] can destroy your house within days. . . . Australian pubs are filled with bikers and rednecks. . . . You'd probably get beaten up if you went there. They all look like savages.[5]

In this case study, despite the material benefits of living in Australia, the migrant still feels out of place there and uses exaggerated language to express his sentiments. He yearns to feel "at home again," with all its comforting familiar securities and predictabilities. He has been unable to leave behind the interpretive framework, with its strong emotional ties that worked so well in Liverpool, and to confidently embrace the unfamiliar culture of Australia.

Symbol

Symbols are at the heart of all cultures. A symbol—such as the Union Jack flag for the British or the White House for Americans—is any object that by its very dynamism or power makes one think about, imagine, get into contact with, or reach out to a deeper, even transcendent, reality, through the dynamism of the symbol itself, and without additional explanations.[6] Symbols are felt or experienced meanings. Whenever I see a photo of my mother and father I experience their presence. In the above case study the powerful negative symbols for the migrant are the blue sky, snakes, and poisonous spiders of Australia. To see the blue sky, for example, is to revive for the migrant their unattractive experiences of their life in Australia. On the other hand, gray skies and rain remind the migrant of the positive, reassuring qualities of Liverpool.

Myth

Contrary to popular belief, myths are not fairy tales or fallacies. A myth is a set of narrative symbols that claim to reveal to people, in an imaginative way, fundamental truths about the world and themselves. These truths are considered authoritative by those who accept them, as in the Exodus myth for the Israelites and the arrival of the Pilgrim Fathers in North America for many nonblack citizens. Myths are stories that inspirationally or emotionally tell people who they are, what is good and bad, and how they are to organize themselves and maintain their feeling of unique identity in the world. Myths provide people with a worldview and their place within it. The truths that myths convey cannot be contained or articulated in ordinary technical language because myths, unlike technical statements, touch the hearts of people. Every organization, whatever its size, will have its myths. The psychologist Rollo May writes that "myths are like beams in a house: not exposed to outside view, they are the structure that holds the house together so people can live in it."[7] Myths provide direction and energy for a people. They are the emotional glue that binds a people together at the deepest level of their collective being. So in times of chaos myths need to be retold and re-owned to give people their sense of bonding and energy to face the turmoil that threatens their existence.

The most powerful and essential myth in every culture is its creation myth, since it provides people with their primary source of identity as a distinct group within the global society, time, and space.[8] The Great Seal of the United States (which is copied on one side of the one-dollar bill) aims to remind Americans that in the minds of the founding fathers, God, or some extraordinary destiny, calls them to participate in a new Exodus, a new journey from poverty and oppression in order to build a new promised land.[9] In times of crisis such creation myths relieve anxiety, providing a sense of group self-worth and uniqueness. Not only are creation myths the most all-embracing of mythic proclamations, addressing themselves to the widest range of questions and meanings and values, but they are the most profound. They are concerned with the relation of the unknowable to the known, for example, the American foundation myth describes the relation between the deity and the people he has called to establish "a new order of things" through the world's greatest experiment in democracy. Often the original reality out of which the absolute created the world is considered to be primal chaos, for example, the "new promised land" of America for the early Pilgrims. Rather than being something negative, chaos is viewed as something positive inasmuch as order can emerge from it.

Ritual

Ritual, a form of storytelling, is the stylized or repetitive symbolic use of bodily movement and gesture to express and articulate meaning within a cultural context.[10] Thus, there are rituals in sports, dancing, traffic, politics, or any human interaction in which meanings that are encased in symbols and myths are visibly expressed and articulated. Ritual action also occurs within cultural contexts in an effort to deal with possible or real tension. We see this in the Western custom of shaking hands as a means to resolve or hide conflict; this is a gesture of set form that, outwardly at least, conveys that peace has been restored.

Ritual is sometimes thought to mean something superficial, empty, and meaningless, a boring ceremony to be endured from time to time. On the contrary, ritual is among the most basic, frequent, and important of human actions, without which we could not remain human. We would be unable to communicate with one another. If there were no rituals accepted by all players in a football game there would be total chaos. Again, when young people do not have rituals that formally symbolize their passage from adolescence to adulthood, it is difficult for them and others in society to know what is expected of them. Ritual is the means by which we seek and establish orderly roles and boundaries for ourselves and for society. It reassures us that we are in control in the midst of a chaotic world, as seen in something so ordinary as the traffic laws that give us a sense of safety when we drive. In brief, ritual has the potential to transform people and their cultural environment; it can create a dedicated, collaborative employee or an office bully.

A fundamental tension in society is that between order and creativity. Without constant openness to creativity people fall victim to the deadening seduction of the social status quo. But to break the power of suffocating order people need actually or symbolically to experience the darkness of chaos, that is, the radical breakdown of order. This abyss of darkness often disrupts us in life when the ordinary support of our cultural or personal security no longer functions: at the death of a friend, a midlife crisis, the loss of employment, or the breakdown of one's marriage. Experiences of this kind can be confusing, even terrifying; but, paradoxically, contact with the unknown is critical *if* there is to be creativity in life or culture. This is why rituals of transition are so important. They help us to acknowledge the chaos with some safety and re-own an old, or embrace a new, mythology that can energize us to move forward. In the sacraments of initiation the symbolism of chaos is a critical stage in the ritual. In baptism the candidate is rescued from the chaos of the darkness of sin and brought to the dignity of an adopted child of God. In the Eucharist we are invited to unite ourselves with Christ in the midst of the chaos of the cross and to embrace with him the joy of the resurrection. We now look more closely at the nature and power of rituals of transition or initiation.

Initiation: Dynamics

Initiation rituals are particular transformative rituals that celebrate important transitions of an individual or group to a new status in life, such as from work to retirement, single to married, conflict to reconciliation, sin to grace, death to life. Old or new myths must be articulated, re-owned or owned for the first time in view of the particular conditions in which individuals or groups find themselves. Initiation rituals are called regenerative when people re-own a myth that has been lost or is in danger of being lost.

In the case study of the dissatisfied immigrant to Australia who wants to return "home," the problem is that he has refused to undergo an initiation ritual or "rite of passage" into a new culture. He rejected the chance to let go the mythology that he lived by in England and adopt an Australian one. He went through the legal formalities of accepting Australia as his home, but his heart had not made the transformation.

In the ritual process of initiation there are the same tripartite psychosocial phases as in patterns of joking (see chap. 1): separation, liminality, and reaggregation (figure 3.1).

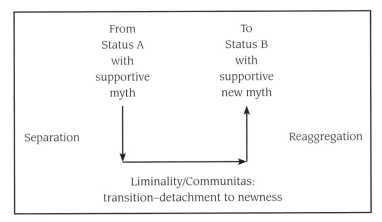

Figure 3.1: A Rite of Passage

Separation

In this brief first stage people are reminded that they are about to make a break with the routine of everyday life. This separation will be marked in various symbolic ways: when people are about to go on vacation they may change from business to informal attire; the baptismal ritual begins, not in the sanctuary, but at the door of the church to indicate to the congregation that something important is to take place; trainees for an elite Marine corps have their heads shaved at the beginning of their training course.

Liminality[11]

This is the intermediary stage between the old and the new status. In the liminal stage, sometimes referred to as the "threshold stage," there is a deliberate ritual status or social leveling. In this liminal stage Marines in training are without roles or status as though, in relation to the society from which they have come or the society into which they are to be incorporated later, they are anonymous, nonpersons. They are in a social wilderness[12]; they have no distinguishing insignia to demarcate them structurally from one another. The purpose of this ritual stripping of former status to the level of cultural nakedness is to dispose them to develop deep, interpersonal relationships with one another and an openness to the mythology of the group they are to join. They must let go of the myths that underpin their former status and be transformed by those of the new status. The liminal stage is sometimes referred to as the *chaos phase* simply because chaos is the breakdown of the culturally predictable order of living. Little wonder that this is a time of significant tension. Hence, the importance of the ritual to guide the process of status change.

There are two types of liminality: spontaneous and normative.[13] Survivors from a sinking ship experience spontaneous liminality; status diversity is totally unimportant to these people as they face the very real possibility of death together, and this experience gives rise to a fellowship or, as it is sometimes called, *communitas*. What binds them together is their common humanity. Normative liminality exists when people deliberately attempt to establish a liminal situation that ideally should lead to a *communitas* experience. The sacraments are examples of normative liminality; they remind us that before God we are all sinners in need of redemption. The ritual of marriage aims to evoke normative liminality by publicly reminding the participants that they are to leave a single state for a lifelong partnership. Often the root metaphor in the liminal stage of ritual is the mythology of death and resurrection—death to the old status and the rising to the new.

The symbols of liminality may be called "anti-normal symbols" because they connote a status for the participants that is nonhierarchical and undifferentiated when compared with normal life. The survivors in the lifeboat instinctively recognize the irrelevancy of titles when faced with possible death—the universal, liminal leveler; the use of first names is an anti-normal symbol. As we will see in chapter 5, Jesus uses the anti-normal symbols of desert, mountaintops, and sea to draw the attention of the disciples, alerting them that some important learning is to occur. The anti-normal symbols help to provide the physical, psychological, moral, and spiritual shocks necessary to evoke reflection and begin the process of transformation.

In the case of the training of Marines, the boot camp conditions are anti-normal symbols to remind them of their duty to learn and interiorize the founding mythology of toughness under extreme conditions, extraordinary bravery, and loyal service to the nation in times of grave risk. If participants are converted to the myths of the new status, as they pass out of liminality they will feel the urge to re-create the world according to their experience of the mythology. Liminality is therefore subversive of the social status quo from which the initiates have come. The incongruous tension between the symbols of "softness" and "toughness" must be resolved by putting aside the former in favor of the latter.

Saint Paul and Baptism

Saint Paul's description of baptism succinctly describes the ritual process of initiation in which there is union with Christ in his death. This is the liminal stage in which the candidate dies to the previous state with its underlying mythology of sinfulness. Then there is the energizing newness of the resurrection. "Do you not know that all of us who have been baptized into Christ Jesus were baptized into his death? Therefore we have been buried with him by baptism into death, so that, just as Christ was raised from the dead by the glory of the Father, so we too might walk in newness of life" (Rom 6:3-4).

Ignatian Spirituality

If in the Ignatian Spiritual Exercises the retreatant is to be open to inner transformation and to a creative apostolic response to *re*-turning to Christ, then the mystery or mythology of Christ's life, death, and resurrection is to be *re*-lived. The retreatant must become one with Christ in a *communitas* experience. The external silence, the complete withdrawal from ordinary duties, and the demanding regime of meditations are anti-normal symbols established to evoke liminality and *communitas* with Christ by an uninterrupted journey through the paschal mystery.

Initiation rituals can also be called grieving rituals. This is especially obvious in traditional cultures where there are normally two levels of oppositional processes at work. In grieving rituals, as in all initiation or joking rituals, we find *disengagement/engagement* dynamics operative in all three stages but especially in the liminality stage. First, there is the process directed at that which has been lost. During funeral rituals in traditional cultures the dead are to be formally *disengaged* from the living; they are given permission, as it were, to leave this world and to become *engaged* in relationships with ancestral spirits elsewhere. Among the Australian Aborigines, although the spirit is independent of flesh in the sense of outlasting their disunion, a spirit is thought to haunt its former home. It must be formally encouraged to move on if it is to become an honored ancestor. The second set of disengagement/ engagement rituals relates directly to the living. They must formally become *disengaged* from the influences of the deceased, who wish to hold them back from moving forward, and *engage* themselves in forming a new set of social relationships.[14]

Reaggregation

The liminal stage is inherently unstable; people cannot live with chaos, that is, without the clarity of the roles and status of daily life, for too long. Hence, the third stage of ritual is the reaggregation process, whereby people move back into an orderly predictable way of life but in a new status and energized by the liminal experience and its resolution.

This is the most difficult of the three stages because people must constantly be applying their newly-owned zeal for creativity without being seduced back into the pre-ritual overpowering experience of the old way of life. Douglas describes the initiated coming out of seclusion as "charged with power, hot, dangerous."[15] Having been exposed to the inspirational creation mythology of their new status, they want to convert the world that they are entering. They are in danger of becoming cynical, however, once they realize the enormity of the obstacles to their enthusiasm. Hence, the need for frequently repeated regenerative rituals of initiation or transformation in order to help people maintain their enthusiasm to keep moving forward.

In summary:

- The separation stage of a ritual of transition is brief, but dramatic, so that candidates are clearly reminded that they are to participate in something of significant importance to them.

- The liminality stage is the subversive betwixt-and-between phase of transition; subversive because those being initiated must detach themselves from their old status with its mythology in order to be open to a new status and its own underlying mythology.

- Liminality is a stage that is simultaneously dangerous and filled with opportunity. It is dangerous inasmuch as candidates can refuse to undergo transformation; it is potentially creative if they are prepared to let go the old status and embrace the new.

- In the reaggregation stage people move back to ordinary everyday life, but energized by their liminal experience.

- Integral to all initiation transitions is the pattern of joking, that is, the process whereby people substitute one set of meanings for a surprising contrary set (see chap. 1).

Carnival: Ritual of Regenerative Joking

Can the subject of . . . reflection for Mardi Gras Tuesday be anything but laughter? . . . We mean the laughter that is not very pensive, the laughter that ceremonious people (passionately keen on their dignity) righteously take amiss in themselves and in others. . . . (Karl Rahner)[16]

Carnival time, such as is found in Rio de Janeiro, Brazil, and in the Mardi Gras of New Orleans, United States, is a ritual of reversal (see chap. 1). Yet it is far more than a comic social "safety valve" for the release of social tension in order to maintain the social and political status quo. Mikhail Bakhtin sees the carnival as profoundly subversive of official institutions and hierarchies, a regenerative initiation ritual.[17] All social decorum disappears. There is an orgy of outrageous dancing, including samba dancing, lavish costumes, singing, unrestrained carousing, and exhibitionism.[18] In a society where there is a strong emphasis on social, religious, and political hierarchy, the carnival is a festival of the poor over the rich and powerful. It "transforms the holistic hierarchy of everyday life into a fleeting moment dominated by magical individualistic equality."[19] The carnival is calling for the transformation of society because it surfaces the dark side of the culture with its oppositional symbols of oppressive hierarchy and equality. In a wildly outrageous liminal moment the incongruity of these two symbols is resolved in favor of equality. Among the anti-normal symbols are the outrageous nature of the behavior and the extravagant style of dress. As a ritual of regenerative initiation, with its tripartite time stages, the carnival permits a brief glance at the axiomatic values of a given culture as well as its underlying dark contradictions.

Ritual Leaders: Clowns, Jokers, Fools, and Comedians

A conceptual distinction is made between "action humor" (clowning, playing practical jokes, acting as tricksters, or shamans) and "narrative humor" (punning and telling funny stories), but in reality, action and narrative humor are usually combined in different ways.[20] Good comedians will not just tell a funny story. They will facially or in other ways act out aspects of the story; so distinctions between clowns, jokers, and comedians can be rather artificial in practice. Therefore, in this book the word "comedian" covers both action and narrative forms of humor. Commonly the words "clown," "fool," "trickster," and "joker" are used to refer to humorists in premodern culture, while "comedian" is a term reserved for humorists in modern and postmodern cultures. However, they ultimately have the same function: to provide either negative or positive humor. In medieval times the court fool was one of the few people who could in comic ways tell the truth about the misuse of political authority. In contemporary times many comedians continue to exercise this prophetic role.

All good comedians have one thing in common. They are able to touch the hearts of their audiences. Yet many comedians—Groucho Marx, Spike Milligan, Peter Sellers, John Cleese—are rather depressive people in their personal lives. They are so in touch with their own inner chaos that they tend often toward despair, although they struggle to be hopeful. Because of this inner brokenness comedians are able to relate to the hearts of their audience at a profoundly deep level. We just feel they understand. They are liminal people projecting in their behavior society's fundamental incongruities or tensions such as order and disorder, good and evil, life and death, hope and despair, body and spirit, rational and irrational, sadness and joy.[21] This is why clowns in Western societies combine both sadness and humor in their makeup and actions—the tear-filled eyes with the upturned mouth of one laughing; one minute they can be crying, the next laughing uproariously. Yet they are able at the same time to transcend these incongruities. Comedians deliberately create disorder in the midst of order to give the appearance of incongruity; they call their viewers or listeners into this incongruous situation to experience its tensions and then invite them to identify the resolution of these tensions. The social status quo is not set in concrete. The following examples illustrate this point.

Charlie Chaplin

In the days of the silent films Charlie Chaplin embodied the best of comedians. His attire and walking style simultaneously mirrored the lowest and the highest of society. With his ample trousers, a gift from the actor Fatty Arbuckle, and oversized shoes he was a tramp, but with his tight-fitting dress coat and bowler hat he appeared to belong to the top rung of society of his time. He exemplified in his films a person who, while never being successful according to the world's measures, could rise above predictable despair. He refused to be crushed by the pomposity and arrogance of government officials; in fact, such figures were reduced to objects of fun and even pity.[22]

King Lear's Fool

William Shakespeare's plays are filled with brilliant clowns and fools who are the conscience of his plays, critics of society. Perhaps the best of his clowns is King Lear's Fool. Stupid, his only reason for existence is to pacify the king. Yet Shakespeare involves the Fool so intimately in the plot that finally it is the Fool who has the answer to the tragedy. Not until Lear loses his sanity, becomes mad and as dim-witted as the gentle Fool, does he finally gain insight. The lesson is valid for all times: the king has to become a fool before he grasps the inner truth of the world.[23]

Comedians are *ritual leaders* because they perform a vital public function of reminding people of foundational cultural symbols and myths. Anthropologist Mary Douglas speaks of comedians as "ritual purifiers." She even proposes that "perhaps the joker should be classed as a kind of minor mystic"[24] because comedians invite their audiences to critique orderly structures and status in society in search of important values and truths about life. Novelist Anthony Burgess succinctly referred to this quality when he spoke at the funeral of comedian Benny Hill. Hill's comedy not only diverted listeners from "headaches, indigestion and paying taxes," but held up "a vision of the truth of what we really are."[25]

Good comedians mock on behalf of humanity the behavior of those who unduly assert authority, who overly insist on rules and obedience to traditions. Like biblical prophets, they hold out irrepressible hope for humanity that life is not necessarily preordained toward defeat, collapse, and tragedy, that fate is conquerable.[26] Comedians are moralists ready to restore balance to that which is disturbed, repressed, or deformed in society or religion.[27] They do not just condemn the world of status, wealth, power, manipulation, and violence, but in some way provide us with a feeling of hope. They are without the power the world applauds; their powerlessness gives them the freedom to challenge the world they disdain, for they depend on no one.[28]

Peter Berger asserts that humor is a revelation of transcendence, a cautious call to redemption, and for this reason "the actions of a clown take on a sacramental dignity."[29] This is what St. Paul is referring to when he describes to the fractious Corinthians his own role as a clown of Christ, without social status and power: "We are fools for the sake of Christ, but you are wise. . . . We are weak, but you are strong. You are held in honor, but we in disrepute. . . . We have become like the rubbish of the world, the dregs of all things, to this very day" (1 Cor 4:10, 13). There have been other holy comedians through the ages who perfectly exemplify the qualities of a true comedian (see chap. 8): the Old Testament prophets, St. Benedict, St. Francis, St. Catherine of Siena, Mary Ward, Dorothy Day, Gandhi, Nelson Mandela, and above all, Christ himself.

Summary

• Through symbol, myth, and ritual a culture provides people with a sense of security in a chaotic and threatening world. Ritual, which is the visible expression of a group's symbols and myths, is a way of resolving the ambiguities, paradoxes, incongruities, and apparently unfathomable tensions of daily life, for example, the tension between order and creativity, health and sickness, life and death. Ritual introduces people to the imaginative possibilities of another way of looking at life.

- Initiation rituals publicly celebrate or mark the transition of an individual or group to a new status. The inner dynamic pattern of initiation rituals follows the same process as that of joking and grieving rituals. Hence, we can speak of initiation rituals as also joking rituals. In the liminal stage of joking people are temporarily thrown into chaos, and incongruities are resolved when a relationship is seen to be meaningful in a previously overlooked way. The crust of conformity is momentarily broken and creative energy is released.

- Comedians are ritual leaders in society; they call people to acknowledge the dark tensions and paradoxes in themselves and their cultures, holding out hope that these can be resolved within the founding of a new mythology.

- The following two chapters apply these theoretical insights to the initiation rituals in the Old and New Testaments.

Chapter 4

Joking Transitions and Laughter of the Heart in the Old Testament

A good laugh is a sign of love; it may be said to give us a glimpse of, or a first lesson in, the love that God bears for every one of us. . . . God laughs, says the Bible. When the last piece of human folly makes the last burst of human laughter ring out . . . in a doomed world, is it too much to imagine that this last laugh will resemble that of God . . . and seem to convey that, in spite of everything, all's well?
  Karl Rahner, SJ[1]

May those who sow in tears reap with shouts of joy.
  Psalm 126:5

This chapter explains:

- the relationship between divine humor and biblical chaos;
- examples of the tripartite joking pattern in initiation rituals in the Old Testament;
- that prophets are God's comedians.

Misery, death, and chaos pervade much of the Old Testament. In vivid contrast, however, there are stunning ritual initiations of people into surprising, even dramatic, experiences of new life.[2] The tripartite stages (i.e., separation, liminality, and reaggregation) in the examples in this chapter show an incongruous disproportion between the level of distress and the spectacular experience of inner peace and renewed vitality, from desolation to startling consolation. At times hearts of stone become transformed into hearts of flesh (Ezek 36:26). There is drama in each ritual, but there is always a positive resolution that is characteristic of humor. This is the joking pattern—from happiness through chaos, real or threatened, to resolution. Consider the example of David's poignant lament over the loss of Jonathan: "How the mighty have fallen in the midst of battle! . . . I am distressed for you, my brother" (2 Sam 1:25-26). Then in his overwhelming sadness David consults God, and the latter calls David to an unexpected new leadership role: "'Go up . . . to Hebron.' . . . Then the people . . . came, and there anointed David king over the house of Judah" (2 Sam 2:1, 4). In each ritual the lesson is clear: God loves us so much that goodness can emerge from the chaos in surprising ways.

Divine Humor and Chaos

As earlier explained, the temporary construction of chaos is an essential ingredient of joking or initiation rituals. In scriptural initiation rituals "chaos" and its many imaginative synonyms, such as desert, sea, pit, emptiness, or mountaintop, contain a special meaning in addition to the sociological one. The word "chaos" was used by the ancient Greeks to describe the amorphous state of primeval matter prior to creation. This concept is integral to the biblical creation myth as well; the earth prior to God's creative act is depicted as formless and void, and concealed deeply under dark waters (Gen 1:2-3). "Chaos" is also found in other parts of the Scriptures, and in its particularly concrete meaning it connotes a barren wasteland (Deut 32:10), emptiness, nothingness in general (Isa 40:17). Yet chaos carries with it the notion of indeterminacy and potentiality. Through God's free creative power and mercy, and with human cooperation, new and vigorous life can spring up, new order and meaning can return to life. Nothingness and potentiality—that is the incongruity of the biblical symbol of chaos. God is a God of surprises. Through God's love and mercy disasters are the catalysts for dramatically new life to emerge. That is divine humor in action. And the lesson is this: through the eyes of faith we are to be constantly open to this action because then, like Job, we will experience laughter of the heart, a peace that is beyond all possible human understanding.

Joking Patterns and Initiation in the Old Testament

The Flood

The deluge story (Gen 6:9–9:17) exemplifies how the Hebrews used the existing Mesopotamian tradition of chaos and adapted it for their own purposes: the deceitfulness of all creation, except the honest Noah; the decision of God to allow creation to return to chaos; God's goodwill toward humankind and creation, which allows new life to emerge.

The pattern of the narrative follows the initiation process. The separation stage (Gen 6:9-22) is marked by the description of the world as "corrupt in God's sight, and the earth was filled with violence" (Gen 6:11). Noah, faithfully believing in God and obeying what must have seemed God's quite absurd directives, builds an ark for his family and selected animals. God promises to establish a special protective covenant with Noah, the second Adam, and his family (Gen 6:18). The actual great flood and its receding indicate the liminal stage (Gen 7:1–8:19). The paradox is: God created the world, yet will destroy it: "He blotted out every living thing that was on the face of the ground, human beings and animals . . ." (Gen 7:23). But Noah and all with him were spared. Then the incongruous situation is resolved: "God remembered Noah. . . . And God made a wind blow over the earth, and the waters subsided . . ." (Gen 8:1). The lesson for God's people through the centuries is that God never forgets his covenants with people; what happened in the deluge prefigures the dramatic time of the Exodus (Exod 2:24) and the Exile. God will allow chaos to occur when his chosen people fail to live up to their covenant commitment, but from this turmoil a loving God will bring new life into being. In the reaggregation stage (Gen 8:20–9:17) there is the joyful experience of God reassuring Noah that a covenant has been established with him and his descendants, with the promise that "never again shall all flesh be cut off by the waters of a flood . . ." (Gen 9:11).

Abraham's Journey

Abraham, our ancestor in faith, is a model for what it means to respond to God's call. Those called must sever their relationship with the world that entraps them in material things and set out on a pilgrimage with God in faith, trusting in the divine humor of forgiveness and generosity. At the heart of the journey there is the ongoing tension between the desire to stop on the wayside and enjoy the human security it offers and the invitation from God to keep striving for promised blessings in the unknown future. Only through ever-developing faith is this paradoxical tension of opposites—this world and God—able to be resolved. Now let us look at the stages of Abram's pilgrimage, in which the joking initiation ritual establishes a model for people of faith throughout history.

The separation stage, with its summons to Abram and promise of blessings, is short and dramatic: "Go from your country and your kindred . . . to the land that I will show you" (Gen 12:1). Abram's response is immediate and positive. The liminal stage is lengthy. It is a journey into the wasteland of unknown temptations and trials. Abram must embrace a new mythology, namely, trust in God at an ever-deepening level. Although he is reassured that God will always be with him, Abram's journey into the unknown leaves him fragile. Quickly he begins to trust himself rather than God. Fearful for his life Abram pretends that his wife Sarai is his sister (Gen 12:10-20). God surprisingly uses Pharaoh, of all people, to help Abram understand the stupidity of trying to be cunning to escape danger, an act that adds to the qualities of divine humor in the incident. The effort to use the maidservant Hagar in order to ensure he has descendants is another example of Abram's failure to trust in God (Gen 16). Abram succeeds in his journey only as long as he learns that faith in God calls him to let go all human certitudes.

The ultimate call to purify his commitment to God is the summons to sacrifice his own son and to trust in the ever-renewing power of God (Gen 22:1-19). The fact that Abraham is ready to take this enormous step testifies to the extraordinary depth that he has reached in his transformation. This is one of the paradoxes of the liminal stage. With God's help, Abraham's yearning for a son has been fulfilled in a remarkable manner, despite the advanced age and doubts of Sarah. Now, however, this is to come to nothing. The beloved Isaac, who is destined to be the very future of God's chosen people, is to be sacrificed. But all the while Abraham still believes in God and that God's ways are not our ways. He passes the test: "he proved faithful" (Sir 44:20).

The reaggregation stage occurs in two parts. First, God blesses Abraham for passing this final test, confirming and establishing the promise given him at the beginning of the initiation journey (Gen 12:1-3; 22:16, 18). God approves of Abraham "in all things" (Gen 24:1). Second, there is to be the ongoing development of salvation history as promised to him and his descendants. So, it has not been just an initiation ritual for an individual to grow in personal faith, but it has been a process through which Abraham becomes "the great father of a multitude of nations" (Sir 44:19). As a sign of Abram's successful initiation into the life of God, his name is changed from Abram to Abraham (Gen 17:5).

Exodus: Archetypal Experience

The initiation pattern of the Exodus, with its comic paradox of chaos and divine intervention, is worth careful examination. It is through this ritual that the travelers formally change from a motley gathering of selfish and ungrateful individuals to God's special people. What could be humanly funnier, more incongruous! The separation phase is the journeying of the Israelites out of Egypt, led by God in a pillar of cloud by day and fire at night, rejoicing that they are at last escaping oppression (Exod 13:17-22). Like all separation stages this phase for the Israelites is filled with dramatic events, such as their escape through the sea and the destruction of the Egyptian army (Exod 14).

In the liminality stage in the desert God allows the Israelites to be tempted, and when they fall they comically think they can survive without God. They say to Aaron, "Come, make gods for us, who shall go before us" (Exod 32:1). Their reliance on other gods and their own strength ends in bickering and fighting among themselves, weariness, and total loss of direction, but God is waiting for them to admit to their self-made chaos. God invites them to acknowledge and embrace the chaos of their failings, but not to linger too long over what they have done. They must face the future with hope and wait to experience his action of uplifting newness in their hearts.[3] Then, they experience a *communitas* with God and one another beyond all human comprehension. They discover in the chaos that if they obey God's commandments and keep the covenant they shall be God's "treasured possession out of all the peoples" (Exod 19:5). They will find "The LORD . . . merciful and gracious . . . , abounding in steadfast love and faithfulness, keeping steadfast love for the thousandth generation" (Exod 34:6-7).

Reflecting on the creative power of the desert, Moses challenges the Israelites never to forget the lessons of liminality in this initiation ritual: "Remember the long way that the LORD your God has led you . . . in the wilderness, in order to humble you, testing you to know what was in your heart. . . . He humbled you by letting you hunger, then by feeding you with manna . . . in order to make you understand that one does not live by bread alone, but by every word that comes from the mouth of the LORD" (Deut 8:2-3).

The reaggregation stage of the ritual is depicted in the book of Joshua. Here is traced the history of the Israelites from the death of Moses to that of his successor, Joshua. The book recounts the Israelite's entry into the Promised Land and its partition among the twelve tribes. Their proclaimed loyalty to God, marking the end of the liminal experience in the desert, is quickly tested in the reaggregation stage. They fail the test by disobeying God. They must learn *anew* that there is but one God and that whenever they cease to offer God total loyalty they must expect chaos: "you will be unable to stand before your enemies until you take away the devoted things from among you" (Josh 7:13). So from bitter experience they relearn the fundamental lesson of the liminality stage: "If you forsake the Lord and serve foreign gods, then he will turn and do you harm, and consume you, after having done you good" (Josh 24:20). The people declare they have learned this basic message by rediscovering and re-owning their fundamental creation myth in the liminality of the desert: "for it is the Lord our God who brought us and our ancestors up from the land of Egypt, out of the house of slavery. . . . Therefore we also will serve the Lord, for he is our God" (Josh 24:17-18).

Job

The book of Job, surely one of the world's finest pieces of literature, depicts the sufferings of innocent people.[4] Many Israelites believe that God rewards the righteous with material well-being, as the book of Proverbs asserts (1:33; 3:1-2), but this contradicts the experience of many God-fearing people, including Job. The author examines the problem in story form and in a series of poems, and ventures some new solutions to the puzzling issue. William Whedbee has cogently argued that the book contains at least two central features of comedy: its perception of incongruity and its basic plot line that finally leads to joy for Job and his return to a harmonious society.[5] The playwright Christopher Fry makes the same claim. He speaks of Job as "the great reservoir of comedy."[6]

The separation stage of Job's experience occurs in the first two chapters of the book. Job is the model of the righteous man, blessed with many children, good health, social respectability, and large flocks and herds. He has shown justice and compassion to widows, orphans, and strangers, that is, toward people especially loved by God but marginalized by Israelite society. For him everything is flourishing. Then disasters begin to hit, including the development of "loathsome sores . . . from the sole of his foot to the crown of his head" (Job 2:7), but his reaction of calm acceptance and patience receives no support from his wife, who demands that he should curse God and die (Job 2:9). Job refuses to change his attitude: "You speak as any foolish woman. . . . Shall we receive the good at the hand of God, and not receive the bad?" (Job 2:10). The storyteller is indicating to listeners that a paradox is about to be presented.

Job's liminality stage begins in chapter 3 and continues through chapter 42. Job's three friends sit with him, silently contemplating the catastrophes that have befallen him, believing they are all in retribution for Job's sinfulness. His secure world has disintegrated because he has lost everything: wealth, health, and family. His whole herd is stolen, his children are killed, and he himself is covered with bleeding sores. No one will approach him for fear of catching the same disease. The rubbish dump where Job sits and the sores that he pitifully scratches with some broken pottery are vivid anti-normal symbols of his personal chaos. Job breaks down, cursing the day he was born (Job 3). He laments his desperate loneliness and his abandonment by God: "so I am allotted months of emptiness, and nights of misery are apportioned to me" (Job 7:3); "I say to the Pit, 'You are my Father,' and to the worm, 'My mother,' or 'My sister,' where then is my hope?" (Job 17:14-15).

Here is the paradox that troubles Job in the depth of his heart. He has done all the right things, despite the protestations of his friends, yet God is punishing him. Puzzled by this incongruous situation, Job cries to God: "If I sin, what do I do to you, you watcher of humanity? Why have you made me your target? Why have I become a burden to you?" (Job 7:20). He gazes nostalgically back to his years of prosperity. His wife encourages him to curse God and his friends berate him and accuse him of insulting God, but Job continues to call on God who now seems utterly inaccessible and uninterested in his plight: "Oh, that I knew where I might find him, that I might come even to his dwelling!" (Job 23:3). Yet, in the midst of his darkness, Job still has energizing hope: "For I know that my Redeemer lives, and that at the last he will stand upon the earth . . . then in my flesh I shall see God, whom I shall see on my side" (Job 19:25-27).

Having put aside his grief Job is open to hear God's response to the bewildering mystery of evil. The world, Job discovers, is alive with the mystery of God's wisdom. In spite of what Job or others might think, God is in charge and holds all creation together. There is to be no return to primeval chaos. Job is reassured that God cares for him far more than all the animals. His sufferings have befallen him in line with God's wisdom, the same wisdom that allows Job to have good health and material prosperity (Job 38:1–40:2; 40:6–41:34). Confronted with evil, human reason alone is powerless to understand; only faith in God makes evil bearable. And the ultimate measure for judging whether or not people are devout is the moral quality of their lives and not the fortuitous status of their material wealth.[7] The incongruous situation that Job has been grappling with from the beginning of the book's narrative is resolved, but in a way unimagined by human reason. A deep inner peace enters Job's soul.

Gifted with this wisdom, Job enters the reaggregation stage, marked by a moving prayer of humility, with gratitude that reflects his inner joy and tranquillity: "I know that you can do all things, and that no purpose of yours can be thwarted. . . . I had heard of you by the hearing of the ear, but now my eye sees you; therefore I despise myself, and repent in dust and ashes" (Job 42:2, 5-6). The fact that his material prosperity is restored is insignificant when compared with Job's newly-found wisdom, this incomparable gift of laughter of the heart.

The lesson that Job learned remains universally relevant. Like Job, we are called to surrender our entire selves to God's all-embracing wisdom and love; we hope that God will give us the same surprising gift of new insight and consolation: "I have uttered what I did not understand, things too wonderful for me, which I did not know" (Job 42:3). No longer does Job's heart faint within him (Job 19:27). Yet despite his newfound wisdom, he is aware that he is but touching the surface of God's loving concern: "These are indeed but the outskirts of his ways; and how small a whisper do we hear of him!" (Job 26:14).

Samson

The story of Samson, a physical giant of a man given to erotic attachments to women, is one of the most cleverly written tales in Scripture (Judg 13–16). It follows the tripartite comic process: from success against the Philistines, to tragic experiences made worse by his own amoral behavior ending in his death, and then an incongruous triumph. Delilah discovers the secret of Samson's astounding strength, which lies in his uncut hair. When his hair is cut, Samson is captured and blinded; but in a last show of strength, as his hair grows, he seizes the pillars that support the house where the Philistines are celebrating, and dies with his mocking captors (Judg 16:4-31). In the chaos of his blindness and captivity—that is, the liminal stage of Samson's journey—he throws himself on the mercy of God and pleads for strength (Judg 16:28). J. Cheryl Exum and J. William Whedbee explain that "Samson's prayer re-establishes his relationship with Yahweh . . . and this restoration of broken relationship is decisive for the comic vision"[8] in the tale. God's desertion of Samson was not irrevocable: God would be swayed by Samson's prayer, which acknowledged his full dependence on divine power. The triumph over the Philistines is not the only sign of the restoration of Samson's good name in the Israelite community; his family buries him in the tomb of his father, a symbol of his full reintegration into the community.

Lament Psalms

As explained in chapter 2 the phrase "lament psalms" does not connote a pessimistic view of life, the bewailing of a tragedy that cannot be reversed. Rather, these psalms are cries from the depths of the heart to God to intervene with compassion to change a distressing situation; God has the power to rescue a sufferer out of "the miry bog" and set his or her "feet upon a rock" (Ps 40:2).

These lament psalms, however, do not describe only the incongruous comic relationship between the creator and humankind. They also set out the tripartite dynamic that needs to be followed in order that we can be transformed by God's unbounding love, a journey from sorrow to rejoicing, from shame to praise. For example, the separation stage in Psalm 13 begins with an address to God, but the psalmist quickly moves into the liminal phase of his journey when the sufferer describes the terrible sadness that he is experiencing as a result of his enemies' oppression: "How long must I bear pain in my soul. . . . How long shall my enemy be exalted over me?" (v. 2). Verses 3 and 4 further portray the psalmist's darkness of shame and fear, all the time waiting for God to hear him. Yet there is the paradox: out of this chaotic experience God is already working to remove the gloom. The psalmist is already singing his praises of God because God will save him: "my heart will rejoice in your salvation" (v. 5). The psalm ends with the reaggregation stage, in which the psalmist experiences—in dramatic contrast to the turmoil evident in the liminal part of the psalm—laughter of the heart or a new inner energy: "I will sing to the Lord, because he has dealt bountifully with me" (v. 6).[9]

There are some similarities between the pattern in the biblical lament psalms and the grieving process as described by Elizabeth Kubler-Ross.[10] Her denial experience falls within the separation phase; the anger, bargaining, and depression come within the liminality phase; acceptance marks the reaggregation phase. Both models of grieving assume that those who grieve move through an experience of chaos or turmoil to an inner peace, requiring a trusted friend or group to accompany them on their journey (in the psalms this friend is ultimately God). Anger in Kubler-Ross's model has its counterpart in the lament psalms. In her model the sufferers may lash out at loyal relatives or friends, even blaming them for the misery they experience. The latter, however, rarely know how to cope with such anger.

The pattern in the lament psalms, however, is significantly different. Here, anger is recognized as a powerful human expression that must not be suppressed. Because the people are united in covenant with God, they have every right to let God know what they feel, even to the point of saying that God helped to cause their sufferings. They know God can "handle it." Thus "You make us the scorn of our neighbors" (Ps 80:6). There are other notable differences; in particular, in contrast to the Kubler-Ross stage of denial, a lament psalm starkly proclaims from the beginning that the psalmist or community is afflicted. So miserable is the sufferer that there is nothing left but to trust God. At the stage when in Kubler-Ross's framework there is a bargaining that leads to depression, in the lament psalm there is a declaration of trust that sparks a hope-filled petition to God: "Give ear, O Shepherd of Israel . . . let your face shine, that we may be saved" (Ps 80:1, 3).

The words of assurance in the lament psalms and in Kubler-Ross's model radically differ. "Acceptance" in the latter seems to mean the same thing as a stoic resignation to the inevitable. But this view is contrary to a fundamental assumption in lament psalms: God can transform every crisis into a stunning new beginning. The task of covenant members is never to give up hope. That is the mark of every true Israelite and Christian in response to divine humor.[11]

By way of summary, like the narrators of the creation and exodus accounts, and like the narrators of Abraham's and Job's initiation stories, the psalmists draw attention to God's comic relationships with humankind. The experience of significant loss is likened to chaos, even death: anger, numbness, loss of identity, denial, nostalgia for the familiar past, guilt over sins, depression, fear of the future, the sense that God has withdrawn his protecting presence. Yet, participation in chaos can be the preface for a transforming experience of God's ever-renewing love, provided we are prepared to detach ourselves from what has been lost. Then the surprisingly new or the unexpected can emerge.[12] Psalm 126 poetically describes this dynamic interaction: "Those who go out weeping, bearing the seed for sowing, shall come home with shouts of joy, carrying their sheaves" (v. 6).

Prophets: God's Comedians

The major initiative for the covenant faith, which is based on three fundamental values—total dependence on God, justice, and love—does not come from the people. It comes from God, who acts through personally selected prophets. Prophets tell in plain words the oldest and best joke in the world: the mighty will be brought down and the lowly raised up. The prophets' task was to lead people to accept the incongruous fact of their own foolishness, on the one hand, and the infinite mercy and love of God, on the other. Yet all the prophets had to experience repeatedly this comic journey in their own lives to testify to their authenticity as ritual leaders of the Israelites.

Moses

There is a humorous aspect in God's choice of prophets—another sign of God's abiding sense of humor in relating to humankind. Consider Moses, who needs extraordinary patience to lead the often rebellious and ungrateful Israelites out of Egypt and through the trials of the desert. Yet Moses is naturally an impatient man with a powerful temper (Exod 2:12; 32:19). Moses, like later prophets, pleads that he is not skilled for the task: "O my Lord, I have never been eloquent, neither in the past nor even now. . . . I am slow of speech and slow of tongue" (Exod 4:10). The Lord humorously replies: "Who gives speech to mortals? . . . Is it not I, the LORD? Now go, and I will be with your mouth and teach you what you are to speak." But Moses is not so easily persuaded: "O my Lord, please send someone else" (Exod 4:11-13). At that point God loses patience and strongly advises Moses to forget his weaknesses and trust him.[13] That a God who creates would engage in dialogue with the created is comic indeed. As a result of this conversation, Moses calls the Israelites to be forever faithful to God's commands (Deut 7:11). But Moses also pleads with God to be merciful to his people (Num 14:19). Hence, the extraordinary paradox of divine humor: despite the enormity of the failings of humankind, our God is a God of steadfast love.

Jeremiah

Because commentators commonly depict Jeremiah as a prophet of disaster, it would seem inappropriate to refer to him as a humorous figure. Yet Jeremiah's response to the call of God to be a prophet follows the comic pattern: "Then I said, 'Ah . . . I do not know how to speak, for I am only a boy'" (Jer 1:6). God is not to be dissuaded: "Do not say, 'I am a boy'. . .; you shall speak whatever I command you" (1:7). The tender-minded young man becomes strong and courageous; the hesitant prophet becomes "an iron pillar, and a bronze wall, against the whole land" (Jer 1:18). This is the newness, the transformation, the miracle born out of Jeremiah's repeated proclamation of his own grief or failure of nerve. At one point Jeremiah bitterly attacks God: "I have become a laughingstock all day long" (Jer 20:7). Earlier he aggressively reprimands

God for having deceived and deserted him in times of personal abuse at the hands of mobs, for he has been flung into prison, beaten, shackled, and even lowered into a well: "Truly, you are to me like a deceitful brook, like waters that fail" (Jer 15:18). Nothing timid here. Yet in acknowledging his own inner weaknesses, Jeremiah rediscovers the energizing or revitalizing embrace of God: "But the LORD is with me like a dread warrior; therefore my persecutors . . . will not prevail" (Jer 20:11). The message is clear. People cannot be God's comedians or ritual purifiers if they are not at the same time journeying inward to acknowledge their own inner chaos and the abiding need of God's love.

Jeremiah is the prophet of creativity out of chaos,[14] of the incongruous message that there can be new life through death, provided the people follow the divinely led comic ritual of transformation. As God's comedian Jeremiah recounts the nation's slide into chaos and then incongruously promises new life beyond human imagination, if only the people will join in the process. He sees the political breakdown of his beloved nation and participates in its complete disintegration. He even encourages his people not to resist the Babylonian invader, because the people have so drifted away from the authentic demands of the nation's creative myth that there is nothing worth holding on to (Jer 5:30-31).

To Jeremiah it seems that the Israelite culture is to be reduced once more to the "primeval chaos from which God had originally redeemed it"[15]: "I looked, and lo, the fruitful land was a desert. . . . Because of this the earth shall mourn . . ." (Jer 4:26, 28). The pivotal symbols of the national culture—Jerusalem, the monarchy, the Temple—to which they are overly attached are to be destroyed. God speaks to Jeremiah: "See, today I appoint you over nations and over kingdoms, to pluck up and to pull down, to destroy and to overthrow" (Jer 1:10). What frightening words! The people have come to believe that no matter how unfaithful they are God will never withdraw his presence from such sacred symbols of their identity and security. How wrong they are! They have lost the detachment of being pilgrims. They no longer hear the call of God to act with justice and love.

Yet the unpredictable or incongruous is to occur—the action of divine humor. In the midst of the people's shattering grief and despair, Jeremiah foretells signs of revitalization of the nation: "Now I have put my words in your mouth . . . to build and to plant" (Jer 1:9-10). A new covenant between God and the revitalized culture will succeed the previous one (Jer 31:31-40) and it will be a richer one, since it will be adhered to in the hearts of believers, not just obeyed out of a sense of duty. The destroyed city will be rebuilt, secure forever, and the gift of personal and intimate union with God will be a sign of the authenticity of his people (Jer 31:34). Even in the Exile's chaos significant pastoral creativity does emerge; the people learn to pray in small supportive groups without the presence of the Temple, and traditional religious practices are updated in the light of the changed situation. For example, the importance of circumcision is no longer tied to the practice as an initiation rite, but it develops into a new symbol of cultural identity.[16]

Isaiah

Second Isaiah is also a mouthpiece of divine humor, using the same tripartite pattern of joke telling. The writer takes up the promise of a regenerated people and culture, calling them away from despair and the nostalgic/escapist dreams of past glory. The prophet reminds them that God did not create the world "a chaos, he formed it to be inhabited" (Isa 45:18), so the Israelites should stop complaining that they do not know God's will for them in the darkness of the Exile. God is a God of order. God has spoken openly and truthfully to the offspring of Jacob about the divine plan for them (Isa 45:19). If only they would listen again to God in a trusting way, letting go their self-pity and selfish ways, then they will discover a transforming freshness in their hearts that has a divine source: "Do not remember the former things, or consider the things of old. I am about to do a new thing; now it springs forth, do you not perceive it? I will make a way in the wilderness and rivers in the desert" (Isa 43:18-19). Then their hearts will rejoice (Isa 66:14). Isaiah depicts the return of the exiles in grandiose terms; it will be an even more dramatic event than the Exodus: "In the wilderness prepare the way of the Lord, make straight in the desert a highway for our God" (Isa 40:3). In the midst of the crisis of the Exile the author recounts the mythology of re-creation. After telling the story of God's creative power at the beginning of the world, when God transformed chaos into cosmos or order, Isaiah narrates once more the incredible victory over the Egyptians at the beginning of the Exodus: "Was it not you who dried up the sea, the waters of the great deep . . ." (Isa 51:10).

Summary

- The Old Testament records the ongoing incongruous struggle between two mythologies: that of a loving and merciful God and of a people repeatedly seduced into idolatry and greed. In the midst of

Egyptian oppression, the Israelites hear the extraordinary comforting assurance of God: "I will take you as my people, and I will be your God" (Exod 6:7); but they continue to cling to false gods. Yet their God will not give up the struggle. God uses the human condition and the Israelite experiences of chaos, such as the Exodus and Exile, to teach us that initiation into the divine life is a transformation through humor. Through this process their hearts can be transformed with new hope and energy. As long as Israelites harden their hearts (Ps 95:8) they will prevent the joking dynamic, with its underlying mythology of detachment and hope in new life, from occurring. Yet all the while God remains "faithful in all his words, and gracious in all his deeds" (Ps 145:13).

- In the lament psalms with their three-stage pattern of praying, we are constantly reminded that no matter how chaotic our condition may be God has the power to do the humanly impossible—to lift us out of "the seething chasm, from the mud of the mire." God can "set my feet upon a rock" and make "my steps secure . . . a new song in my mouth" (Ps 40:2, 3).[17] Lament psalms, writes Claus Westermann, transform the experience of liminal chaos into a way of approaching "God with abandonment that permits daring and visioning and even ecstasy."[18]

- From chaos to order, from weariness to rest, from suffering to joy, from sinfulness to justice—this incongruous theme runs constantly through the Old Testament. The prophets arise to remind people that this is the message of the Lord, and each time the people respond positively they will relive the transformative ritual of death to life, of sadness to the inner joy of the heart.

- The next chapter identifies examples of the same tripartite ritual joking pattern in the New Testament, the first example being the initiation of Mary as the Mother of God. She ponders within her heart this paradoxical experience—she, an unknown village girl, is to be the Mother of the Messiah: "My soul magnifies the Lord . . . for the Mighty One has done great things for me" (Luke 1:46, 49). Such is divine humor!

Chapter 5

Transformative Joking in the New Testament

Paradox is the language of the incalculable. We are doomed to live by paradox, by the hope that rises from the tomb of Christ.
David Power[1]

The resurrection of Christ is . . . an expression of God's laughter at death, a laughter which proves infectious for human beings . . . "Death is swallowed up in victory. Death, where is your victory? Death, where is your sting?" (1 Cor 15:54-55).
Karl-Josef Kuschel[2]

This chapter explains:

- that to live the paradox of Christ's detachment and exaltation we need to follow the ritual joking pattern of initiation established by him;
- that this tripartite ritual pattern is evident in significant events of the gospels, such as the Annunciation, the Transfiguration, and ultimately in the life, death, and resurrection of Christ.

Saint Paul goes to the heart of Christian rituals of initiation with their joking dynamic when he describes baptism. It is the personal reliving of the passion, death, and resurrection of Jesus himself (Rom 6:3-4). There is death of the mythology of enslavement to sin and the acceptance of its opposite, the person of Christ (Rom 6:5-11). This chapter examines several other examples of initiation rituals. At times, as in the parables, Jesus uses these rituals to teach his followers what conversion should mean. On other occasions he himself participates in these rituals as he journeys toward his death and resurrection. As in the examples from the Old Testament we notice all the time the underlying joking dynamic in these rituals.

In the following examples note the variety of "anti-normal" symbols, that is, symbols with unexpected meanings (see chap. 3) used to indicate the liminality or chaos stage: the startling appearance of an angel at the Annunciation, mountaintops, desert roads, a pig pen, journeying, a storm-swept lake, and a cross. The geographical sites are exposed, away from the spaces set aside for everyday orderly living. Again, as in the Old Testament, the emphasis is on inner transformation, not on the mere external submission to the ritual. It involves the dying to oneself and embracing Christ in faith: "Those who find their life will lose it, and those who lose their life for my sake will find it" (Matt 10:39). A perfect comic expression of divine humor! Finally, notice that there are ritual leaders in the events. It might be an angel in the case of the Annunciation, the Father at the Transfiguration, or Jesus with the disciples in the storm and on the road to Emmaus. Jesus himself shows, however, that it is not sufficient for people to have a liminal transformative experience. That conversion must be carried over into daily living, otherwise there is a dangerous vacuum in a person's life: "[The unclean spirit] says, 'I will return to my house from which I came.' When it comes, it finds it empty, swept, and put in order. Then it goes and brings along seven other spirits more evil than itself, and they enter and live there; and the last state of that person is worse than the first" (Matt 12:44-45).

Joking Pattern and Initiation in the New Testament

The Annunciation

The Annunciation is a ritual of initiation whereby Mary passes from being a young, unknown Jewish virgin to being the mother-to-be of the Savior of humankind. Since this is to be a dramatic shift of status for Mary, with unimagined consequences for herself and the universe, the ritual is filled with profound theological symbolism.

The separation stage in the Annunciation event is brief (Luke 1:26-27). The initiation, as in all previous rituals in the Old Testament, is to be led by God, in this event with the angel Gabriel as God's intermediary. The salutation "Greetings, favored one! The Lord is with you" (Luke 1:28) is not a simple conventional greeting, but it is messianic in structure and purpose (see Zeph 3:14-17), an invitation to celebrate at the coming of messianic times. The words "favored one" refer not just to Mary's personal holiness, but they point to the ultimate source of her blessedness, namely, that she is to be the Mother of God.[3] The mythology that is to infuse the initiation ritual is being stated from the very beginning.

The angel's greeting throws Mary into a chaos experience and the liminality stage (Luke 1:29). Her predictable world is dramatically disturbed and she wonders what it all means; then the angel, seeking to reassure her, must have intensified rather than calmed Mary's anguish of heart. Now the divine humor is dramatically active because the angel reveals what Mary's new role in this ritual is to be: she is to be the mother of the Davidic Messiah as earlier foretold in history (see 2 Sam 7:8-16). At this point Mary is deeply troubled because she is a virgin (Luke 1:34). Then the angel reveals something unimagined in the past, that the child is to be the unique Son of God through the power of the Holy Spirit. The paradox at the heart of Mary's liminal experience is resolved—God is to be the father. Humanly speaking this is nonsense, but from God's perspective "nothing will be impossible" (Luke 1:37).

How is Mary to react? From a merely human viewpoint? If so, then God's invitation to change roles does not succeed. If she responds in faith, then her entire vision of the future—and that of the entire world forevermore—will change. She immediately chooses the second option. The incongruous challenge is resolved for her through her act of faith (Luke 1:38). While remaining a virgin and through divine initiative Mary is to be simultaneously both the mother of Jesus and his first disciple. The ultimate human contradiction is that God is about to enter the world, with its violence, sinfulness, and corruption, fulfilling the messianic prophecies that he would suffer and die as its deliverer.

The visitation to Mary's cousin Elizabeth (Luke 1:39-45) is the third stage, the reaggregation, in the ritual of initiation: Mary is fulfilling her first duty of sharing the Good News with others. The speed, enthusiasm, and the physical dangers she is prepared to undergo on the four days' journey are confirmation that she is radically converted to her new role. Her song of praise in response to Elizabeth's greeting eloquently expresses her newfound laughter of the heart. The reaggregation stage concludes with the departure of Mary about three months later (Luke 1:56).

Jesus: Initiation as the Anointed Prophet

The threefold ritual pattern is strikingly evident in the initiation of Jesus himself into his public ministry as the greatest of all prophets.[4] There are two steps in the separation stage (Matt 3:13–4:1): the first is Jesus moving alone away from familiar Galilee to the Jordan to be baptized; the second break with the past is his passing "into the wilderness to be tempted by the devil" (Matt 4:1). Each step removes him further from his normal surroundings and supportive kinsfolk.

Significantly, Jesus travels into the desert, the liminality stage (Matt 4:2-11), the very sacred Israelite paradigm of marginality, trials, and the simultaneous experiential discovery of human weakness and the power of God. Jesus fasts, dramatically symbolizing the letting go of his former identity and disposing him to receive a new one. Now Jesus is confronted by the devil as the "cultural monster" whose temptations are the catalyst of much learning and self-growth. In response to each temptation Jesus expresses his solidarity (*communitas*) with Moses and symbolically with all the prophets who succeed him through the centuries down to John the Baptist. Jesus passes the tests: "Absolute loyalty to God, solidarity with the prophets, an ability to see through the devil's tricks, recognizing and driving away evil are all essential characteristics of the authentic prophet. Matthew's audience sees that Jesus has full and flawless possession of these faculties."[5]

Two scenes follow the temptation as Jesus enters into the reaggregation stage of newness. The first is the appearance of the angels who "came and waited on him" (Matt 4:11), representing "the virtually unmediated presence of God," and symbolizing "God's certification of Jesus' status as prophet, just as the Voice from heaven at the baptism declares that Jesus is God's Son."[6] In the second scene (4:12-25), Jesus takes up his role as the Son of God and prophet: he proclaims his mission, as foretold by the prophet Isaiah; summons his first disciples; preaches; and heals the sick. He not only has divine approbation as a prophet, but the people now publicly endorse him. He is the fully anointed prophet.

Sermon on the Mount: The Beatitudes

The separation stage of the ritual in which Jesus proclaims the Beatitudes is short: "he went up the mountain" (Matt 5:1). Then Jesus moves into the liminality stage, symbolized by being on a mountaintop, where he articulates, by listing the Beatitudes, what is required to enter the kingdom of God according to the new covenant. The common theme in the blessings is this paradox: those who die live a new life! Blessings are to be bestowed, not because of a person's worldly good luck, but because of self-denial, or what the world considers folly. The Beatitudes stress the joy of participation in the kingdom of God, especially in its fulfillment at the end of time, rather than rewards in this earthly life. Followers of Christ will be rewarded with these blessings of an entirely new way of being and living, on the condition that they are prepared to enter daily into their own rituals of personal transformation.

The second Beatitude in Matthew's gospel is: "Blessed are those who mourn, for they will be comforted" (Matt 5:4). The mourning here refers to a supernatural grief in contrast to worldly sorrow. When we enter into our own inner chaos of personal sinfulness, we discover that we are nothing without the power and loving presence of God in Christ, the one who alone can ultimately hold back the forces of evil.[7] This all-important self-knowledge is a gift of God, as is the invitation to grieve and to let go of whatever is holding us back from moving forward in faith. The description of the true Christian is incomplete if we emphasize only the need to reflect on loss. Those who mourn, says Jesus, are to be called blessed, not precisely because of their sorrow for sin, but because of what it produces, namely, "they will be comforted" (Matt 5:4). The ultimate comfort promised is the consolation that will come from sharing in the life of the kingdom of God in its fullness, when God "will wipe every tear from their eyes. Death will be no more; mourning and crying and pain will be no more" (Rev 21:4).

The evangelist Luke refers several times to weeping. For example, Jesus says: "Blessed are you who weep now, for you will laugh" (Luke 6:21); "Woe to you who are laughing now, for you will mourn and weep" (Luke 6:25). Those who weep are people who trust in God, for they weep for their sins. Those who do not weep now will do so at the end of time when God reveals his power and majesty; although they will weep then, it will be too late, for their arrogance will have condemned them to eternal death.

Luke uses the word "laugh" in the Beatitudes in two different ways (see chap. 3). People are depicted to be visibly laughing in the Old Testament, but it does not necessarily point to a genuine gift of humor. It is a sarcastic laughter springing from a lack of deep faith in God, for example, when people laugh cruelly at the sufferings of Job (12:4). This is the same type of faithless laughter that Jesus is condemning; it is synonymous with an arrogant refusal to accept God as one's creator, and Jesus as one's Savior (Luke 6:25). Those who resist Jesus' will here on earth are deprived of inner peace or the laughter of the heart that alone comes from Christ and will be rejected in the life to come: "There will be weeping and gnashing of teeth when you see Abraham and Isaac and Jacob and all the prophets in the kingdom of God, and you yourselves thrown out" (Luke 13:28). But those who weep for, or grieve over, their sins in this life acknowledge God as their creator. Their laughter of the heart is not hollow; it is genuine because it is rooted in the gift of detachment. Through detachment we experience the relativity of all created things and the ability to discern what does or does not matter. So, laughter as used here by Jesus means the joy that comes from recognizing the sheer stupidity of trying to ignore God by being sinful.

Matthew marks the newness of the reaggregation stage with the words, "when Jesus had finished saying these things" he "[came] down from the mountain" (Matt 7:28; 8:1). There follow three healing incidents (Matt 8:2-22), illustrating the energy for his mission that his followers will also possess if they interiorize the message of the new covenant.

Healing of Bartimaeus

This is a short event in the life of Christ (Mark 10:46-52), but as a ritual of transition for Bartimaeus, as an instructive example for others, it is full of symbolism. The separation stage of the ritual begins by describing Bartimaeus, who is a blind beggar, "sitting on the roadside" (Mark 10:46). This phrase connotes that, because of his blindness and economic condition, he has become a social outcast. (Poor people, especially those who were ritually unclean, had to remain silent and accept their fate—which, as it was falsely believed, was God's punishment for their sins.) Even for his family and friends Bartimaeus has socially ceased to exist. Hearing Jesus approaching, Bartimaeus cries out for healing, but the crowd condemns the arrogance of someone who was supposed to remain silent (Mark 10:48). The crowd has followed Jesus and listened to his words on compassion and justice, but they remain blinded by their prejudice against people like Bartimaeus. Jesus will have none of this fundamentalist and violent nonsense. He calls Bartimaeus to his side.

The liminality period begins. Symbolically, Bartimaeus detaches himself from his past identity as a beggar by throwing off his cloak and running to Jesus, an act that signifies the chaos stage for Bartimaeus. The cloak is his only symbol of official identity; it is the equivalent of a license to beg. Without it he is bereft of any identity that could give him some minimum of protection: "So throwing off his cloak, he sprang up and came to Jesus" (Mark 10:50). Jesus, the ritual leader, asks what Bartimaeus needs: "My teacher, let me see again" (Mark 10:51). Jesus heals him. The newness of the reaggregation phase for Bartimaeus is briefly, but touchingly, described: "Immediately he regained his sight and followed him on the way [road]" (Mark 10:52). The words "on the road," in contrast to the opening verse where Bartimaeus "was sitting by the roadside," symbolically mean that he is again part of the community. His social exclusion has ceased. Bartimaeus would have been filled with joy, energized with laughter of the heart.

The Storm

This incident, although briefly recorded, reinforces the need for Christ's disciples to think no longer in mere human terms but rather through the eyes of faith. The separation stage is clearly identifiable: Jesus climbs into the boat and is followed by his disciples (Matt 8:23). The liminality or chaos phase is described in graphic terms: "the boat was being swamped by the waves" (Matt 8:24). Then the paradox—Jesus, like Jonah in a similar situation, is asleep despite the noise, water, and tossing of the boat. Jesus is awakened by the desperate cries of the disciples, for they are perishing (Matt 8:25). The disciples not only doubt the promise of Jesus, but they rebuke him for what they see as his failure to care for them (Matt 8:26). Jesus then uses the occasion to teach them a fundamental lesson: if they truly have faith they will not doubt his concern (Matt 8:26). And to prove his point he calms the storm.

Implicit in the account are the different reactions of two ritual leaders—Jonah and Jesus. In the fictional story of the Old Testament Jonah is sent by Yahweh to warn Nineveh of its great evil and its consequences, but he boards a ship to escape the task. The storm hits the boat and he is thrown overboard by the crew because they believe he has caused their misfortune. Jonah eventually accomplishes his mission but remains reluctant to the end. Jonah is an anti-normal symbol of what a true prophet should not be: self-centered, nasty, and relishing the destruction of Nineveh. Jesus, however, is willing to carry out God's wishes without reluctance, for "something greater than Jonah is here" (Luke 11:32).[8] The reaggregation phase is marked by the wonder that the disciples experience after witnessing the calming of the waves: "They were amazed, saying, 'What sort of man is this, that even the winds and the sea obey him?'" (Matt 8:27).

The Transfiguration

The Transfiguration is to be a ritual of initiation for Peter, James, and John; they are to experience in a spectacular way the true identity of Jesus as the Messiah and also the nature of his mission. Jesus' glorification is to be his resurrection, but only after suffering and death (Matt 17:1-9). Yet despite the startling nature of the event, Peter's reactions are very human and instructive for subsequent generations of believers who hesitate to enter into a transformative experience with Christ.

The separation phase is the ascent of the mountain (Matt 17:1); this is to remind the disciples that something extraordinarily important is to take place on the mountaintop, the liminal space. Jesus at prayer is suddenly and radically altered: "and his face shone like the sun, and his clothes became dazzling white" (Matt 17:2). The fact that his face shines like the sun and his clothes are so brilliantly white indicate symbolically that this is no ordinary human event. Jesus is in the presence of God. He is mirroring the radiance foretold in Isaiah (6:1-3), just as Moses had reflected the brightness of God at Mount Sinai (Exod 34:29-35). Moses and Elijah, representing the Israelite law and the prophets, converse with Jesus about his passion that is to occur at Jerusalem. As Moses and Elijah begin to disappear Peter is terrified at what is happening and wants to control the situation. Thinking in human terms he wants all three to be, as it were, frozen in time, by being made to reside in three tents of equal dignity: "Lord, it is good for us to be here; if you wish, I will make three dwellings here, one for you, one for Moses, and one for Elijah" (Matt 17:4). His speaking is cut short.

The liminal experience of transcendence is to continue no matter how much Peter fears what is happening: "While he was still speaking, suddenly a bright cloud overshadowed them, and from the cloud a voice said, 'This is my Son, the Beloved; with him I am well pleased; listen to him'" (Matt 17:5). Again the bright cloud is a culturally paradoxical symbol representing the presence of God (Exod 13:22; 24:15-18), and God the Father confirms that Jesus is truly the Messiah (Matt 17:5). Jesus is superior to the other two great messengers, Moses and Elijah, who, as they represent the old covenant that is to end, leave the scene. The disciples must now listen to Christ as the voice of God.[9]

The profoundly moving incident in its liminal stage is filled with divine and human comic contrasts:

- Jesus is to be the "suffering servant" as foretold by the prophet Isaiah (52:13–53:12), yet he is to be glorified at his resurrection following his death (Matt 17:9). Through their initiation Peter and his two companions must let go of any dream that Jesus will be a political revolutionary.

- In the midst of such an intensely powerful, supernatural experience Peter is so distracted that he amusingly wants to build three temporary shelters to honor the equal importance of Moses, Elijah, and Jesus. But it takes the intervention of God the Father to remind Peter that Jesus is *the* prophet, superior to all previous prophets, because Jesus is God's Son. Again, the disciples are reminded that they must abandon any idea that Jesus is merely a human prophet.

- Despite the fact that the incident is so divinely significant and filled with such biblical symbolism, Jesus remains humanly concerned for his disciples who are overcome with fear. Jesus comes to reassure them by touching them and inviting them to "'Get up and do not be afraid.' And when they looked up, they saw no one except Jesus himself alone" (Matt 17:7-8).

The reaggregation phase is symbolized by the disciples' discovery that Jesus is now alone, back to his normal physical self. Their descent from the mountain symbolically indicates the ending of this reaggregation phase (Matt 17:9).

Parable: Two Confused Sons

The parable of what is normally called the "Prodigal Son" is a dramatic illustration of divine humor: the paradox of a loving, compassionate God earnestly reaching out to embrace self-centered humanity.[10] We respond positively only if we acknowledge before God our own failings and pride; if we fulfill this requirement we will successfully be initiated through God's overwhelming mercy into union with Christ. Jesus explains in detail the journey of one son who does this in a rather spectacular way, but the description of his elder brother is equally instructive because, unlike his younger brother, he refuses the opportunity for transformation.

Younger Son

The separation phase of the prodigal son's transformative journey is concise (Luke 15:11-12): the brash, self-centered adolescent, acting within his rights according to the custom of the time, asks for his share of his father's property and then leaves for a distant country where he squanders his wealth on "dissolute living" (Luke 15:13). He views his father purely in economic terms, as a source of money. Then follows the liminal phase. Utterly destitute and alone, the younger son is forced to accept what is culturally one of the lowest and most shameful employments for a Jew—working with pigs. Thus the pigpen is a powerful anti-normal symbol of the chaos in this adolescent's journey into mature adulthood. In this liminal stage he begins a process of conversion by acknowledging that his troubles are his own fault. He recalls his father's love and compassion, which in his self-centeredness he has long ignored. This energizes him to go to seek forgiveness and reconciliation, but he does not expect his father will openly receive him. Hence, he will offer himself to his father as just another hired laborer. But the father, seeing his son in the distance, runs to him and embraces him—a gesture of profound compassion and forgiveness. The actual running is itself a cultural symbol of incongruity because no man of his social standing would do such a thing.

The reaggregation stage of the initiation of the young man is marked by the feast of celebration called by his father. The lesson to Jesus' listeners is this: the heart of Christ's message is that God's love is unconditional and God is constantly inviting us to let go of our attachments to worldly things. We must abandon our secular myth of self-centered desire for power and material things and embrace God's message of Christ's unqualified love and concern for those who are marginalized. If we do so, we also will rejoice with an inner peace that cannot be measured in merely human terms.

Elder Son

The elder son's failed journey of initiation into maturity is in striking contrast to that of his brother. Something of his selfishness is indirectly depicted at the beginning of the parable. By custom the elder son must act as the mediator in disputes between younger brothers and their father, but this one fails to do so. People listening to Jesus would have known this and have developed a negative view of his behavior. But worse is to come. Hearing of his sibling's return, the elder son is overwhelmed by destructive jealousy and envy of his brother. Jealousy is the sadness that arises when a person either fears losing or has already lost a meaningful status or relationship to another rival. On the other hand, envy is the sadness a person experiences because of what someone else has and the desire to possess it. Jealousy and envy can lead to violence. The elder son is jealous because he fears he will lose the capital goods he thinks belong to him (Luke 15:29). He is envious because his brother now possesses what he lacks: a mature adult relationship with their father.

Despite his protestations of maturity, the elder son has not grown up to be a responsible person. He wants his brother punished for his earlier adolescent selfishness, so he attempts to belittle his brother and thus destroy the joy of his father; but the father will not be seduced into destroying the mature relationship that he and his younger son have established. The elder son, refusing to even begin an initiation ritual of transformation, remains consumed by his envious and jealous feelings. In addition, by custom the elder son should be the host of the party, but he even refuses to enter the house, thus publicly insulting the dignity of his father and his reconciliation with his brother. Yet the father still encourages his elder son to begin the journey of conversion, for the words about his failure to accept his brother are not harsh, but a kindly invitation to acknowledge his own need of conversion (Luke 15:31-32). As we are not told if the elder son accepts his father's invitation, the story ultimately ends on a sad note.

Servant Leadership: Initiation of the Disciples

The evangelist John describes at length (chaps. 13–17) the final efforts by Jesus, prior to his crucifixion, to prepare his disciples for leadership. Jesus wants to ensure in the time left to him that the disciples understand the heart of his message. During the Last Supper he invites the disciples to join him in a ritual of profound significance: leaders in the new covenant need to be on a transformative journey of dying to self in order to be one with the risen Christ.

The separation stage is so dramatic that his disciples should have immediately sensed that something important was to happen. Jesus "got up from the table, took off his outer robe, and tied a towel around himself" (John 13:4). This action contains two culturally discordant symbols: a ritual of foot washing is to take place, but it should have been done prior to the meal, not during it. And Jesus dresses as a servant. No master or teacher would ever wash the feet of their servants or students, nor would they ever kneel before them. It was strictly forbidden by the culture.

In the liminal stage Jesus washes the disciples' feet and dries them with a towel. He wishes to teach his disciples by example that leaders must not rule through fear and coercion, but through humility and compassion. Humility and empathy for others develop only when we realize we ourselves are fragile as human beings. We need each other. By adopting the status of the lowest of servants Jesus is proclaiming that he also belongs to fragile humanity. As he acts, so must they. But Peter, as the representative disciple, sees the cultural absurdity of what is happening; Jesus is acting both as host and as servant, so Peter vigorously reacts by refusing to have his feet washed: "You will never wash my feet" (John 13:8). Jesus cannot be allowed to act in the lowly ways of a servant. Host, yes, but not servant! Then Jesus categorically states that unless Peter submits he has "no share" with him (John 13:8). Peter resolves the situation by effusively declaring he is totally for Christ and his message (John 13:9).

The ritual's reaggregation stage is marked by the return of Jesus to the table and the replacing of his robe (John 13:12). He then explains the symbolism of the ritual. The disciples are to be so united in love for one another that "whoever receives one whom I send receives me; and whoever receives me receives him who sent me" (John 13:20). He later says: "I give you a new commandment, that you love one another. Just as I have loved you, you also should love one another" (John 13:34). This is comically turning the culture upside down. Instead of behaving with authoritarian power toward others, as their culture would approvingly demand, they are now to be known for their humility, patience, willingness to serve others, mutuality of love: "By this everyone will know that you are my disciples, if you have love for one another" (John 13:35). Servant leadership now means that the disciples are to influence people not through their ability to control them by fear but through their own personal example. They will be sustained in this new behavior only to the degree that they are themselves open to the forgiving and merciful love of Christ; they cannot do this depending on their own power alone (John 15:6-11).[11]

Jesus: Initiation as Savior

Again the threefold ritual pattern is clear in Matthew's account of the passion and resurrection. There are several steps in the separation stage, each marking a further movement of Jesus away from his established role as only a preacher of the kingdom to that of the suffering Savior: the anointing in anticipation of his burial (Matt 26:6-13), the drama of the Last Supper (Matt 26:17-19, 26-29), and the distressing actual and anticipated loss of friends, Judas and Peter (Matt 26:14-16, 20-25, 30-35). The narrative reveals an ever-deepening sadness in Jesus as he begins the pilgrimage of withdrawing from a world of loving crowds, supportive friends, and an exciting ministry of preaching and healing. Now Jesus becomes the divine fool, a mock king entering Jerusalem on an ass, to be displayed in purple, beaten, and laughed at. By his behavior Jesus challenges the corrupt power structures of his day, but few will heed the message.

There are many scenes in the liminality stage as well, each one a further experience for Jesus of deepening, painful marginality. It begins with the trial of the agony in the garden. The Gethsemane experience, as described by the evangelist Mark, needs to be considered separately because as a "mini" transition ritual for Christ within the larger drama of his death and resurrection, it is impressively rich in symbolism. The separation stage is short. Mark describes Jesus going with his three companions "to a place called Gethsemane" (Mark 14:32). Jesus then experiences initial distress and agitation (vv. 33-34).

Then Jesus goes further into the liminal stage alone, symbolized by the garden, and the depth of his personal chaos is painfully portrayed by the description of throwing himself onto the ground in prayer (v. 35). Has he the strength to take up the ministry of suffering, even unto death, as the Father wishes of him? He is tempted to retreat to his former status of being the teacher enjoying the companionship of his disciples (v. 38), but he finds them asleep and of no help in his anguish. He returns to the heart of the garden and prays even more earnestly (v. 39), but twice more he seeks support from his friends to no avail. They are asleep. This is a "Disabled God"—divine humor at its most profound.

Mark significantly comments on the failure of the disciples to help Jesus: "and they did not know what to say to him" (v. 40). They cannot extend compassion simply because they themselves have not as yet become fully converted to the saving message of Christ. They do not know what to say because they have not yet owned up to their own inner need for compassion. And so they refuse to offer Jesus the gift of fellowship (*communitas*) that would have consoled him in his loneliness; by sleeping the disciples escape in a very human way the challenge to respond. They leave Jesus a "Disabled God"—personally alive to the enormity of the gap between the mission given him by the Father and the frailty inherent in his human nature when he is faced with the sufferings he is shortly to experience. It is the Father, not the three disciples, who hears the anguish of Jesus and consoles him. And Jesus is so transformed by this that he takes up his role of the Messiah with renewed energy: "Get up, let us be going. See, my betrayer is at hand" (v. 42).

Yet the process of transformation is not complete. At his trial Jesus must make a choice: to be loyal to the monstrous powers of the Sanhedrin and the civil authority represented by Pilate *or* to assume the role of the suffering servant as portrayed in the messianic psalms and prophecies (Matt 26:57-68; 27:1-31). Fundamentally, the option in the chaos is God *or* the world. As in his earlier initiation as the anointed prophet, Jesus passes the test, expresses his total loyalty to God, and continues his pilgrimage.

The crucifixion, death, and burial of Jesus conclude the liminality stage, a stage in which Jesus experiences marginality to an extreme degree (Matt 27:32-56): mocked, stripped of his clothes, crucified between two rogues, with a few remaining friends "looking on from a distance" (27:55). Yet in the midst of this darkness, the humanly, impossibly new begins to break through. Jesus recites the lamentation of Psalm 22, which, though it recounts the sadness of total disaster, also expresses its opposite, that is, hope in the saving power of God. In the chaos of his dying, Jesus is already being initiated into the new life of hope that comes only from a God in whom he has total trust:

> My God, my God, why have you forsaken me? . . .
> For he did not despise or abhor the affliction of the afflicted . . .
> All the ends of the earth shall remember and turn to the Lord . . .
>   (Ps 22:1, 24, 27)

As in the desert, Jesus triumphs over evil. The gospels portray various signs that follow the death of Jesus. The Temple veil tears apart "from top to bottom" (Mark 15:38), but this is a literary artifice of the writer to emphasize that with Jesus' death we are now able to approach God directly by a "new and living way," namely, through the flesh and blood of Jesus our Savior (Heb 10:19-21). This is the newness that immediately follows Jesus giving himself to the Father at his death.

Clowns, as explained earlier, frequently move back and forth from a world of suffering to one of joy (see chap. 3). In themselves they hold together these two opposing experiences: "the self-contradictions and incongruities that the clown incarnates are held together in a single, mysteriously particularized human being."[12] Yet clowns become the objects of abuse because the lessons they offer us about ourselves are not to our liking. Such is the lot of Jesus, for at the crucifixion those "who passed by derided him" (Matt 27:39). They starkly acknowledge the incongruous situation before them—someone who claims to be the Son of God dies on a cross; someone who trusts in God is ignored by God (Matt 27:40-44).

Yet death is not the final word. The evangelist Matthew uses dramatic symbols to describe the resurrection scene of Christ (Matt 27:62-66; 28:1-20). He writes of the earth quaking, boulders splitting apart, bodies of saints rising from their tombs after the resurrection of Jesus (Matt 27:53-54). These anti-normal symbols are a literary device of Matthew, who wants to make a strong contrast between the death of the old and the birth of the new as a result of Christ's death and resurrection. These contrasts between old and new, between death and resurrection, mark the shift from the liminal to the reaggregation stage. Jesus is the first to rise from the dead in the new covenant, but we also will follow him when the present world ceases. The raising of "bodies of the saints" symbolizes the fulfillment of the new life that will be ours at the end of time, when "the heavens will be set ablaze and dissolved" (2 Pet 3:12). We also will be raised from the dead and united with Christ in the "new heavens and a new earth, where righteousness is at home" (2 Pet 2:13).[13]

From death to life, from renunciation to joyful newness—Christ as the ritual leader of his own death sets the pattern for authentic initiation. This is divine comedy at its most extraordinary expression. For us there can never be life, for any individual or group, without a dying to that which is irrelevant or an obstacle to fulfilling the mission of the Father in Christ. Detachment is humanly costly, and without the abiding support of the Holy Spirit, it is impossible to achieve. The challenge is frightening, but there can be no human shortcut to achieve apostolic individual or community resurrection: "The saying is sure: If we have died with him, we will also live with him; if we endure, we will also reign with him" (2 Tim 2:11-12).

Mary's Initiation as Mother of Believers[14]

Following the birth of Jesus, and the mysterious expressions of joy that surround this, Mary's role as the first believer and disciple of her Son is sorely tested in two recorded incidents of liminality: the disturbing prophecy of Simeon and losing the child Jesus in Jerusalem during the Passover festival. As Abraham's faith is tested prior to his acceptance of the role of "the great father of a multitude of nations," (Sir 44:19), so also with Mary before she is offered a new role as her Son dies before her. The tone of Simeon's prophecy (Luke 2:33-35) is ominous because the child is to be a cause of bitterness and division throughout Israel; there is to be much suffering *before* there is peace, and Mary is to share in this. The first painful experience occurs when she and Joseph lose Jesus during the Passover festival and three days later find him in the Temple. The puzzlement she shows in trying to understand the independent behavior of Jesus illustrates that she has much yet to learn about her Son's role (Luke 2:41-50). There is a mother's anguish in her rebuke: "Child, why have you treated us like this? Look, your father and I have been searching for you in great anxiety" (Luke 2:48). Little wonder that she needs time and space to ponder the meaning of this event. She is again being asked to view things from God's perspective and to let go any human effort to understand what is happening. The paradox is that on the one hand, Jesus is behaving like any other precocious boy, but at the same time he self-identifies as the Son of God. Only Mary's deepening faith can resolve this incongruous situation. Her initiation into a deeper faith journey is to continue.

Within the crucifixion sequence Mary is invited by Jesus into a short, poignant ritual process of her own. The evangelist John alerts his listeners that there is to be an important interruption to the narrative. The focus shifts from Jesus to two other people, Mary and the Beloved Disciple, whom many identify as John. The beginning of this short transformative ritual is marked by the statement: "Meanwhile, standing near the cross of Jesus were his mother . . . and the disciple whom he loved standing beside her" (John 19:25-26). One can imagine Mary, as all mothers of dying children would, clinging to Jesus, not wanting him to die. Poets, artists, and mystics have tried for centuries to portray the grief of the suffering mother at the foot of the cross. The author of the thirteenth-century hymn, the *Stabat Mater*, depicts the scene:

> At the cross her station keeping
> stood the mournful Mother weeping . . .
> through her heart, his sorrow sharing . . .
> now at length the sword had passed . . .[15]

The scene is filled with symbolism and meaning. Mary at the wedding feast at Cana is concerned about the embarrassment to her hosts if it becomes known that there is no more wine. Jesus listens to her pressing petition for help and changes the water into wine. Because of Mary's intercession Jesus for the first time reveals his glory, and his disciples learn to believe in him (John 2:1-12). Now Mary is to be given the same intercessory role for all humankind. It is a second annunciation when Mary is given a new role: "Woman, here is your son" (John 19:26). No longer is Mary to be the exalted mother of the Son of God only. Now she is to be the mother of all who come to believe in Jesus down through the ages; the disciple John symbolizes the countless number who will see Mary as their ever-present intercessor with her Son. In the midst of her lament of bitter anguish she is to be the support and model of detachment for every gospel community seeking to love Jesus and to mourn over its own sinfulness and failings. When Mary is assigned to the care of the disciple John (John 19:27), she "becomes most nearly conformed" to the detachment of her son, writes Hans Urs von Balthasar. As Jesus is "the only one sent away and abandoned by the Father," so he "leaves her standing," sent away; he "settles her someplace else."[16]

Mary's presence in the midst of the small believing community, gathered in the upper room in Jerusalem while waiting for the coming of the Spirit, symbolizes the reaggregation stage of this ritual of detachment (Acts 1:14). Mary is actively fulfilling her new role. She was central to the birth of Jesus, so also is she to be present in her new role at the birth of the church itself at Pentecost, supporting and encouraging those who now believe.

The Emmaus Story

The incident, with Luke as narrator, of the appearance of Jesus to two despondent disciples on the road to Emmaus unfolds according to a clear tripartite pattern of initiation.[17] During the separation stage two former followers of Jesus are moving away from Jerusalem, escaping from the place in which their hopes of Jesus as the Messiah have been irrevocably crushed (Luke 24:13-35). They cannot take any more! Deeply disappointed, they have had enough!

Jesus, the skillful grief and initiation leader, joins them during the liminal stage, but they fail to recognize him. Their inability to identify Jesus is caused more by spiritual blindness than by anything unusual about Jesus' appearance. This fact adds to the drama of the event, for it highlights their need for conversion. Jesus, pretending to be ignorant of the reasons for the travelers' sadness, invites them to express their feelings: "'What are you discussing with each other while you walk along?' They stood still, looking sad" (Luke 24:17). They are shocked to discover a stranger "who does not know the things that have taken place" (Luke 24:18). This is a comic scene. Jesus is the only one in the group, in fact, who knows the full meaning of what has taken place. We know that the stranger is Jesus, and we wonder when the disciples will recognize him. All their anger and sadness tumble out at great speed, leaving them breathless. Jesus listens patiently before he begins to challenge them. He presents them with several key sacred symbols of Israelite cultural history: Moses, the prophets, and the messianic text (Luke 24:25-27). Now they must make a choice: continue to hold on to their wrong beliefs, *or* accept what has been said and move forward out of chaos into the future in faith and hope. They choose Christ because they recognize him in the breaking of the bread, experiencing a fellowship (*communitas*) with him and a laughter of the heart that words cannot fully articulate:

"They said to each other, 'Were not our hearts burning within us while he was talking to us on the road, while he was opening the scriptures to us?'" (Luke 24:32).

The reaggregation stage in the Emmaus story is brief but filled with movement and excitement (Luke 24:33-35). The disciples are so transformed and energized by discovering Jesus in their midst that they leave immediately to share their experience with "the eleven and their companions gathered together" (Luke 24:33). This energy is in vivid contrast to their earlier sadness and testifies to the depth of their conversion.

The Ascension of Jesus

The account of Jesus' ascension into heaven contains three distinct phases. Even at the very end of his life on earth Jesus invites his disciples to join him in his final transformative phase. He has frequently told them that he is leaving the world and "going to the Father" (John 16:28); "for if I do not go away, the Advocate will not come to you; but if I go, I will send him to you" (John 16:7). Despite the fact that Jesus repeats himself, the disciples fail to hear. They are so attached to the physical presence of Jesus that they become trapped in the liminal stage; they will need to be encouraged through faith to let Jesus go in order for them to become his witnesses in the world.

The separation stage is marked by a definite break from the scene in which Jesus appears to his disciples, reassures them that he has truly risen from the dead, and leaves them final instructions (Luke 24:36-49). He then "led them out as far as Bethany, and, lifting up his hands, he blessed them" (Luke 24:50). Luke identifies the site in the Acts of the Apostles as Mount Olivet (Acts 1:12). Olivet is one of those exposed liminal sites, like the road to Emmaus, symbolizing that Jesus is calling his disciples to enter into a conversion experience: "he was lifted up, and a cloud took him out of their sight" (Acts 1:9). The cloud symbolizes the presence of God and reaffirms for the disciples that something beyond the normal is occurring.

The scene shifts to the disciples and an incongruous situation. The disciples are stunned by the experience and keep looking up to the sky hoping that Jesus will return. Their fear is further intensified by the sudden appearance of "two men in white robes" (Acts 1:10). The men, probably to be understood as angels, unexpectedly appear to challenge the disciples to resolve their fears of the unpredictable by reaffirming their faith in the return of Jesus at an unknown time in the future (Acts 1:11). They now make a firm act of faith and return to Jerusalem to await the coming of the Spirit.

The actual movement away from Olivet is the reaggregation stage; sustained by the transforming experience of the Ascension the disciples will await the coming of the Spirit at Pentecost with the supportive prayer of their faith community, which includes "Mary the mother of Jesus" (Acts 1:14).

Paul and Initiation

Saint Paul's writings on Christian initiation are intimately connected to his own personal experience of conversion. It is God who calls and leads people to conversion (1 Cor 3:5), but Paul emphasizes the creative potential of acknowledging his inner chaos as a condition of this conversion: "So, I will boast all the more gladly of my weaknesses, so that the power of Christ may dwell in me. . . . for whenever I am weak, then I am strong" (2 Cor 12:9-10). Christ is the new energizing power in his life. At another point Paul describes the rich potential of inner desolation as the springboard for accepting the creative newness of Christ's life, provided there is trust in the overwhelming power of God: "We are afflicted in every way, but not crushed; perplexed, but not driven to despair . . . always carrying in the body the death of Jesus, so that the life of Jesus may also be made visible in our bodies. . . . So death is at work in us, but life in you" (2 Cor 4:8, 10, 12). We also enter into the regenerating life of the risen Christ by acknowledging our unconditional dependence on him; there is then such oneness with him that we can say with Paul: "I have been crucified with Christ; and it is no longer I who live, but it is Christ who lives in me" (Gal 2:19-20). From our nothingness we become one in Christ, in his power, in his love. It takes the courage of faith, born of love, to confront our own inner darkness.

Paul's personal experience of the dynamic of detachment/newness is further revealed in his letter to the Philippians. The Christian community at Philippi is struggling to survive in the midst of a pagan majority who fail to understand or accept their way of life. In these circumstances it is imperative for Christians to be of one mind and heart in support of one another (Phil 2:1-4), not to be acting selfishly. This will be possible only if they daily relive Christ's initiation as Savior—his dying and rising.

Authors commonly conclude that Paul at this point incorporates into his letter a christological hymn that is not his own, except for some modifications (Phil 2:6-11).[18] Its striking description of the initiation of Jesus as Savior, with its dynamic of detachment and final exaltation, is a model for the embattled Philippians. It is divided into two parts: the detachment (*kenosis*) or humiliation of Christ in three verses (Phil 2:6-8) and the exaltation of Christ by the Father in the three following verses (Phil 2:9-11). Jesus Christ, though preexistent divine and equal with God, does not take advantage of his divinity for his personal enhancement; he wills to give himself entirely in the service of humankind. He does not avoid suffering, but recognizes as God and man that he is uniquely qualified to become our redeemer. For this reason God "highly exalted him" (Phil 2:9). The symbols of incongruity are: Christ as God, yet a slave in status, without rights, or power; and death on the cross. The *communitas* experience, a consequence of his detachment, is the sharing in the Father's own power over sin and death. This process of detachment, bonding with humankind in all its chaos, and exaltation is set out in figure 5.1.

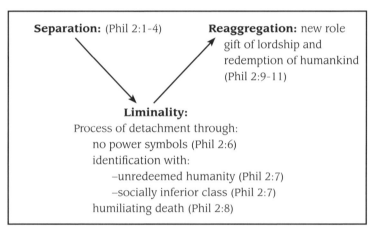

Figure 5.1: Initiation of Jesus as Savior

Paul frequently refers to himself and other believers "as fools for the sake of Christ" (1 Cor 4:10). The message of Christ by worldly standards is incongruous: "For the message about the cross is foolishness to those who are perishing, but to us who are being saved it is the power of God" (1 Cor 1:18). In a satirical way Paul says: "For Jews demand signs and the Greeks desire wisdom, but we proclaim Christ crucified, a stumbling block to Jews and foolishness to Gentiles . . ." (1 Cor 1:22-23). He then explains why in worldly terms Christ's message is nonsense. Christ bypasses those with power and embraces the weak; powerlessness is the model of true power and foolishness becomes the wisdom of God: "But God chose what is foolish in the world to shame the wise; God chose what is weak in the world to shame the strong; God chose what is low and despised in the world, things that are not, to reduce to nothing things that are, so that no one might boast in the presence of God" (1 Cor 1:27-29). Paul asks the Corinthians to reflect on the paradox of his own life. They know well his many weaknesses, yet the power of God shines through (2 Cor 12:10).

Summary

- Jesus admonishes those who refuse to grieve in this world, despite all that he has done to call them to this: "we wailed, and you did not weep" (Luke 7:32). We will be authentic followers of Christ only if we grieve over our failings and become open to the newness of heart that comes from God. The joking paradigm is the very foundation of this imperative of grieving: "Very truly, I tell you, you will weep and mourn, but the world will rejoice; you will have pain, but your pain will turn into joy" (John 16:20).

- In his lifetime Christ used many examples through teaching and personal action to describe how this ritual of grieving into newness is to unfold. Detachment, which is the letting go of all that would hinder individuals or communities from a committed relationship with God, is at the heart of all authentic grieving. Jesus is *the* model of detachment, for he "emptied himself, taking the form of a slave . . . and became obedient to the point of death—even death on a cross" (Phil 2:7, 8), in order that, through his resurrection, we might share in the new fruits of his victory over death.

- Christ was adept at using humor as a medium of cultural and personal transformation for himself and his followers. Contemporary evangelizers are to do the same, but in order to do so they need to understand how humor is used in their own cultures. The following chapter identifies four models of culture with their particular forms of humor.

Chapter 6

Understanding Humor in Cultures

> *The more thoroughly and substantially a human being exists, the more he [or she] will discover the comical.*
> Soren Kierkegaard[1]

> *[W]hatever is true, whatever is honorable . . . think about these things.*
> Philippians 4:8

This chapter explains:

- four models of culture: premodern, modern, postmodern, and paramodern;
- the different expressions of humor that characterize each model;
- that prophetic humor is an integral quality of paramodernity.

The task of evangelization is to present the Gospel message in order that it becomes a deep transforming force within a particular culture. This transforming action involves a twofold process: liberation and enrichment. Evangelization endeavors to liberate a culture from all forms of domination or injustice that demean the dignity of people. And it aims to identify whatever is already good in a culture and endow it with the richer meanings of the Gospel. Even before the Gospel is preached God is working in the cultures of people. There are, says Justin Martyr (ca. 100–165), "seeds" sown by the Word of God, or "glimmers of tran-scendence," in all religions and cultures.[2] The task of evangelizers is to transform through the power of the Spirit these seeds so that the whole culture becomes "a new creation" (2 Cor 5:17).

This process of transformation is slow because cultures are so com-plex that they are difficult for evangelizers to comprehend or interpret. Humor, though, is a quality of all cultures. When we understand how and why people use positive or negative humor in different cultures, we begin to grasp the values they cherish and the issues that distress them. Whatever is good in their humor are "seeds" or "glimmers of transcen-dence" so that when people express positive humor in their lives they are already revealing something of divine humor. The task of the evangelizer is to build on these glimmers of transcendence through the enlighten-ing power of the Gospel. The pastoral advice of St. Paul is relevant here: "whatever is true, whatever is honorable, whatever is just, whatever is pure, whatever is pleasing, whatever is commendable, if there is any excellence and if there is anything worthy of praise, think about these things" (Phil 4:8). Of this we can be sure, claims Paul, that anything and everything that is "honorable" or "commendable" comes from God.

To help evangelizers, therefore, this chapter explains four models of culture and the positive or negative qualities of the humor that charac-terize each one. An anthropological model is constructed to illuminate complex social realities by highlighting major social patterns and initially reducing the importance of details or nuances. In a particular society it is possible for all the models to be simultaneously present, with one model being more dominant than others. Also, a person may draw on one model and then another within a short time period, depending on the situation.[3] The four models to be explained in this chapter are: pre-modern, modern, postmodern, and paramodern. More attention will be given to the last two because they are particularly relevant in the contemporary world. Readers may find it useful at this point to refresh their understanding of the different uses of humor, particularly humor as subversive and confirmatory, as explained in chapter 1.

Premodern Cultures

Examples of cultures approximating to this model are the Israelites as described in the book of Leviticus,[4] cultures in many parts of Africa, Southeast Asia, the South Pacific, rural South America, groups based on fictive kinship, and the Catholic Church prior to the Second Vatican

Council. Fictive kinship systems, such as mafia, gangs, police forces, military units, and sporting clubs, are groups in which members relate to one another according to the norms of biologically defined families, that is, the imperative to maintain group loyalty.

Elements

A premodern culture is one in which behavior is highly traditional. Personal identity is inseparable from the group into which an individual is born, such as the extended family, clan, or tribe. When the evangelist Matthew wanted to define who Jesus was, he started by listing a long genealogy (Matt 1:1-17). Many peoples of the world would understand his logic. Language is concrete, dynamic, and filled with imagery.

Founding myths exalt stability and the sacredness of tradition, not change; the culture is a gift of the gods/ancestors so it must not be questioned. The fear of being mocked, laughed at, or punished by spirits and other group members if one goes against tradition enforces conformity to the group's norms. Because tradition is pivotal, harmony and unity must be maintained in the group at all costs, even if the objective norms of justice are broken in the process. To be expelled from the group, as Cain found after murdering Abel (Gen 4:10, 12-13), is the most severe form of punishment possible because the individual then loses social identity and rights. Respect for patriarchal values is also a strong force maintaining the social status quo. Sin is the breaking of detailed rules established particularly to maintain the clarity of roles and boundaries within the culture; sexual sins are especially evil because if control over the body is broken there is real danger that the social body will be fractured as well.[5]

Humor: Confirmatory

Rituals of initiation are especially important in premodern cultures because they define roles and expectations about ways in which tradition is to be maintained. In the liminality stage the emphasis is on instilling in initiates the understanding that belonging to the group demands unquestioning loyalty to the group and its tradition. Since these rituals aim to enforce the cultural status quo, subversive prophetic humor is discouraged. Rituals of reversal in which public figures are ridiculed, for example, at carnival times, are permitted provided that they aim to release community tensions and not threaten the cultural status quo. Ritual leaders, such as clowns and priests, have a high social status only if they remind people of pivotal traditional values in the culture.[6]

Pastoral Response in Premodern Cultures

Since people have a sense of a spirit world but frequently see those spirits as fickle and vengeful, the pastoral response is to stress the loving and forgiving aspects of God's humor, as in the parable of the Prodigal Son. Additionally, the threefold stages of rituals of transition are an integral quality of premodern cultures and can be used in catechesis as foundations for explaining the Christian rituals of initiation. In explaining the Scriptures, the pastoral response should emphasize the role of subversive prophetic humor. Premodern cultures, with their emphasis on group loyalty, can oppress individuals who dare to challenge aspects of these cultures. Since storytelling is a quality of this culture model, the parables are a useful way to teach the importance of prophetic humor.

Modern Cultures[7]

This culture model is particularly applicable in Western countries and in other parts of the world, such as contemporary Russia, Japan, and China, where the capitalistic ethic has been adopted.

Elements

At the heart of modernity's mythology is the preeminent position of patriarchy and of the person rather than the group, in addition to the belief that human progress is unstoppable. Modernity encourages secularism in which there is no place for God or worship, optimistically exalts science, and claims the human mind can discover truths of universal value through the application of scientific and technological methods alone. Individuals, groups, and nations are destined by nature to compete for survival. Only the strong should survive.

Humor: Confirmatory

Modernity discourages subversive prophetic humor and emphasizes humor that confirms the optimistic belief in the perfectibility of human nature. Negativities such as violence, oppression, greed, and death are ignored lest people question the optimistic view of the world around them. Humor reaffirms the existing political and hierarchical power structure. Even in democracies festivities are commonly controlled to reinforce national identity and hide brutal realities. A stroll through the streets of Disneyland or Disney World offers visitors the chance to experience the mingling of nationalism and the comic fantasies of modernity. The streets—spotless and patriotic—are full of warmth and sometimes even cloying coziness; they are places in which the harsh reality of the outside world, when admitted, is scaled down to safer, softer dimensions.[8] Even rituals like the English Last Night of the Proms do not escape a strong nationalistic influence. So also for sport. Soccer now engages nations in a worldwide rivalry, second only to the Olympic Games in the amount of ritual action surrounding the national teams. Historian David Cannadine argues that one of the reasons why witty and comic Gilbert and Sullivan operas remained so popular in Britain well into the twentieth century was because they did not address social problems, encouraging instead the orderly traditions of flag saluting, foreigner hating, and aristocrat respecting.[9]

Popular comedy sitcoms such as *I Love Lucy*, *Leave it to Beaver*, *Father Knows Best* (a paragon of idealized family life, with its gray-suited head of the household), and *The Brady Bunch* mirror the mythology of optimism and patriarchy. The ideal "normal" family is one in which the father/husband is in charge and the wife is at home, dedicated to domestic chores and ensuring her spouse is welcomed back after a tiring day at work. Everyone knows their place in the social and family hierarchy, and if perchance they stray from their "rightful" roles they will be back once more to "normality" by the end of the show. These sitcoms rarely, if ever, deal with suffering in any real sense, but if they do it is done briefly and all is resolved happily in the end.

Prophetic humor that is subversive of the cultural status quo is not to be tolerated in societies structured for modernity. In terms of the ritual model of biblical humor—separation, liminality, and reaggregation—humor in modernity avoids the liminal or chaos stage. Prophetic humorists are placed socially at some distance. In a world of individualism, consumerism, and competition for power, people are not to be reminded of the fleeting nature of the world and social injustice. Woody Allen acknowledged the second-class social status of the comedian in modernity: "When you do comedy, you are not sitting at the grown-ups' table."[10] It was the same in Shakespeare's time. As soon as Prince Hal becomes Henry V, he puts Falstaff, the teacher and support of his jokes in his pre-kingly days, behind him: "I know thee not, old man: fall to thy prayers; How ill white hairs become a fool and jester."[11] When Charlie Chaplin's film *Monsieur Verdoux*, a critique of capitalism, was released in 1947 it evoked protests in many American cities. Not surprisingly, during the era of McCarthyism, Chaplin was accused of "un-American activities" as a suspected communist and forced into exile.

Pastoral Response in Modern Cultures

The mythology of this culture model contains much that is contrary to the gospels and Christian tradition: the denial of suffering and death, individualism to the neglect of social responsibility, the weakening of belief in the afterlife and God. Parables such as The Rich Man and Lazarus and the Good Samaritan, along with examples of Jesus as Servant Leader and advocate of gender equality, are important for explaining the gospel message of justice and human solidarity. The prophetic witness of "holy fools," such as Dorothy Day, Mother Teresa of Calcutta, Nelson Mandela, John Paul II, and groups that challenge modernity's mythology by their radical approach to life, is crucial. Evangelizers can use occasions of personal and group suffering as opportunities to explain Christ's abiding love for them testified by his life, death, and resurrection.

Postmodern Cultures

Postmodernity's mythology was a complex reaction to the cultural revolution of the 1960s. The most common characteristic of this dramatically quick and radical cultural movement was the symbolism of antiauthority and anti-institution. It was essentially an attack on boundaries, limits, certainties, taboos, roles, systems, style, ritual, optimism, and respect for the orderly world of modernity. The modernity that had given birth to the mass carnage of two world wars and the disastrous potential of atomic warfare was seen to be morally bankrupt. The multifaceted world of postmodernity contains two oppositional mythologies, which I term "anti-order" and "pro-order" mythology. Different behavior patterns, including dissimilar approaches to humor, reflect these two mythologies.

Elements of Anti-order Postmodernity

Adherents of anti-order mythology reject modernity and yearn to continue the cultural revolution. Reality is meaninglessness, chaos without hope, a world in which God, rationality, and history have no place. There is a bleakness and an inescapable sadness that can lead to personal and group depression.

Superficiality

In anti-order postmodernity there is nothing beneath the glittering surfaces of a culture, no hidden meanings. Postmodern art mirrors these assumptions with its rejection of the aristocratic aloofness of the art of modernity from everyday life of people. This leads to the embrace of kitsch and popular culture so evident in the works of artists like Andy Warhol and writers like Kurt Vonnegut.[12] Thus pop art in the 1960s and 1970s rejects the objective norms of art and humor of modernity and exalts superficiality. For example, there is Claes Oldenburg's incongruous giant plastic French fries and ketchup, Jim Dine's toothbrushes and tuxedos, and Andy Warhol's soup cans from the psychedelic supermarket, his gaudy Marilyn Monroes. Warhol deliberately cultivated the banal in his art to illustrate the shallowness of life: "Just look at the surface of my films and paintings. . . . There's nothing behind it."[13] Warhol and his followers expected people to laugh at the sheer banality of all this.

No Universal Truths

In an anti-order postmodern culture universal truths such as justice and compassion do not exist. Thus traditional institutions, for example, governments and churches, which are constructed on the assumption that there are universally valid truths, no longer have any social legitimacy. In the case of religion, people form their own mixture of beliefs, selecting what appeals to them personally and rejecting the rest.[14]

Narcissism

Narcissists are focused only on themselves and though narcissism exists in modernity, it is more markedly present in postmodernity. There is a constant and exhausting search among postmodernists for new satisfying personal identities, but there is no way of proving they have any validity. This idea of self as "continuously revised biographical narratives"[15] is an attempt to achieve some fleeting personal meaning; examples are artistic performers like Madonna and Michael Jackson. Between 1978 and 1986 Madonna "imaged" herself as rebellious, exhibitionist, and overly sexual. At one time she mixed male and female dress codes and body language. Then she identified with sadomasochism, homoerotic imagery, and bisexuality.[16] This ongoing, even manic, narcissistic search for sustained meaning in life in the midst of a rapidly changing world can produce very fragile, insecure, cynical, and depressed people.

No Solidarity

There is no meaningful basis for collective agreement or action since the only "thing" that exists is the self, but the true self is unknowable. Individuals join an organization primarily for their own ends and any commitment to serve the common good is considered a waste of time.

Anti-order Humor: Negative

Because anti-order postmodernity cultivates cynicism about anything that appears good and decent, its humor can be openly negative, violent, and bitterly ironic. No one has any obligation toward society or anyone else, so people are free to attack anything and laugh at whatever causes violence. Even in the widely popular comedy series such as *Monty Python*, *Saturday Night Live*, and *Mr. Bean*, cynicism and sadistic elements are common. Blatant sadism accompanied by foul language is especially evident in the chic lyrics of the widely popular rapper Eminem, who can sell seven million albums and grip the attention of mainstream white American youth culture.[17] Frequently the objects of his violence are women and gay people, but shocking though the language is, Eminem is ironically articulating the violence of millions of people trapped in poverty and oppression.

The American situation television comedy *Married . . . With Children* (started in 1987) depicts a family and neighborhood that violates every ideal of romantic love, kinship, friendship, community, where life is mere routine and banal, uncaring, with manipulation, distrust, treachery, betrayal, mixed with comic violence. Bundy, the central figure, is a misanthropic women's shoe salesman with a miserable life. He loathes his job, his wife is lazy, his son is dysfunctional (especially with women), and his stereotypically dumb blonde daughter is mindless and promiscuous. All characters have one thing in common—they are all entertainingly tasteless and coarse. The comedy is filled with irony, because while it is humorously focusing on the dysfunctional family, it is in fact but a mirror of contemporary society.

Another popular postmodern television show is *Cheers*, a humorously depressing portrayal of failure and loss, disappointed expectations, cynical motives, fading ideals, disloyalty, betrayal, all in contrast to the utopian optimism of modernity.[18] An equally well-liked sitcom in the 1990s was *Seinfeld*, a comedy that focuses on the daily trivial, uninspiring experiences of four unmarried characters in their thirties from white, middle-class New York. There is nothing heroic in their behavior. Despite the fact that the characters are well past adolescence they lead lives that are narcissistic, unashamedly devoid of all concern for others. In the last episode, for example, they witness the mugging and theft of a weak and overweight man and, refusing to come to his assistance, they laugh at his size. *Seinfeld* is a mirror of the "anti-order" postmodern society and beneath its funny surface is a biting satire on the fundamental weaknesses of postmodernity.[19]

Dada: Prototype of Postmodern Humor

Dada is commonly considered to be the original archetype of how postmodern art in its many forms, including humor, should go about being radical. Dada was one of several art movements in the early twentieth century that aimed to annoy the self-important middle classes of Europe and North America. Founded on principles of irrationality, incongruity, and irreverence towards accepted aesthetic criteria, Dada used a number of methods to disturb bourgeois fantasies, using materials not normally associated with sophisticated art, for example, a urinal, a bottle rack, a comb. Art became a juxtaposition of incompatible or heterogeneous fragments for ironic or parodic effect, as opposed to the principle of orderly and focused presentation.[20]

Fight Club was released in the cinemas in 1999, not long after the tragic shooting at Columbine High School in Colorado, and was quickly acclaimed as an icon of American pop culture. Two new male friends start a fistfight in a parking lot and discover the joys of pain. Fighting makes them feel alive again. Other young men imitate them and they establish the "Fight Club," which soon develops into an underworld organization in which violence is a way of life. Instead of moral revulsion viewers are encouraged to laugh at violence as though it is something normal. An earlier film, *Pulp Fiction*, had a similar banal and "humorous" approach to brutality. The film is filled with violence, which the film's characters deal with by laughing at it. Violence and murder become events that produce a comic effect as the two main characters are depicted as regular guys who just happen to make their living as hit men.

In summary, humor in anti-order postmodern cultures is such that the world in all its chaotic disorder is simply taken for granted as inevitable. In terms of the ritual model of biblical humor there is separation and liminality, but no reaggregation. Hope is unreal; only the despair and reality of the liminal chaos are acceptable themes in humor. Hence, there is no place in this negative humor for the prophetically subversive, with its promise of hope in "a new heaven and a new earth" (Rev 21:1).

Elements of Pro-order Postmodernity

At the heart of pro-order mythology is a revitalized commitment to modernity, with its optimistic view of human perfectibility through individual effort, patriarchy, and exaltation of unrestrained capitalism typical of the nineteenth century. Hence, the rise of what is variously termed "economic rationalism," "ncocapitalism," "ncolibcralism," or "the new Right." The ideological assumptions are: profit is the sole measure of value; sustained economic growth is the best way to distribute wealth; free markets, unrestrained by government interference, result in the most efficient use of resources; low taxation for the wealthy and reduction of government spending, especially in favor of those who are poor; breaking up of trade unions; the privatization of public services; the emphasis on "law and order" as a way to control crime, for example, mandatory sentencing and zero tolerance strategies; the demonizing of refugees and asylum seekers.[21] The achievement of wealth is again implicitly a sign of God's especial love; poverty is a sign of God's punishing displeasure.

Pro-order Humor: Confirmatory

The Cosby Show, one of the most successful American television comedy series from 1984 to 1992, is a pro-order comedy. The series revolves around the day-to-day events of an African American upper-middle-class family, the Huxtables: the father (Bill Cosby) a respected obstetrician, the mother a successful attorney, and their five children. Secure in a sheltered atmosphere of love and affluence the children live trouble-free lives. The sitcom is an updating of the previous successful comedy, *Leave it to Beaver*, and mirrors the optimistic qualities of modernity. The premiere of *The Cosby Show* coincided with President Reagan's landslide reelection, and many of the qualities of the Huxtable family fit well into the conservative pro-order agenda of the Republican party.

Pastoral Response in Postmodern Cultures

In the tripartite process of initiation rituals, humor of anti-order postmodernity, unlike modernity, emphasizes the liminal or chaos stage, but not the reaggregation stage. The chaos offers no hope for individuals or society. Catechesis can begin with the despairing qualities of the chaotic world, but with the help of Scripture people can be then encouraged to see in Christ's death *and* resurrection the gift of hope that gives ultimate meaning to life. It is a time also to introduce people to the spirituality of chaos and hope in the lament psalms. The catechetical challenge of pro-order postmodernity is similar to that posed by modernity. Chapter 8 will explain some pastoral responses to the violences and negativities of postmodernity.

Paramodern Cultures

Readers would be forgiven for thinking that there is little or nothing particularly positive in postmodernity. In fact, however, there are positive movements in reaction to the negativities of postmodernity, so much so that we can speak of a new culture model emerging, which I call paramodernity. The model critiques, on the one hand, the excessive optimism and rationality in modern culture and, on the other, the built-in pessimism and self-destructiveness of much postmodernist thinking. Paramodernity is a model that takes the best of postmodernity and looks to the future. The main constituent and interrelated elements of the mythology of paramodernity can be summarized under the following headings.

Spirituality

Paramodernists speak of a yearning for a spirituality, although there is often a vagueness about what it means. It is generally agreed that it is "something" that gives an uplifting, intimate, and exciting meaning to personal life. The response to the search for a spirituality, however, is less and less thought to be found in traditional mainline churches. People will draw from any source that they feel responds to their need for meaning.

Dialogue

Dialogue is an interaction between people in which each one aims to present herself/himself as she or he is and seeks also to know the other personally and culturally. Dialogue is an attitude of listening with respect and friendship; when this is present people will be open to hear what God is saying in the hearts and cultures of people. It is authentic if three conditions are met: if people feel they understand the positions of others, if they also feel that others understand their points of view, and if there is a readiness on the part of all to be open to change.

Interdependency/Solidarity

Instead of a machine-like universe of the culture of modernity, there is a growing acceptance that the world consists of interrelated living organisms that are essentially cooperative and characterized by coexistence, interdependence, and symbiosis. Touch one relationship and all are affected to some degree. Humankind must adopt the same qualities to survive. Hence, the increasing emphasis on building solidarity and interdependence between peoples and the whole universe. Solidarity is a profound, moral sense that stresses that our well-being depends on the well-being of others.

Otherness and Storytelling

Paramodernity is noted for its emphasis on the rights of peoples of minority cultures to exist and to tell their own stories of human survival and creativity. Founding myths of nations are important, but paramodernity claims that everyone—individuals and groups—has the right and the need to retell for themselves and others the narratives of their own journey. Through storytelling we not only define our identity but are also helped to become agents of our own lives; an untold life is not worth living.[22] This emphasis of otherness encourages respect for multiculturalism, which opposes the view that immigrants must adopt the host society's customs and values so that there is just one story. The challenge for a truly multicultural society is to retain the uniqueness of different traditions, with their particular ways of expressing humor and celebrating life, while simultaneously creating a new entity in which these traditions are able to be shared and respected by all.

Myth

Paramodernists are revitalizing the importance of myths (see chap. 3) in our lives because the cold logic of modernity's rationality has led to devastating violence. Myths, with their emphasis on imagination and intuition, are able to express the hidden and eternal factors integral to daily living that cannot be articulated in ordinary literal or empirical language. The renewed interest in the importance of myths is being accompanied by a revitalized awareness of the importance of positive humor to keep one's balance in the midst of otherwise humorless situations. Both myth and humor require imagination and intuitive flexibility. Humor and meditation workshops are increasingly popular because they help participants to put on hold the use of rational thinking and allow them to remain comfortable with just waiting for intuitive insights to emerge from the unconscious.

Supportive Groups

To counteract the dehumanizing impact of postmodern society people seek supportive friendships in small groups. These groups provide opportunities for members in search of meaning to tell and to listen to stories of life's experiences.

Deconstructionism

According to the philosopher Jacques Derrida, deconstructionist methodology is a process "of unceasingly analysing the whole conceptual machinery"[23] of language and structures in society in order to examine the ways they manipulate power to the disadvantage of people. Positive subversive humor is again recognized as an important way to identify and critique oppressive power structures in society. This is one of the aims of Umberto Eco's book *The Name of the Rose*, which first appeared in English in 1983. Although it is acclaimed as the quintessential postmodernist novel with its considerable irony, its fondness for quotation, and its playful use of history, it has paramodern qualities. The conspirators in a fourteenth-century Benedictine Italian monastery fear that if comedy, with its subversive qualities, were to be restored within respectable academic circles, the entire framework of hierarchical power in the church and society would collapse. The novel imagines a lost book by Aristotle in support of humor; murders mysteriously occur to prevent its finding, but eventually the monastery is destroyed, as is the book. The novel brilliantly reminds contemporary readers that it is common for people in authority to fear the revolutionary power of positive subversive humor. Hence, their desire to control the use of humor in order to protect their power.[24]

Death and Evil

One gift that paramodernity receives from postmodern culture is the increasing acknowledgement of the reality of death and evil that is a reaction to modernity's denial of both. The writings of Michel Foucault, Zygmunt Baumann, and Jean Baudrillard significantly dwell on this point. Evil here means the destruction of people either by killing or by the development of conditions that materially or psychologically destroy or weaken their dignity, happiness, and ability to fulfill fundamental human needs.[25] Postmodernists alert us to this reality and the fact that we ourselves can be the agents of oppression. In the words of Alexander Solzhenitsyn, "the line dividing good and evil cuts through the heart of every human being."[26] People are increasingly prepared to campaign against oppression using, among other aids, positive humor. For example, during the time of the communist control of the Eastern bloc countries, the underground press regularly circulated humorous skits and jokes critiquing the oppressive behavior of their rulers. It was risky but widely successful. Movements protesting against violence have been common in history, but over the last seventy or so years the application of nonviolent methods has given birth to a different way of confronting and even overthrowing an unjust order, such as in the civil rights movement in the United States, South Africa, and Poland. Nonviolence proves that violence can change events, even radically, but violence does not grant power to people.

Humor: Prophetic

As explained above, anti-order postmodernists believe that there is nothing that can be done about evil but to accept it and try to survive if possible. Despair and ultimately suicide are the logical conclusions to such a negative view of life. Humor in paramodernity, by contrast, accepts the reality of evil, yet believes personal and group transformation is possible. The uplifting experiences of compassion and justice can happen. In terms of the paradigm of initiation rituals, namely separation/liminality/reaggregation, paramodernists claim that people can proceed in a transformative way through all three stages. The evils of society can be critiqued *and* resolved; that is, subversive prophetic humor is possible in word and action. The following are some examples of paramodern prophetic humor as developed in plays, films, and books.

Plays

"Theatre of the Absurd" is a term created by the literary critic Martin Esslin[27] for the plays written mainly in the 1950s and 1960s by writers such as Samuel Beckett, Arthur Adamov, Eugene Ionesco, Jean Genet, and Harold Pinter. The authors were deeply influenced by the traumatic events of the Second World War and the growing fears of nuclear disaster. For them the world no longer had any meaning for people, especially following the loss of faith in the existence of God; but people needed to be encouraged to rediscover that life can have a purpose. Authors like Beckett and Ionesco were visionary because their writings survived the tumult of posmodernity and fit well within the paramodern model.

Theatre of the Absurd aims to reinstate the importance of myth and ritual so that people can again celebrate the awesome beauties of the world and the universe as a whole. It does this by shocking people out of their complacent and mechanical lives. Conventional and stereotypical language patterns are ridiculed to make people conscious that there are far more powerful ways of communicating than through traditional language. Rational thinking does not move beyond the superficial things of life. Plotless, illogical, and without discord, the plays dramatically diverge from what is considered to be conventional theatre. Often the scenery has no connection with the play and the dialogue is commonly plain nonsense. Nonsense, however, provides a glimpse of the infinite. Eugene Ionesco writes of the liberating impact of the absurd: "Humour . . . is the only possibility we possess of detaching ourselves . . . from our . . . malaise of being. . . . Laughter alone does not respect any taboo, laughter alone inhibits the creation of new anti-taboo taboos; the comic alone is capable of giving us the strength to bear the tragedy of existence. The true nature of things, truth itself, can be revealed to us only by fantasy, which is more realistic than all the realisms."[28]

The best known writer in this tradition is Samuel Beckett (1906–89). In his *Waiting for Godot*[29] he adopts the techniques of vaudeville and farce: hat-swapping, Laurel-and-Hardy-like banter. The play's two protagonists, who are tramps, suffer from mildly comical physical ailments: Vladimir has a weak bladder and smelly feet. The tramps' wordplay and jokes, some good, some deliberately feeble, are sprinkled throughout the play. The men wait under a tree by the side of the road for someone or something that never appears. Nothingness, emptiness, repetition, boredom, for better or worse, Beckett refined these attributes in his writings, but the result is far from depressing. He depicts his characters in situations of acute decay and deprivation because that is where some kind of hope can be rediscovered, where people have no place to go except upward.

Films and Books

The comedy films of Woody Allen require special mention. Allen uses positive relaxing humor to entertain, but at times he also brilliantly employs prophetic humor specifically to highlight the moral void left by postmodernity and the need to seek objective moral standards. The human soul has the potential for goodness in the midst of complex pressures to the contrary.[30] In *Annie Hall* (1977) Allen critiques the world of the 1970s, with its conflictual politics, drugs, narcissism, religion, celebrities. He does this without losing the attention of his audiences through the dazzling and sophisticated mixture of humor and philosophy.[31]

Several highly successful recent books and films, *Star Wars* among them, are popular with all age groups. Mythological or allegorical language and scenes present the stark reality of evil in the world. Unlike their postmodern counterparts, however, these books and films claim that evil can be overcome through personal transformation and integrity. Their plots follow the tripartite pattern of ritual, with its inherent joking dynamic, and all stages are important. Here are some examples.

The Lord of the Rings

There is positive subversive humor in J.R.R. Tolkien's *The Lord of the Rings* books, which have been popularized in films in recent years. The theme is the evil of the misuse of power and how good eventually triumphs. Sauron seeks total power for himself, but to do so he desperately needs to find a ring that has been lost in battle. Anyone who has the ring is in danger of being seduced into its evil power; the only way to stop this from happening is to destroy the ring. The main hero in the saga, Frodo Baggins, is the symbolic antithesis of corrupting power. He is a very ordinary hobbit and this is his subversive, humorous quality. He is the biblical embodiment of St. Paul's famous self-discovery, namely, that God chooses those who are foolish in the world's assessment in order to shame the wise (1 Cor 1:27). Because Frodo is so ordinary—he does not seek power and lacks any selfishness that the ring could attach itself to—he has the dangerous task of destroying the ring. He succeeds, despite the efforts of evil forces to kill him and capture the ring. The subversive and socially incongruous lesson is clear: every individual, provided they are selfless, can resist evil and consequently be of help to others. The theme is a warning that people can easily convince themselves it is right to do good things by committing evil.

Harry Potter

A similar theme is to be found in the extremely popular *Harry Potter* books by J. K. Rowling. The young orphan Harry Potter lives with a very disagreeable family and is in constant conflict with evil wizards, in particular Lord Voldemort. The latter has lost his power but seeks to regain it, with the assistance of his former followers, through all kinds of evil measures. Evil is synonymous with a self-centered desire to dominate others and is opposed by those who have power and are prepared to use it for the good of others. The headmaster of Harry's school is Dumbledore, a wizard motivated by kindness and compassion, and because of this he is feared by Voldemort.

The Simpsons

The Simpsons is the longest-running cartoon series on American prime-time network television (with translated editions in other countries as well), aired for the first time in 1989. It recounts the animated adventures of Homer Simpson and his lower-middle-class family. Homer, the father, is a lazy, unintelligent, beer-drinking safety inspector for the local nuclear power plant in the fictional city of Springfield. Marge, his wife, is a somewhat spacey woman with a huge beehive hairstyle; and Bart, their ten-year-old son, is a borderline juvenile delinquent. Lisa, the middle child, is a gifted, sensitive, and perceptive saxophone player. Maggie is the voiceless toddler, observing all while sucking her pacifier. In addition, there are other equally dysfunctional members of the community.

The Simpsons first appeals to children because the cartoons are immense fun; but, like Jonathan Swift's *Gulliver's Travels*, it is primarily written for adults as an allegorical satire. Children and adolescents especially love the antics of Bart, who so readily and unashamedly manipulates and ridicules his parents and other adults. One of the program's writers comments: "We're really writing a show that has some of the most esoteric references in television. . . . We're writing it for adults and intelligent adults at that."[32] *The Simpsons* is richly laced with satire, sarcasm, irony, and caricature[33] as the authors seek to expose reality as it is—chaotic and violent. Hypocrisy, the incompetence of pop psychology, modern child rearing, commercialism, consumerism, fundamentalism in religion, environmental abuse, corporate greed, and the deceits of American education are all uncovered in stark and often parodied ways. Homer tells his daughter Lisa that it is quite acceptable to steal things "from people you don't like." Reverend Lovejoy lies to Lisa about the contents of the Bible to succeed in an argument. There are plenty of disreputable characters in Springfield, but the most loathsome is Mr. Burns, the owner of the nuclear power plant and a cruel example of the worst form of contemporary neocapitalism. Speaking to a group of school children he says: "Family, religion, friendship: These are the three demons you must slay if you wish to succeed in business."[34]

continued on next page

The spectacular emphasis on violence in its many forms is especially evident in the television comedy that Lisa and Bart regularly enjoy—*The Itchy and Scratchy Show*. The interaction between a cat and mouse is not confined to slapstick mixed with a little violence, but the violence is carried to extremes of stark gruesomeness. The creators of *The Simpsons* get away with it because it is in the form of a cartoon and, more particularly, because viewers condone violence in many areas of contemporary life. The writers know this and are focused on mirroring back to their audiences what society has come to accept as normal: that violence is condoned even for children, provided it does not affect the interests of individual viewers. Bart says to Lisa at one point when she is becoming squeamish about the violence they see on television: "If you don't watch the violence, you'll never get desensitized to it."[35]

So satirically and bluntly true to life is the show that Carl Matheson, a professor of philosophy, concludes that *The Simpsons* is filled not just with normal irony but with what he terms "hyperirony."[36] The show appears to condone in comedic form pervasive and blatant violence, but in fact it is morally critiquing the social, capitalistic, and physical brutality that American people and others accept as normal. Yet, unlike much postmodern literature and films, this series, while accepting the evil in the world, recognizes that people are capable of goodness at times. I agree with Mark I. Pinsky, a theologian, when he writes that overall it is a "funny show about a family as 'real' as the faith lives of many Americans. It is a show that does in fact give hope and joy and, yes, inspiration to millions."[37] While uncovering hypocrisy in religion, *The Simpsons* recognizes its indisputable role in American life. Homer does go to church and he speaks to God from time to time, but his image of God is rather confused. God for Homer is like a parachute that he hopes he will never have to open, but he needs God just in case. Homer's God is more forgiving and compassionate than the God of Homer's local minister. Lisa and her mother Marge at times do become the social conscience of the family and others (including viewers), reminding them that in the midst of a neocapitalist world of greed the fundamental virtues of compassion and justice can and should be lived.

These examples assume that it is possible to triumph over evil, especially through collaborative action. It will take an internal conversion on our part for this to happen, but, contrary to the destructive pessimism of the worst elements of postmodernity, redemption is possible. The examples given are brilliantly constructed and are aimed at different audiences. The Theatre of the Absurd and the films of Woody Allen are directed at a highly sophisticated audience; *The Simpsons* appeals to young people as well as to a more discerning section of adult viewers. All have one common characteristic—they create a reflective liminal space in which the social, political common characteristic and economic status quo can be critiqued, and alternatives to suffocating conformity have opportunities to emerge. For this reason humor in paramodernity is both subversively positive and prophetic.

Pastoral Response in Paramodern Cultures

The resurgence of positive humor, with its acceptance of the tripartite ritual dynamic, provides a welcome cultural support for evangelizers to explain how the Christian message of the paschal mystery can be a response to people's deepest yearnings for personal and social transformation. Examples will be given in chapter 8 of how people are using this cultural support in pastorally creative ways.

Summary

- When people express positive humor in their lives they are already revealing something of divine humor. The task of the evangelizer is to build on these glimmers of transcendence through the enlightening power of the Gospel.

- The ritual of humor in premodernity follows the tripartite process of initiation rituals, but the emphasis in the reaggregation stage is to reinforce the wider cultural status quo; humorists as ritual leaders affirm the traditional cultural myths. Rituals of humor in modernity, however, bypass the chaos of liminality in order to reinforce the optimistic fantasy of a future without suffering. Humorists in modernity are regarded as socially inferior whenever they dare to uncover the chaos of personal and social failings.

- Postmodernity is of two kinds: anti-order and pro-order. The former rejects the certainties and optimism of modernity; since the achievement of meaning in life is an illusion, despair is the logical consequence. Negative humor flourishes in anti-order postmodernity, with its bleakness and hopelessness. Pro-order postmodernity is a revitalization of modernity; hence it aims to affirm, not to challenge, the status quo in a prophetic way. The paramodern model, in which humor is of the prophetic type, critiques the excessive optimism about human progress in modern culture and the built-in pessimism of postmodernity.

- The next chapter traces how Christians have accepted or rejected the use of positive humor over the centuries.

Chapter 7

The Churches and Humor: Reflections

"[T]he lack of humour and irritability into which we in the contemporary Church and contemporary theology have so often slipped is perhaps one of the most serious objections which can be brought against present-day Christianity.
Cardinal Walter Kasper[1]

From the Reformation onwards laughter and humour were almost completely eclipsed in Christian writing.
Stephen Pattison[2]

This chapter explains:

- the theology of the transformation of cultures, that is, inculturation;
- the meaning of "functional substitution" as a pastoral method;
- the church's ambivalent relationship historically to culture(s) and humor;
- the role of prophetic humorists in the church.

This chapter very briefly considers the attitudes of Christians over the centuries toward cultures. Since humor is part of every culture this review will also reveal how it has been regarded in theology, worship, and pastoral ministry. Historically, we can identify two opposing theologies: "redemption-centered theology" and "creation-centered theology,"[3] which have had a profound influence on our appreciation of cultures and humor. The former discourages even positive humor, but the latter encourages it in theological reflection, pastoral action, and worship. Redemption-centered theology assumes that nature, including the human body, is inherently corrupt. Since all cultures, the products of human actions, are morally depraved there is no possibility that God is revealing to us something of his own divine goodness in cultures. There are no glimmers of transcendence in cultures. God is a God who counts our failures, threatening us all the time with punishment. With little room for God's loving mercy, redemption-centered theology is depressing theology that condemns, or at least discourages, humor in worship and preaching.

Creation-centered theology is built on the belief that we are prone to sin, and evil does exist in the world, but through the grace of God we can struggle to act justly and compassionately. As explained at the beginning of the last chapter, God's Word is being spoken within cultures even before, and while, the Gospel is preached. Evangelizers, declares Vatican II, "can learn by sincere and patient dialogue what treasures a bountiful God has distributed among the nations of earth. But at the same time, let them try to illumine these treasures with the light of the gospel, to set them free, and to bring them under the dominion of God their savior."[4] Thus when people express prophetic humor in their lives, such as acting justly in cultures where it is considered a weakness, God's humor is being revealed: "Truly I tell you, just as you did it to one of the least of these who are members of my family, you did it to me" (Matt 25:40).

The task of the evangelizer, as explained in the opening paragraphs of the last chapter, is to illumine this humor through the enlightening power of the Gospel. This process of transforming cultures is termed inculturation, a theological term used in the Catholic Church beginning in the early 1970s.[5] There are four mysteries of faith involved in inculturation:

- The incarnation of Christ continues within the lives and cultures of people. Aylward Shorter comments: "The Christ who took human flesh is the Word in whom all has been created. This means that he is at the heart of all human cultures, that he is responsible for whatever is true and good in them and that he makes them vehicles of salvation."[6]

- Christ's death is reenacted as cultures die to what is not of God.

- The power of the resurrection elevates attitudes, values, and customs that are in conformity with Christ's message.

- The creative Spirit of Pentecost energizes people and cultures to share their love of Jesus with others.

Christianity, Cultures, and Humor

We use the term "functional substitution" for the particular method of inculturation that enriches with gospel values the glimmers of transcendence in a culture. It is a process whereby over a lengthy period of time a Christian meaning is gradually substituted for a non-Christian symbol, myth, or ritual. Functional substitution assumes that symbols can change their meanings only slowly. It respects the dignity of people because, while they may accept intellectually a new understanding of truths or rituals, it takes much longer for their hearts to feel comfortable with them. Jesus himself uses functional substitution. He preaches in the synagogue and shows himself to be a good Jew by frequenting the Temple. At the same time, however, when he uses traditional religious rituals, he endows them with new meanings; for example, at the Last Supper the traditional Passover meal is given a much richer mythological significance. Jesus helps his listeners to discover what is good and to be retained in traditional Jewish mythological life, and what needs to be changed through the introduction of new meanings.

When we view Jesus' method of preaching and witness from a humor perspective, we see that he respects the cultural ways of the people. He employs relaxing humor in his parables to put people at ease. When they are relaxed he uses prophetic humor to teach his message according to the pattern of functional substitution. For example, he testifies that he is a prophet, a role that the Jewish people were accustomed to for centuries, but moves on to explain he is the greatest of all prophets. He uses the tripartite initiation ritual, with its inherent joking pattern, that the people are familiar with from their religious traditions, but always explaining that the mythology of the new covenant must be a substitute for the former covenant between Yahweh and the Israelites (see chap. 5).

In the Acts of the Apostles St. Paul is at pains to use functional substitution in his pastoral ministry. He has a positive and open attitude toward what is good in the cultures of Gentiles, as displayed in his

Areopagus speech to the philosophers and leading politicians in Athens (Acts 17:22-31). Acknowledging the existence of an altar dedicated to an unknown god, Paul respectfully explains that this God is now revealed to be the creator of the world and is present to us in Jesus Christ who is risen from the dead. In good functional substitution style Paul constructs his speech step-by-step according to the rules of Greek rhetoric that were familiar to his listeners. He first focuses on winning over his audience by pointing out that he is not speaking about a new divinity, but one whom the Athenians have worshiped for a long time without knowing it (Acts 17:22-23). Paul then states the facts that his listeners are likely to accept (Acts 17:24-26): this God is the creator of the whole universe and of humankind, not residing in temples, and with no need for sacrifices. This is followed by his key point: it is necessary for people to search and find this God in whom "we live and move and have our being" (Acts 17:29). Next Paul spells out the consequences: the need to stop worshiping idols and the necessity to repent and be transformed by this God (Acts 17:30-31). In addition to quoting Scripture in support of his statements, Paul turns to the Greek poet Aratus: "For we too are his offspring" (Acts 17:28). This reference to a local poet would have impressed Paul's audience. Functional substitution does not mean cloaking over difficult truths. Like Jesus, Paul does not hesitate to point out what is not of the Spirit in cultures. At the end of his speech Paul does not apologize for speaking of the resurrection, just as in his letter to the Romans he castigates those who have failed to recognize God in his creation and have fallen into idolatry and depravity (Rom 1:18-23).[7] Overall, Paul's speech had positive results: though some scoffed at Paul's message, others believed and still others were prepared to at least hear him again (Acts 17:32-34).[8]

Centuries later, Pope Gregory the Great (540–604) exhorts St. Augustine of Canterbury (d. 604) to adopt this pastoral approach of functional substitution when evangelizing in England: "[Do not] destroy the temples of the gods, but only the idols housed therein. . . . [S]et up altars and place relics of the saints [in those same temples]. . . . The people will see that their places of worship have not been destroyed and will, therefore, be more inclined to renounce their error and recognize and adore the true God for the places to which they will come will be familiar to them and highly valued."[9] Christianity throughout Europe was gradually able to absorb and transform pre-Christian elements of indigenous cultures, such as wells, caves, mountains, and stones, through this process of functional substitution.

It is possible to identify three very broad periods in which the churches, in particular the Catholic Church, have reacted to cultures in ways that reflect creation-centered and redemption-centered theologies. When churches used creation-centered theology, they encouraged respect for different cultures, including their humor. Functional substitution was then an acceptable pastoral method of evangelizing. More commonly over the centuries, however, an acceptance of redemption-centered theology led to a rejection of cultures and their ability to reveal glimmers of transcendence. When this happened functional substitution was considered to be a dangerous compromise with local cultures and to be avoided.

Partial Respect: First to Fifteenth Centuries[10]

Up to the Peace of Constantine (ca. 312) evangelizers faced considerable hostility, either from Jewish communities or from Roman officials. But evangelizers during this time, despite the opposition, successfully used functional substitution in their teaching of the faith. In the third century Tertullian turned to Roman juridical language to explain aspects of the faith; thus, baptism is the breaking of a contract with the world and the entering into a new one with God in Christ. His listeners, attuned to juridical language, would then more readily have understood what baptismal renunciation and the profession of faith in Jesus means. Early Christian martyrs depicted Christ on the walls of catacombs as a crucified man with the head of an ass. This crucifix represented a mixture of animal, human, and divine qualities, and symbolized also the incongruous position of early Christians, who became fools for Christ, with a foolishness wiser than the wisdom of the world.[11]

But this openness to cultures remained rather selective because there was little encouragement given to relaxing humor. For early Christian writers the emphasis was on the need to be serious. Perhaps they were too influenced in part by the disdain that great classical scholars such as Plato, Aristotle, and Cicero showed toward the comic.[12] They were, however, also influenced by redemption-centered theology, with its belief that the world is a place of sin and evil; in this vale of tears we must spend our time in prayer, good works, and repentance for sin. As Jesus, it was assumed, never laughed we also must not laugh. The world would soon come to an end and there was no time to be distracted by the frivolity of humor. "The Christian," wrote St. Basil (ca. 330–79), "ought not to laugh nor even to suffer laugh-makers."[13] In the same century St. Ambrose believed that laughter is a sign of pride, but tears point to a heart that is truly penitential.[14] Saint Benedict in the sixth century admonished his monks not "to speak idle words, or such as to move to laughter," but he seems rather grudgingly to have allowed some moderate laughter: "Do not love great or excessive laughter."[15] Much later, Hildegard of Bingen, a gifted Rhineland mystic of the twelfth century, was less flexible, for she argued that laughter was proof of the sinful state of humanity.[16] Saint Bernard of Clairvaux (1090–1153) condemned all jesting. Fortunately St. Thomas Aquinas (ca. 1225–74) would later strongly support at least positive relaxing humor; in order to relieve the mind and tensions of life he allowed jesting, sporting, and playing of games.[17]

Following the Peace of Constantine in the early fourth century the church was allowed to function freely after years of persecution, but it often uncritically embraced many negative aspects of the imperial culture in its official worship and lifestyle. Whenever it did so it lost its sense of humor and therefore its ability to laugh at its own pomposity and misuse of power. Ecclesiastics accepted the symbols of the hierarchically structured imperial system but failed to measure them by the standards of the Gospel. Hence, bishops adopted the power or authority symbols of royalty; priests emphasized their authority over people and downplayed their role as servants within the community. Worship left the home and entered grand and impersonal basilicas; the ceremony of the imperial court provided models for glorious displays.[18] The church and its officials became increasingly wealthy, women were increasingly excluded from leadership positions, and undesirable aspects of Roman legalism began to have a deep negative impact on Christian living. Sin—which had earlier been thought of as a fracturing of the relationship of love and trust between members of the community, and as a violation of the covenant relationships between the community and God—was now presented too rigidly in legal terms as the breaking of an impersonal divine and ecclesiastical law. There is little room here for an appreciation of divine humor.

Whenever the church became uncritically involved in the imperial culture, it lost its evangelical flexibility and openness to functional substitution. Evangelizers found it hard to distinguish what was of the faith and what pertained to its particular cultural expression. As the Dominican theologian Yves Congar commented: "There existed an imperialism which tended to confuse unity and uniformity, to impose everywhere the Roman customs and rites, in a word, considering the universal Church as a simple extension of the Church of Rome."[19]

By the Middle Ages the divinity of Christ had become overemphasized to the detriment of his humanity, and in this atmosphere redemption-centered theology began to flourish. Liturgies under the control of clergy became remote from the people, who were expected to be passive on-lookers. Mass was offered *for* the people, not celebrated *by* the people, and by the time of the Reformation the Mass had become an elaborate performance: "there is a very rich façade, but behind it a great emptiness yawns."[20] In terms of our explanation of the different types of humor, liturgies had become confirmatory, that is, they confirmed the widening gaps between a distant, punishing God and the people, between power-centered clergy and laity.

Rituals of Reversal

During this period, however, the church did tolerate some expressions of positive humor that verged at times on the prophetic, for example, a pagan festival that had been at least partly Christianized through functional substitution. The festival of Shrove Tuesday on the eve of Ash Wednesday, and the carnival period that extended from the New Year to Lent, were formally incorporated into the church's liturgical calendar. These became substitutes for the ancient Roman feasts of Saturn, the Saturnalias, during which there was much licentiousness, and slaves dined with their masters, whom they freely mocked.[21] Through a process of functional substitution the church built on these festivals but sought to purify them of their sexual excesses.

Mikhail Bakhtin describes the festivities in the church during the carnival period as expressive rituals of folk humor in which ordinary people were able to assert their distaste for the oppressive, hierarchical, and clerical power structures in the church and society itself.[22] These comic, sometimes cruel, rituals of reversal were a way of resisting the official, serious culture, in which humor was seen to be a dangerous subversive process (chap. 1). One notable example of these rituals was the Feast of the Fools, sometimes called the Feast of Innocents, which thrived in parts of Europe during medieval times and the Renaissance. During this ritual of grotesque buffoonery, ordinary pious priests and respectable townspeople appeared in lewd masks and sang offensive lyrics. Lesser clerics with painted faces strutted around in the sacred vestments and courtly costumes of their superiors while mocking the rituals of the church and court. In Bohemia clerical merrymakers turned their vestments inside out and danced with vigor.[23]

The composition of satirical verse and the preaching of burlesque sermons were an integral part of these rituals, and no person in authority escaped mockery. In 1431 the Council of Basil condemned the Feast, but it continued until the sixteenth century.[24] The official church recognized that if "organized religion hoped to remain organized, only seriousness would keep it solidly together";[25] laity and ordinary clergy had to be kept in their place. Expressions of humor only threatened the orderly hierarchical structures of ecclesiastical (and secular) society. Protestant reformers, such as John Calvin, in subsequent centuries would also recognize the dangers of humor to the established order. Carnival festivities left the church and found a more welcome home in the streets and taverns.

Holy Fools

From time to time individuals recognized that humor can be a graced prophetic expression of God's presence in their lives. They sought to convince others of this insight, even to challenge the institutional church and secular society to be true to the Gospel message. Their lives became rituals of reversal in that their personal asceticism, love of poverty, and concern for people on the margins were in incongruous contrast to the values prevailing in society and the church, such as abuse of power, clericalism, and exaltation of wealth. Saint Benedict of Nursia (ca. 480–547), for instance, reacted prophetically to the growing chaos within civil and ecclesiastical societies. As the Roman Empire crumbled and Europe became subject to destructive invasions from outside, Benedict, influenced by people like Basil, the father of Eastern monasticism, fostered a fraternal and socially-conscious monasticism centered on the local church. Benedict's rule, again in opposition to the individualism, materialism, and authoritarianism of the feudal system, offered an alternative vision of society founded on the kingdom values of interdependence, love, and justice. He dreamt of communities in which class discrimination would have no place.

Over time Benedict's brilliantly humane, lay-inspired, and egalitarian movement itself fell victim to clericalism, individualism, and materialism, but new "jokers of God" would then emerge. Saint Francis of Assisi (1181–1226) had a profound sense of the divine humor so evident, he believed, in all creation and in the life and death of Jesus Christ. Inspired by a creation-centered spirituality he looked on all creatures as sisters and brothers united in the vast friary of the universe. So far from being serious distractions, all creatures are revelations of God's paradoxical love for all creation. Saint Francis's lifestyle and spirituality subversively questioned the rigidity of ecclesiastical and secular structures. His reaction to the moral ills of his time, such as the growing gap between the rich and the poor, and the corruption of ecclesiastical political life, came only after his deep conversion to Christ the Suffering One who gave meaning to all Francis did. His emphasis on a spirituality open to lay people in a world of clericalism and his continued stand against the vanities of the world made his life an example of prophetic humor. He was a clown of God whose followers actually became known as God's minstrels and jesters.

In the last two centuries of the Middle Ages, with their growing complexity and the ongoing corruption of the church, other prophetic figures emerged. People such as St. Catherine of Sienna (1347–80), Gerhard Groote of Deventer (1340–84), and Julian of Norwich (1342–1420) became contemplatives, mystics, critics, and reformers.[26] Meister Eckhart (1260–1329), a Dominican mystic, believed that we are to be joyful in the presence of creation simply because God is filled with joyfulness as he contemplates what has been created. Eckhart even says that the "whole Trinity laughs—and gives birth to us."[27] Little wonder that Eckhart filled his sermons with jokes. The heart of his message was that poverty had to be found in the soul itself, an interior abandonment to God, who in turn would fill the soul with a joy that words could not describe. This gift of inner conversion, Eckhart said, was open to everyone, including lay people. This was dangerous thinking in a church that claimed an elite spiritual and professional status for clergy and members of religious congregations. It was largely Eckhart's success with lay people that brought down on him the envy and hostility of ecclesiastical authorities, and finally his condemnation.[28] A little later another mystic, Julian of Norwich, was equally forthright when she recorded her visions: "Then I saw our Lord royally reign in his house, [filling] it with joy and mirth. . . . It is God's will . . . that we seek him willfully, gladly and merrily, without unskillful heaviness and vain sorrow."[29] Close to death she was tempted by the devil, but chased him away by laughing at him.

Another, more controversial, figure was Girolamo Savonarola (1452–98), an Observant Dominican who was hanged and burned in Florence as a schismatic and heretic. At a time of the spectacular corruption of the papacy (the Borgia pope, Alexander VI, had openly bought his election in 1492), Savonarola denounced clerical lechery and simony. Against political oppression, he promoted a Christian social teaching: people who are poor are to be protected against exploitation and unjust taxes. While his humor in the cause of the Gospel was prophetic, he had little time for the lightheartedness of relaxing humor.[30]

Prophetic Publications

Dante Alighieri's (1265–1321) *The Divine Comedy* is not only a world-renowned literary masterpiece, but it is also a gem of prophetic humor. The author is not aiming to condemn human nature and the gift of humor. On the contrary, he yearns to rearticulate the heart of the Gospel message for people of his time through an imaginative poetic reflection on his own journey to God. Assisted by the insights of philosophers such as Aristotle and St. Thomas Aquinas, Dante ponders with joy the God-given rich potential of the human mind to discover truths, but then reflects on the causes of evil within the world of his time. It is not just the failure of individuals to be open to the mystery of God's love in Christ, but the church itself is corrupt, even at the level of the papacy. He draws attention to the prophetic lifestyle of St. Francis, a social critic of papal opulence. He depicts St. Peter contemplating the papal corruption of his recent successors. The comedy aspect, which pervades the entire poem, is the emphasis Dante gives to the simple but profound truth that human beings owe their existence to a joyful creator[31] and achieve happiness and dignity when, in returning to their true origins, they contemplate God in the "court" of heaven. Positive humor exists when the incongruity of God's abiding love for his sinful creatures is recognized. And it is subversive when people see that this love conflicts with existing unjust and oppressive political and ecclesiastical structures.[32]

Geoffrey Chaucer (1343–1400), in his unfinished *The Canterbury Tales*, highlights in a humorous though earthy and satirical way the immorality and religious laxity of the clergy and religious congregations in the contemporary Catholic Church. With a deep love of the church he portrays characters to emphasize the qualities that should ideally be in the church. One of his characters in *The Canterbury Tales* is the well-fed prioress of a convent who is more interested in showing compassion to animals than to those around her. She is so concerned for these pet animals that she insists they are to be fed only the very best meats. Chaucer, of course, in humorously describing the prioress, is critiquing the wider failure of the church to live according to gospel values.

In brief, through most of the Middle Ages the church tolerated a significant degree of relaxing and prophetic joking behavior, particularly in saintly individuals, in the liturgy, and in the religious plays in which audiences were expected to laugh. These varieties of joking helped people to question and dispel only some of the rigidity and haughtiness of ecclesiastical figures.[33] But by the end of the Middle Ages, the liturgy had come to mirror the belief that the church was synonymous with its hierarchy, its institutions, and its authority over temporal society. The church was no longer seen as the People of God and the Body of Christ made visible in liturgical assemblies.[34] Humor that prophetically dared to challenge this was increasingly seen to be dangerously subversive and in need of control.[35]

Condemnation: Sixteenth to Twentieth Centuries

During the Reformation, unlike the dour John Calvin (1509–64), Martin Luther (1483–1546) had a raucous sense of humor; but they both accepted redemption-centered theology, hence their emphasis on soberness, thrift, industry, the fear of the world as the source of sin, and somber liturgies. There was no room here for the spontaneity of humor. These attitudes also reinforced the Catholic Church's growing rigidity in worship. As noted above, from the Renaissance onward the Mass became increasingly a grand spectacle that overemphasized the divinity of Christ and the centrality of the church as a hierarchical institution, rather than as a community of people in the pilgrimage of life where social rank is unimportant.[36] Baptism from the sixteenth century onward came to be seen primarily as an initiation into the church as an institution, not as a sacrament of initiation into the life of Christ. The clampdown on the importance of humor in society and religion also coincided with the rise of the ideology of the divine right of kings, the growing centralization of the Roman Church, and the evolution of the modern totalitarian state.[37] Laity within the Catholic Church were to be the passive receivers of the expert ritual leadership of clerics and were required to go about saving their souls in a dangerous and evil secular world through faithfulness to a set of intricate rules and customs.

The new age of European colonial expansion coincided with the Reformation. Both Catholics and Protestants assumed that non-European cultures in the New World were inferior to their own and therefore obstacles to missionary activity. The faster these cultures could be destroyed, the better. The missionaries—true children of their times—viewed the indigenous cultures and religions with the same intolerance and prejudice as the conquistadors.[38] They ignored the results of the critical debate so clearly described in the Acts of the Apostles, namely, whether or not the Gentile converts should become Jews and accept circumcision (Acts 15:1-35). The Council of Jerusalem had decisively rejected the view that the converts had to become Jews in order to be Christians (Acts 15:28-29). The converts did, however, have to refrain from eating food that had been "sacrificed to idols and from blood and from what is strangled" (Acts 15:29). This latter requirement was pastorally understandable because most meat sold at that time had been killed in the temples as part of ritual sacrifice.[39] Despite the unequivocal clarity of this decree, missionaries refused in practice to accept it. To such missionaries, conversion simply meant accepting the European cultural expression of the faith. There was to be no dialogue with cultures; functional substitution was unnecessary and theologically wrong. Only the soul mattered. Christians were to show compassion, for example, through medical and educational services; but such efforts were accidental to the main evangelizing thrust, which was the conversion of the individual soul to God.

The Congregation for the Propagation of the Faith in the Catholic Church in 1659 tried to stop this foolishness, but to no avail. Condemning the stupidity of exalting the cultures of Europe, it urged evangelizers to respect the customs of people: "Admire and praise the customs that merit praise. . . . Do not rashly and excessively condemn the unworthy."[40] Fine and courageous words! But they were ignored, as was quickly evident in the Roman condemnation of the Jesuit Matteo Ricci's flexible approach to evangelization in China in 1742.

Holy Fools

Throughout this long period in which the Catholic Church actively discouraged any critique of its corruption, extraordinary men and women emerged to challenge this situation in various ways. People such as St. Angela Merici (1474–1540), St. Ignatius of Loyola (1491–1556), St. Teresa of Avila (1515–82), St. John of the Cross (1542–91), Mary Ward (1585–1645), St. Vincent de Paul (1580–1660), who in their desire to give themselves to the radical demands of the Beatitudes, became fools for Christ, many establishing religious congregations that still exist today. Saint Ignatius begged his followers: "Laugh, and grow strong!"[41] He challenged the assumption that the only authentic forms of religious life could be monastic and mendicant. He succeeded, but attempts by women to do the same met insurmountable ecclesiastical barriers. Saint Philip Neri (1515–95) lived in Rome at a time when it was one of the most corrupt of renaissance cities. Surrounded by ecclesiastical opulence, Neri lived a life of poverty and did not hesitate to joke openly at church officials who were abusing power. His lifestyle and comic behavior were forms of prophetic humor.

Saint Angela Merici and Mary Ward: Holy Fools

Saint Angela Merici, the founder of the Ursulines, had the idea of forming apostolic religious congregations before Ignatius Loyola. Confronted with the breakdown of family life in northern Italy, Angela felt that an appropriate pastoral response was to form women within the family circle, not in any institution or within a cloister. For this she needed uncloistered women prepared to live right where the problems were to be found, that is, with families themselves if necessary. They were to wear no religious habit, earn whatever money was necessary to maintain their apostolate, and take no public vows, but a private vow of chastity only. Members were to be united by bonds of mutual love, not by preset and inflexible community structures. Though Angela Merici's plans were initially accepted by papal authorities, her followers were soon forced to accept the monastic cloister, solemn vows, and habits.

Mary Ward and her followers faced the same appalling fate. Mary planned to evangelize in England during the days of persecution. She recognized that the cloister, habit, and choir would be incompatible with this aim, so she wished to adapt the Jesuit Constitutions and formation programs to the needs of women but to be in no way dependent on the Society of Jesus. As she wrote: "There is no such difference between men and women that women may not do great things . . . I would to God all men understand this verity, that women . . . might do great things."[42] Her imaginative designs were too much for ecclesiastics unwilling to grasp the idea that women not having a cloister could work in an apostolate. Mary persisted, suffering in consequence considerable personal hardship for her prophetic stand, but failed to have her insightful vision for the congregation approved. Mary was accused by the Office of the Inquisition of being a heretic and was briefly imprisoned by civil authorities in Munich. [43]

Despite her many trials, St. Teresa of Avila maintained a sense of humor firmly founded on her trust in God's Providence. The closer Teresa came to God, the more she became amazed at the humanly nonsensical thought that God, her creator and redeemer, loved her beyond anything she could imagine. Agents of the Spanish Inquisition harassed Teresa because she dared to write that individuals could have an exclusive relationship with God that did not necessitate the mediation of the church. Here was an incongruous situation—a woman daring to teach the church that was controlled by men, men who believed women could not think rationally or have the ability to teach.[44] At one stage in the midst of physical danger Teresa joked with God, telling God in no uncertain terms that she had had enough. When God replied that this was the way he treated his friends, she retorted that it was no wonder he had so few friends. Not surprisingly Teresa strongly disapproved of sad nuns: "I am more afraid of one unhappy sister than a crowd of evil spirits . . . What would happen if we hid what little sense of humor we had? Let each of us humbly use this to cheer others."[45]

Prophetic Publications

Great Renaissance authors, such as Erasmus, Cervantes, Rabelais, Boccaccio, and St. Thomas More, were able to focus their subversive comic gifts with good effect on the major weaknesses of the church. Desiderius Erasmus (1469–1536), whose *The Praise of Folly* appeared in 1511,[46] and Francois Rabelais (1494–1553) both taught "first Europe and then the world to laugh afresh. . . . As priests living in the world, both brought men and women to laugh at what they saw as ugliness and error within the Church."[47] Erasmus directed his cutting humor against decadent scholastic philosophy which, he believed, had entrapped Christianity. He complained of its arid rationalism, its rigid systematization, its authoritarian moralism, and its pretentious verbiage. He detested the self-importance and snobbishness of theologians, monks, and princes of the church, and at the same time he sought equality for men and women in the church and society.[48] For Rabelais, not to laugh is to stop being human. Laughter, he believed, has the capacity to be a vigorous force for moral good, but it must always be under control. Like Erasmus, Rabelais claimed that Christian truths could be protected by humor, "and that laughter is the means of reducing heresy and error to the kinds of worldly madness which Christians can contain."[49]

Pilgrimages and Humor

Christian pilgrimages began early in the Christian era, particularly to places made sacred by the life of Christ. The pattern of the journey followed the tripartite process of initiation rituals, the lengthiest being the liminal phase. Anti-normal symbols (see chap. 3), such as the same penitential dress for all, fasting, and frequent prayers, were important.

Often people experienced such personal joy on reaching the sacred sites that many were tempted to remain. As the centuries passed more and more sacred sites became the object of pilgrimages, especially shrines to the Mother of God and particular saints. Despite their serious purpose, pilgrimages were accompanied by much humor and celebration. Eventually, however, ecclesiastics became wary of pilgrimages and sought to control them because during the relaxed liminal experiences people could begin to question religious and political power systems. Victor and Edith Turner comment: "There is something inveterately populist, anarchical, even anti-clerical, about pilgrimages. . . . Pilgrimages are an expression of interrelatedness, the spirit bloweth where it listeth. From the point of view of those who control and maintain the social structure, all manifestations of communitas, sacred or profane, are potentially subversive."[50]

Tentative Respect: 1900–

Writing of this period, Stephen Pattison says that the efforts "to integrate laughter into Christianity are refreshing and welcome, but often uncritical and peripheral to the main Christian tradition."[51] Pattison is right but there are nonetheless significant theologians, novelists, poets, and movements within the churches that seek to reinstate humor at the heart of theology and Christian life.

Theologians and Writers

Among these influential theologians and writers are: Soren Kierkegaard (1813–55), a Danish Lutheran theologian, though a little before this period; Karl Barth (1886–1968), a Swiss Protestant theologian; Reinhold Niebuhr (1892–1971), an American Protestant theologian; and Harvey Cox, an ordained Baptist minister and currently (2006) Professor of Divinity at Harvard University. Barth has a particularly sensitive appreciation of the need for humor in Christian living. For him self-humor is ultimately founded in the glory and beauty of God. We see ourselves for what we are—sinners but thinking ourselves to be saints—but because God loves us so much this incongruous situation evokes a joy, a laughter of the heart within us.[52] Niebuhr, in an important essay published in 1946, gives a detailed theological analysis of the nature of human and supernatural humor. Human humor has limitations because by itself it can never be a substitute for faith-inspired humor, since it is only through faith that we can perceive the disproportionate gap between our sinfulness and the forgiving love of God. Only then is true inner peace possible. At one point Niebuhr writes: "Faith is the only possible response to the ultimate incongruities of existence which threaten the very meaning of our life. . . . Man's [and woman's] very existence in the universe is incongruous. That is a problem of faith, and not of humour."[53] Harvey Cox has written a popular book on the necessity of humor for Christian living.[54] Laughter is hope's last support, "and where laughter and hope have disappeared man has ceased to be man."[55] He persuasively argues that "man will grasp his divine origin and destiny only if he regains the capacity for festive revelry and the ability to fantasize."[56] For Cox, play and prayer are intimately related because both are acts of disciplined fantasy.

There are some brilliant novelists and poets in this period who use their writings as a medium to reflect on the impact of divine humor on the lives of their characters and the world in general. G. K. Chesterton (1874–1936), a great admirer of Geoffrey Chaucer's comic writing ability, in his engaging novels (e.g., *The Innocence of Father Brown*) and other publications aims to view all things from the divine perspective. C. S. Lewis (1898–1963), in a lighthearted way in *The Screwtape Letters*, helps people to focus on the use of comedy in order to convey important Gospel truths. The novels of Flannery O'Connor (1925–64) are dramatically different in humorous style from those of Lewis. The characters in her novels, which contain significant violence, are often bizarre, and at first sight there is nothing comic about them. Yet she reminds readers of the fragility and brevity of life and that the grace of God can effect wonders within the most unlikely people. The novels of Graham Greene (1904–90) are not violent but contain the same message of incongruity: God's forgiveness in the midst of sinfulness. In Greene's novel *The Power and the Glory* (1940) the main character is a priest who is caught up in the anti-Catholic turmoil of the Mexican revolution of the 1930s. Despite the enormity of the ugly suffering that surrounds him, the priest discovers and feels God's goodness shining through the lives of people who are poor and helpless. He even finds it possible to pity the person who is to betray him. But as he is about to face execution the priest feels that his own sinfulness is a terrible disappointment to God. When he cannot get to confession he believes that he is now damned by God. The overall thrust of the story, however, is not pessimistic because salvation depends not on formulas or good actions but on faith and ultimately on God's loving mercy and forgiveness.

Two poets are especially influential in this period: Gerard Manley Hopkins, SJ (1844–89), and Thomas Stearns Eliot (1888–1965). Though

Hopkins wrote in the nineteenth century, his influence was far more profound in the following century. In "The Wreck of the Deutschland," Hopkins portrays God as both masterful and merciful. Influenced particularly by the incarnational qualities of the *Spiritual Exercises* of St. Ignatius Loyola, Hopkins describes that the way to God is through the various stages of the spiritual life, through prayer and penance, pain and suffering, sacrifice and imitation of Christ. In one of his most moving poems ("That Nature is a Heraclitean Fire and of the Comfort of the Resurrection") Hopkins refers to the human person who, having been made one with Christ by grace in this world, will even in his or her body be one with Christ hereafter in the glorious triumph of the resurrection. To highlight the incongruity of this extraordinary gift from God, Hopkins graphically describes the human person as a "joke," a "patch" (an archaic word for a fool), a "poor potsherd" (that is, a fragment of broken pottery), and "matchwood." But through Christ's merciful love this broken piece of creation is an "immortal diamond."

By contrast, Eliot in his early writings favors a redemption-centered theological stance. In *The Waste Land* (1922) Eliot bleakly depicts the contemporary world as a sterile land in which even death has no meaning; it is a land consumed by lust, selfishness and bereft of joy. The Western civilization has a death wish. But in *Ash Wednesday* (1930) and subsequent poems Eliot begins to shift toward a creation-centered theological position; he claims that belief in Christian values and the traditional wisdom of the church is the way to survive and be reenergized. The mercy of God in Christ is able to break through the terrible darkness of the world. This change in emphasis is particularly evident in *Four Quartets* (1943), in which Eliot senses a budding peace that has not existed in the world for over a century. The garden and the laughter of joyful children finally prevail over the bleakness of the desert and the grieving of people.

Papal Thinking

The Catholic Church in this period made significant efforts to reinstate creation-centered theology with its incarnational foundations and respect for the cultures of people. Under Pope Leo XIII (1878–1903), the theology of St. Thomas Aquinas from the thirteenth century was reintroduced into the church. People were encouraged to reflect on human nature and society as a way to discover key insights about life, even about the divine nature itself. Sadly, this renewed concern for the totality of the person, and thus indirectly for the importance of cultures and humor in people's lives, did little to change how evangelization was to be conducted. While ethnocentric attitudes of missionaries were condemned, no action was taken to break down the all-pervasive emphasis of Eurocentric culture in a centralized ecclesiastical administration, in worship, and in seminary and religious life formation.

Pope Pius XII (1939–58) claimed that "the rights to one's culture and national character . . . are the exigencies of the law of nations dictated by nature itself."[57] He insisted that the Catholic Church "cannot belong exclusively to any particular people, nor can she belong more to one than to another." [58] In 1951 the same pope reminded evangelizers that their "office does not demand that they transplant European civilisation and culture, and no other, to foreign soil, there to take root and propagate itself."[59] In fact, however, the church continued to belong exclusively to Europe in its expression of life and administration, and with its supporting redemption-centered theology. A theology of the local church, which encouraged an appreciation of cultural diversity and the freedom necessary to foster the localized earthing of the Gospel through dialogue, did not exist. Consider this simple example. Before Vatican II there were three liturgical festival days mandated for the universal church to celebrate in September: the grape, wheat, and olive harvests. These perfectly fit the temperate European climate but fit neither the tropics nor the countries below the equator!

Vatican II brought a dramatic change in favor of creation-centered theology and its pastoral implications. The Holy Spirit speaks to us through human cultures, as the opening paragraph of a major document prophetically states. The Church in the Modern World summarizes the council's more flexible, apostolic relationship between the Gospel and cultures: "The joys and hopes, the griefs and the anxieties of [people] of this age, especially those who are poor or in any way afflicted, these too are the joys and hopes, the griefs and anxieties of the followers of Christ."[60] The church is to be not a huge, uniform monolith of Eurocentric cultural characteristics but a fraternity of local churches, each of which seeks to give life to the universal church, in accordance with the native genius and traditions of its own members.[61] The whole person, soul and body, is the object of evangelization; thus the search for justice is integral to evangelization.[62] Through a process of dialogue and exchange between the Gospel and cultures, local expressions of worship and theology should emerge. The creation-centered model is to be the theological foundation of this dialogue and exchange.[63] Finally, the council recognizes the merits and salvation potential of other Christian traditions and even other religions: the Holy Spirit can be speaking to us through these different traditions and religions.[64]

Several prophetic theologians, such as Yves Congar, Teilhard de Chardin, and John Courtney Murray, helped to prepare for the council long before it was ever called. They were marginalized or silenced for championing creation-centered theology, but their learning eventually deeply influenced the documents of the council. Nothing, however, could have happened without the leadership of Blessed Pope John XXIII (1958–63) who courageously called the council. This pope, by his own good humor and commitment to the mystery of the incarnation in daily life and cultures, changed the face of the papacy in the eyes of the world. In his opening speech to the council, John XXIII unequivocally condemned the anti-world paradigm—that people are to be changed by the church, not the church by people and cultures in dialogue with the Gospel and tradition. He said: "we sometimes have to listen . . . to . . . persons who . . . are not endowed with too much sense of discretion and measure. In these modern times they can see nothing but prevarication and ruin. . . . We feel we must disagree with those prophets of doom." He continues: "Divine Providence is leading us to a new order of human relations. . . . And everything, even human differences, leads to the greater good of the Church."[65]

Within ten years of the closing of the council the word "inculturation" was to be frequently used by both Pope Paul VI (1963–78) and particularly by Pope John Paul II (1978–2005). The Apostolic Letter *On Evangelisation* (1975) of Paul VI is rightly called the "Charter of Inculturation." "What matters," he wrote, "is to evangelise human culture and cultures (not in a purely decorative way as it were by applying a thin veneer, but in a vital way, in depth and right to their very roots)."[66] Other ecclesiastical documents from Rome and episcopal conferences reiterated this pastoral principle, giving particular emphasis to the social teaching of the church. John Paul II stated that Vatican II is to be "a sure compass by which to take [their] bearings"[67] and spoke frequently of the need for prophetic action for justice in the world and church. Pope Benedict XVI, in his first encyclical *Deus Caritas Est*, supports the theology of Vatican II. For example, in explaining the notion of *eros*, the love between a man and a woman, he does not condemn it as those motivated by redemption-centered theology have done through the centuries; he sees it, when disciplined and purified, as "a certain foretaste of the pinnacle of our existence, of that beatitude for which our whole being yearns."[68] This is creation-centered theology, acknowledging that what is good in human love is a manifestation of the presence of God, a faint mirror of God's love (*agape*).[69]

With documents such as these the Catholic Church is set to reclaim the role of humor, both as a source of spirituality and as a method of evangelization in cultures. At the same time, however, a vigorous restorationist movement has appeared in the church. Restorationism is an ill-defined, but nonetheless powerful, movement within the church toward the uncritical reaffirmation of pre–Vatican II structures and attitudes. It has developed in reaction to the stress resulting from the theological and cultural turmoil generated by the council and the modern world at large. Integral to restorationism is an anti-world stance that takes many forms, some fanatically aggressive, such as fundamentalist movements, others less so. Restorationism does not encourage prophetic humor and even relaxing humor in liturgies needs to be rigidly controlled.[70] For example, in 2001 Rome issued *Liturgiam Authenticam*, a document asserting that Rome has the right to intervene in liturgical matters. John Allen, a liturgical commentator, writes: "[The document] strikes at the heart of Vatican II ecclesiology by centralizing power in the curia and by insisting that local cultures adopt an essentially Roman style of worship."[71]

Other Christian Churches

Although generalizations are risky when trying to categorize evangelicals in the United States, it can be said that their theological roots are firmly in redemption-centered theology;[72] cultures, other than the dominant American culture, cannot have within them any glimmers of transcendence. Evangelicals have traditionally emphasized the conversion of the individual believer and not of cultures, as Jerry Falwell said in 1964. However, he later modified his views: "Preachers are not called to be politicians but to be soul winners. Our only purpose on this earth is to know Christ and to make him known."[73] Since the destruction of the Twin Towers in New York in 2001, groups of Evangelicals have intensified their support for a radical American nationalism. Nothing, they believe, could possibly be good in cultures where people do not accept the American way of life.[74] Less rigid Evangelicals, however, now speak of evangelization in ways that resemble the incarnational language of inculturation.[75]

Still, in other Christian Churches there have been significant developments over the last thirty years towards accepting creation-centered theology through inculturation. In 1982 a document on mission and evangelism was produced by the World Council of Churches, which also used the term: "Inculturation has as its source and inspiration the mystery of the incarnation. . . . Inculturation . . . occurs when Christians express their faith in the symbols and images of their respective culture."[76] Various Protestant theologians, such as Jürgen Moltmann, have further supported this approach with their emphasis on the cultural implications of the Gospel.[77] In 1985 the Church of England published a stimulating report called *Faith in the City*, which focused on questions such as belief and belonging, justice in education, health, welfare, order, and law, having in mind particularly people on the social and economic margins.[78] It was a trenchant criticism of the policies of the neo-capitalist government and its denial of the rights of people who are poor, but it was criticized for its lack of a strong theological base that would make the connection between faith and the city. That is, it was strong on diagnosis and planning but weak on incarnational or creation-centered theology.[79] This was corrected in a follow-up publication in 2006 called *Faithful Cities: A Call for Celebration, Vision, and Justice*.[80] In introducing the report Rowan Williams, Archbishop of Canterbury, refers to the fundamental expression of divine humor, namely the Judeo-Christian tradition of recognizing our God above all as one who is faithful, no matter how often we forget this in our lives. Our task is to mirror this faithfulness in justice and celebration. In relating to cultures the church has always to ask: do human actions "show something of what God is like and thus something of what humanity, made in God's image, might be"?[81]

Summary

- Inculturation, as a pastoral method of evangelization, assumes that the Word of God is actively present, although in an incomplete way, in all cultures. This presence or glimmer of transcendence is a foreshadowing of the fuller revelation of Jesus Christ in the Scriptures and tradition. Whatever is good in cultures, including positive humor, comes from the Spirit. This is at the heart of what is termed creation-centered theology; its opposite, redemption-centered theology, assumes that there can be nothing good in cultures prior to evangelization.

- The evangelizing approach of the churches to cultures has been ambivalent. When the Catholic Church accepts or tolerates a creation-centered approach, positive humor is considered to be an integral quality of personal and cultural transformation. From the Reformation to the 1960s a redemption-centered theology significantly influenced all the churches so that nothing good was assumed to exist in cultures prior to evangelization. Humor was considered to have no place in evangelization of people and their cultures.

- In the Catholic Church creation-centered theology was revitalized with the advent of Vatican II. Dialogue with all cultures has been seen as an integral requirement of evangelization and worship. However, following the turmoil generated by the combined influence of the theological and cultural changes of the council and the cultural revolution of the 1960s, a restorationist movement is encouraging a revival of a redemption-centered theology. In mainline Protestant churches there are efforts to emphasize the importance of creation-centered theology, but its influence remains marginal.

- In the final chapter positive movements are identified that are signals of divine humor breaking into contemporary society. The challenge is to build on these movements through a pastoral process of functional substitution.

Chapter 8

Laughing with God:
Transformation through Humor

> *The [religious] groups that will find a voice [in postmodernity] will be
> those that are able to encode their messages, their symbols, in ways that
> adapt them for the new media.*
> David J. Lyon[1]

> *I have considered the dialogue with the cultures of our time to be a vital
> area. . . . In order to evangelise effectively, it is necessary to have reso-
> lutely an attitude of exchange and of comprehension. The power of the
> Gospel must penetrate to the very heart of different cultures.*
> John Paul II[2]

This chapter explains:

- that in acting justly and in love we are joining in the laughter of God;
- the relationship between dialogue and cultural transformation;
- by examples how positive aspects of humor in paramodernity can be transformed by the Gospel.

We speak of God's "divine humor," which is our human attempt to describe God's surprising love and forgiveness in relating with us (see chap.
3). The psalmist grapples with this concept in his own matter-of-fact way:
God "sits in the heavens and laughs" (Ps 2:4) at the stupidities of those

who act as though God does not exist. The Almighty laughs at the antics of the wicked, for God sees that their day is coming. God continues to laugh at our human stupidity, at the times we forget we are God's creatures acting as though we are above the One who fashioned the world out of nothing. So, writes theologian Karl Rahner, "God laughs. . . . He laughs the laughter of divine superiority over all the horrible confusion of universal history that is full of blood and torture and insanity and baseness."[3]

But it is not a harsh laughter, for it is inspired by love, compassion, and mercy. God is our parent who will not abandon us, who pursues us in Christ with a love beyond all our possible dreaming. This is the ultimate in divine foolishness: that we are God's children, revealed through God's human face—Christ: "When we cry, 'Abba! Father!' . . . we are children of God, and if children, then heirs, heirs of God and joint heirs with Christ" (Rom 8:15-17). As any good parent loves a child, God as our parent is not a revengeful, but a merciful, loving one.

When we laugh at our own follies we are laughing in our hearts with God. Our laughter "is praise of God because it is a gentle echo of God's laughter, of the laughter that pronounces judgment on all history."[4] Ultimately we can come to know our laughing God, as far as this is possible to humankind on earth, by being transformed into the image of Christ, the visible presence of the Father. We know this transformation is happening when we are struggling to have the same mind "that was in Christ Jesus" (Phil 2:5): respecting the dignity of others and the universe, loving one another, acting justly and with mercy in the midst of a postmodern world that commonly considers such values a sign of weakness. We are then "fools for the sake of Christ" (1 Cor 4:10), joining in God's laughter.

Paramodernity, Functional Substitution, and Dialogue

By the words "transformation through humor" we mean the process whereby the incongruous expressions of divine humor—God's love, mercy, justice, compassion—become actively present within our own hearts and cultures. The pastoral challenge is *how* to foster this transforming presence so that the "new creation" (2 Cor 5:17) becomes a living reality. The answer lies, as it has in the past, in the process of inculturation (see chap. 7). As John Paul II writes: "The Christian message must be planted in such a way that the particular values of each people will not be rejected but purified and brought to their fullness. In the Third

Millennium Christianity will have to respond ever more effectively to this *need for inculturation.*"[5]

In this emerging cultural model of paramodernity, positive humor is increasingly prophetic. It raises issues such as: the need for spirituality in our lives; the realization that, although potential for evil exists in every human heart, it can be overcome through individual and collaborative effort; the need for storytelling as a way to achieve a sense of identity and dignity; the need for objective moral values. In vivid contrast to the negativities of postmodernity these concerns are signals or glimmers of the divine humor breaking into our cultures, waiting to be "purified and brought to their fullness" through a particular process of inculturation that we call functional substitution (see chap. 7). Functional substitution identifies what is good in cultures, and therefore from the Spirit, and aims to enrich this with the treasures of the Gospel: "For everything created by God is good, and nothing is to be rejected, provided it is received with thanksgiving" (1 Tim 4:4).

The ability to engage in dialogue with people and cultures is a valued quality in paramodernity. It is also a basic requirement for evangelizers wishing to proceed with the process of functional substitution. Through dialogue we can discover together the actions of God in our midst. This dialogue cannot be rushed; it must proceed with patience and a deep respect for people, with wide consultation, and with willingness to have trust in people and especially in the presence of God,[6] "for it is God who is at work in you, enabling you both to will and to work for his good pleasure" (Phil 2:13). The World Council of Churches in 1979 described dialogue as "witnessing to our deepest convictions, whilst listening to those of our neighbors."[7]

There are several kinds of pastoral dialogue that often overlap in practice. First, there is "life/religious dialogue" in which people are concerned for others and are willing to share their faith, joys, anxieties, and hopes.[8] Second, "justice dialogue," especially with people who are poor and marginalized, searches for ways to develop just relationships.[9] And third, through "theological dialogue" people seek to deepen their understanding of their respective religious traditions and spiritual values, particularly in light of contemporary cultural realities.[10] Each type of dialogue is founded on positive values that are alive in paramodernity and through them people are able to help purify and bring to their fullness in Christ the innate goodness of these values. The relevance of each type of dialogue will now be examined in light of some particular values in paramodernity.

Life/Religious Dialogue

The following examples illustrate how some esteemed values of para-modernity, for example, a renewed emphasis on storytelling, supportive small groups, spirituality, myth and ritual, and multiculturalism, can be enriched with the power of the Gospel message.

Storytelling

In paradoxical reaction to the individualism, loneliness, and rootless-ness of postmodernity, people are discovering the positive experience of storytelling. Storytelling in which myths are retold and applied to life may take one of three forms: identity stories, revitalization stories, and fictional stories.[11]

Identity Stories

People can fashion their identity through storytelling by telling their own experiences for the first time, or they may turn to the narratives of others as a model to guide them.

While people may be repelled by the institutional church or formal religion, they may still be open to stories within the Christian tradition in their search for identity. This tradition is filled with stories of people—Jesus of Nazareth, St. Paul of Tarsus, St. Francis of Assisi, St. Teresa of Avila, Dorothy Day, Martin Luther King Jr., Blessed Mother Teresa of Calcutta—who provide road maps through darkness to light. As people ponder the very different lives of these pilgrims they come to recognize that God's love is also searching for them in their own unique experience of life. God will respond, not in some prepackaged style, but in ways that respect each person's qualities and journey.[12]

Revitalization Stories

Storytelling is important in times of crises for individuals, families, ethnic groups, and nations because it reaffirms a sense of identity and self-esteem. Contrary to the postmodern disdain for history, paramod-ernists claim that there are truths, including especially painful ones, that need to be retold. The recalling of horrific experiences of individ-uals and groups in the Holocaust reminds the living that everyone is capable of evil. To forget this is to put the future in jeopardy. There is a risk, however, that storytelling of this kind can lead to ethnic or national violence against outsiders, a problem that is so evident in recent years, for instance, in the ethnic cleansing in Rwanda and Serbia.

People's need for hope in the midst of their life crises provides evangelizers with the opportunity to introduce them to scriptural accounts of the transformative rituals that move from grieving into new life (see chaps. 4 and 5). These stories give a deeper meaning to the sadness in their lives. They also help people to avoid falling victim to personal and group despair.

Fictional Stories

In fictional stories listeners and readers are able to hear words that articulate their own sense of sadness and hope. They are then encouraged to recognize the importance of their own stories in their search for significance and security. The great novelist J.R.R. Tolkien wrote that fictional stories are "prophylactic against loss" in a way that permits the loss to be named. It is through the quasi-experience of loss, which fiction evokes, that listeners and readers are able to gain a certain therapeutic permission to reconnect with truths from which they may be sheltered in daily life.[13] Tolkien writes profoundly on this point:

> Probably every writer making a secondary world, a fantasy, every sub-creator . . . hopes that the peculiar qualities of this secondary world are derived from Reality, or are flowing into it. . . . The peculiar quality of the "joy" in successful Fantasy can thus be explained as a sudden glimpse of the underlying reality or truth. It is not only a "consolation" for the sorrow of this world, but a satisfaction, and an answer to the question, "Is it true?"[14]

As people search for meaning in their lives, the parables in the Scriptures can provide them with stories that are rich in meaning. Pope Benedict XVI, in his encyclical *Deus Caritas Est*, frequently refers to the parable of the Good Samaritan to illustrate God's universal love, especially for people who are marginalized. In my own ministry of working with staffs of Catholic hospitals, many of whom have lost contact with their own churches, I am frequently edified by the way in which they identify with the characters and lessons of the parables. The parables act as catalysts for them to share their journey of faith, but they must be explained in interesting and interactive ways. One such way is through the use of the art of miming. I have watched people with learning disabilities in L'Arche communities mime the parable of the Good Samaritan; both they and onlookers have been deeply moved by this narrative form in ways that words could not achieve.

Supportive Small Groups

People increasingly gather in small support groups of all types, from abuse prevention to prayer fellowships to Alcoholics Anonymous, because they can achieve some control over a perplexing world. Storytelling is the main form of communicating within a small group; it has the benefit of allowing members to maintain their own individuality while discovering that others have similar concerns, thus leading to a collective story and a common worldview. People no longer feel alone because their problems are not unique to them. The more frequently they retell their life experiences the more they discover new layers of meaning and hope in their lives.[15]

In the United States an estimated 40 percent of the population belong to such groups. Robert Wuthnow, who has studied these groups, concludes that they are causing a quiet revolution in American society by changing people's attitudes to community and by redefining spirituality.[16] The communities are less demanding on their members than in the past and there is more recognition now of their emotional needs. Many are searching for a spirituality, although this term is understood very broadly to signify a search for meaning in life, which may or may not be a direct seeking for God. When religion is the center of concern people develop a more personal relationship with God. Wuthnow, however, highlights a critical postmodern weakness of self-centeredness of the groups;[17] they will not survive if members are concerned only with their personal needs and fail to recognize the needs also of others.

This is the opportune time for the Christian insight of "community for others, not for me." There is a fast growing small-group movement within the Roman Catholic Church, based on the pilgrim model of the church emphasized by Vatican II, which is also a reaction to the spiritual sterility of postmodernity. Pilgrims have little room for the baggage of titles or formal dress. Every member of the group has a particular ministerial role based on baptism; clerics are not singled out for special status or influence beyond what their sacramental duties require of them. These small groups have a variety of names: Basic Christian Communities (BCCs);[18] "churches from below," which are common in South America and the Philippines; "house churches"; small Christian communities (SCCs), as in the United States. Four main activities have been identified in SCCs: prayer, faith sharing, reading and discussing Scripture, and spirituality.[19] The study of Scripture and faith sharing need to go together because participants with different backgrounds and experiences are able to unearth different riches of divine humor within the Scriptures. It is important, however, that members have access to well-presented and up-to-date Scripture commentaries and theological expertise. Without this, small groups are in danger of falling into scriptural fundamentalism, of formally or informally cutting themselves off from the institutional church, or of uncritically accepting postmodern narcissistic values. Karl Rahner foresaw the importance of this movement toward small faith-based communities shortly after Vatican II ended:

> The Church of the future will be one built from below by basic communities as a result of free initiative and association. . . . [The] Church will no longer exist . . . [by] recruiting new members simply because the children adopt and maintain the life-style of their parents and are baptized and indoctrinated by the Church.[20]

Small Group Community: L'Arche

On one occasion when visiting a L'Arche community for lunch, I noticed a person with severe learning disabilities being invited to set the table under the encouraging and watchful eye of an assistant. Her face lit up as she struggled to respond to the invitation. At the same time, the assistant's face also expressed her joy as she observed the community member respond to the very best of her ability. Before coming to the community, the person with disabilities had been socially excluded by a neocapitalist society because she was economically unproductive. She could receive but not give. The founding myth of L'Arche, which contradicts this self-centered philosophy, assumes that people with disabilities are the primary teachers of assistants who work with them. I could see this happening in the incident of the table setting. By their simplicity and vulnerability, people with learning disabilities remind us of an important reality—the need to recognize within ourselves our own need for love and trust. Jean Vanier, the founder of L'Arche, describes the contemporary Gospel relevance of this philosophy:

> Our [postmodern] societies . . . seem to favour people who are aggressive, individualistic, powerfully competitive, needing success and influence, but who tend to lose a sense of what it means to be human and to live together. L'Arche is a school of love. Without love

continued on next page

our world will disintegrate. . . . So many [of our assistants] have been transformed by our people [with learning disabilities], by their simplicity, their trust flowing from their littleness. . . . No matter how seductive our world may be, there is something in L'Arche that reveals to assistants the fundamental beauty of their humanity, [that the mutuality of love is] more fulfilling than competition, success, power and riches. . . . [People with learning disabilities] heal us and reveal to us the face of God. . . . They are the ones who in a special way bring life and tenderness to the community.[21]

Spirituality

One of the most remarkable examples of paramodernity is the world-wide meditation movement. William Johnston, SJ, one experienced in integrating Western and Eastern contemplative traditions, describes what is happening: "everywhere we see Christians of all ages and cultures sitting quietly in meditation. Some sit before a crucifix or an ikon in . . . meditation. . . . Others recite a mantra to the rhythm of their breath. Others, influenced by Zen or yoga . . . open their minds and hearts to God in the universe."[22] People are weary of being bombarded with words, of having even their leisure time preprogrammed by business entrepreneurs of modernity. Others are fatigued by an overuse of words in liturgies. They want to be silent, to develop a contemplative dialogue with God in their inner selves, and to kindle in the deepest recesses of their being the faith-inspired laughter of the heart. They yearn for an experience of God beyond words or rational thinking in response to the invitation: "Be still, and know that I am God!" (Ps 46:10). They desire to see the world through God's eyes, and this will surely lead to a humorous attitude toward life in general and an inner peace.

Karl Rahner claimed that "the devout Christian in the future will either be a 'mystic,' one who has 'experienced' something, or [they] will cease to be anything at all."[23] This summarized a conclusion of Vatican II:[24] all are called to contemplation, that is, at least to an awareness of the abiding presence of God in Scripture, doctrines, liturgy, and the universe. Walter Burghardt, SJ, defines contemplative consciousness as simply "taking a long loving look at the real,"[25] at God's presence in the midst of the human and cultural condition. All are invited to enter into this journey, but after the sixteenth century, contemplation was thought to be a rare gift available only to some members of enclosed congregations. Meditation then became synonymous only with discursive and affective prayer, discursive emphasizing rational reflection and affective the movement of the will.[26] But contemplative prayer is the normal development of listening to the word of God. There are two kinds of contemplation: infused knowledge and love, a pure gift of God that is unattainable by human effort; and contemplation in the broad sense, which is simply a form of active prayer, shaped from simplified attempts to be attentive and to be open to the divine influence.[27] The Holy Spirit is active in both forms, inspiring people to be aware of the loving mystery of the Trinity in their lives and the reality of their human and cultural condition. Here we discover the incongruity of divine humor—the fact that, "In this is love, not that we loved God but that he loved us and sent his Son to be the atoning sacrifice for our sins" (1 John 4:10).

Two forms of contemplative prayer in its broad sense have become especially popular in recent times: centering prayer under the influence of Thomas Keating, OCSO; and Christian meditation, designed by John Main, OSB. These practices aim to go beyond rational and imaginative reflections by disposing the heart to be attentive to the loving, joyful inner presence of God in whatever way this is manifested, even if it should lead to contemplation in the fullest sense of the word.[28] In Christian meditation John Main encourages people to begin their prayer with a mantra, a prayer phrase or word, and he suggests the word *Maranatha* (an Aramaic word meaning "O Lord, come!") to help them relax and avoid distractions.[29] Both prayer forms are ways of learning self-surrender to God's overwhelming love and follow the three-stage ritual of joking. For example, in the first stage of centering prayer the person simply relaxes in quiet, preparing the body and spirit to become aware of God's presence. The person then without hurry or anxiety identifies a single word, such as "Jesus," that articulates a response to God's presence. In this liminal stage there is the joking pattern of detachment and being open to the surprising newness: the letting go of whatever is holding the person back from being fully open to God's presence, and then the letting in of this presence. The more this quiet dynamic develops the more the soul is transformed in faith and love by God's abiding power. Whenever distractions occur there is a return to the particular word that evokes the presence of God. The third stage is the conscious return to daily life by, for example, reciting a simple prayer such as the *Our Father*.[30]

Myth and Ritual

The Rite of Christian Initiation of Adults (RCIA), as developed in the early 1970s following the restoration of the catechumenate in the church, highlights the importance of appreciating the tripartite process of ritual (see figure 8.1),[31] with its dynamic of conversion and accompaniment by sponsors acting as ritual leaders of the process. Readiness to enter the first, relatively short, stage of the rite (pre-catechumenate) is assessed according to several criteria, such as evidence of initial conversion and the intention to request baptism. The heart of RCIA is the catechumenate, the liminal stage, which may last about five months. It fosters a small-group gathering where catechumens, their sponsors, and catechists form a faith community. Catechumens are challenged to shape their personal faith stories in line with the mythology of Christ and the church. It is in this stage that catechumens discover the paradox of divine love for each person. The liminal stage concludes with the full initiation rituals of baptism, Eucharist, and confirmation.

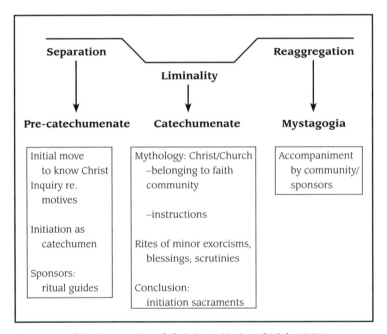

Figure 8.1: Joking Pattern: Rite of Christian Initiation of Adults (RCIA)

During the third stage of the ritual neophytes, while being accompanied and mentored by their sponsors, are slowly inducted into the life of their parishes and are encouraged to go forth to continue the mission of Jesus Christ in the world around them. This stage is often referred to as the period of *mystagogia*. The word is derived from an ancient Greek word meaning a deepening understanding of the mysteries of the faith. *Mystagogia*, like the liminality stage, is lengthy, depending on the progress of the neophytes. There is wisdom in prolonging this stage of reaggregation. Mary Douglas brilliantly writes of the third stage of initiation: "It is consistent with the ideas about form and formlessness to treat initiates coming out of seclusion as though they were themselves charged with power, hot, dangerous, requiring insulation and a time for cooling down."[32] Initiates, with their newfound enthusiasm, need time to adjust to the realities of parish life, with its failings as well as its strengths. Without adequate accompaniment it is possible for initiates to fall victim to cynicism.

Multiculturalism

The constant risk in the development of a multicultural society is that one or more ethnic groups will seek to dominate other groups. There is need for dialogue to allow people to express their cultural uniqueness while developing at the same time conversations among all ethnic groups in the community. The difficult challenge, to respect ethnic rights on the one hand and the rights of the wider common good on the other, is evident in the New Testament. Saint Paul fought hard at the Council of Jerusalem to defend ethnic rights and succeeded (Acts 15:1-21), but he also defended the need for people to act for the wider common good: "There is no longer Jew or Greek, there is no longer slave or free, there is no longer male or female; for all of you are one in Christ Jesus" (Gal 3:28). When faced with this challenge the pastoral team of St. Anne's Parish, Manurewa, New Zealand, decided to establish a process of dialogue with members of the thirty ethnic groups in their parish. The framework for the dialogue is based on two complementary liturgical liminal spaces: private and public. In the private space people have the right to celebrate events such as weddings, funerals, and family rituals that respect their cultural diversity, but in the public space, for example, at Sunday Eucharists, no one ethnic group dominates, for it is here that the different ethnic groups celebrate their oneness in Christ: "But now that faith has come . . . you are all children of God through faith" (Gal 3:25-26).

Justice Dialogue

People who are involved in justice dialogue aim to identify and bridge the gaps between the justice imperatives of the Gospel and the reality around them. In the examples that follow we see "the little people of

God," those considered of no social, political, or economic importance, paradoxically defying the powers controlling them, but in ways that respect the dignity and rights of others. In this they reflect the divine humor with its preferential love for people on the margins of power. Notice also that the initiators of the following projects believed that the way a problem is defined powerfully affects what is actually done about it. Inaccurate perceptions of, and defective attitudes toward, poverty invariably result in bad policies and unjust practices that are harmful to people. Governments motivated by neocapitalist philosophy (see chap. 6) fail to recognize the structural barriers that imprison people in poverty. People become the agents of their own liberation from poverty if the right structures are developed to allow them the freedom to act. Integral to the success of these programs are the human qualities of their initiators—their willingness to relate to people not as cogs in an economic machine but as people with God-given dignity.

Self-help Movements

Challenge 2000

For the first time in over a century, because of the radical introduction of the neocapitalist policies of governments, an identifiable socioeconomic underclass has emerged in New Zealand, once a model for its equitable distribution of wealth. A skilled organizational consultant, Kitty McKinley, deeply felt the inner pain of people, especially youth, who were caught in the cycle of poverty. In 1989 she established *Challenge 2000* as a charitable trust to provide people with skills to raise self-esteem and gain employment. Inspired by her passion for social justice, her belief in the inner worth of every human person, and her trust in Providence to supply financial support, people have joined her crusade. Today *Challenge 2000* is a twenty-four-hour youth agency, employing specialist staff, as well as volunteers, that primarily works with young people and families in their communities, schools, churches, and peer groupings. It did not surprise me to discover when I visited Kitty and her coworkers that, despite the daily pressures of their work, there is much laughter of heart among them.

Fiji Credit Union

Following the end of my studies at Cambridge University in 1963, I visited the headquarters of the credit union movement in Fiji. A credit union is a group of people who pledge themselves to save together and then lend their savings to one another at the lowest possible interest rates. While waiting to meet the founder of the movement there, Marion Ganey, SJ, I asked a Fijian, also hoping for an appointment, what he had obtained from joining his credit union. This is what the man said:

> Before I joined my credit union I was not a man. I could not save any money. I felt like nothing. One day I decided to do something about this, so I went to the capital city to speak to the big official in the agricultural department for advice to improve my coconut trees. I borrowed money to pay the fare but when I got to the door of the office I froze. I am nothing. I turned around and went home, now more in debt than before. Then a credit union started in my village. I joined it. After several months I had saved one dollar a week. Then one day I woke up and I said to myself: "I am a man now. I can save money like everybody else!" So, off to the capital again, using a loan from my credit union. I got to the door of the office and I walked in. Then I banged on the desk demanding advice. The man was startled, but he was good because he said he would come to my village to help me and others. He did. Now we have money for schooling, for medicine. I thank God for my credit union. I can do things for my family. I am proud of myself and they of me. I am so happy. Now I know what Jesus means when he says he comes to save us. I am saved from poverty, from feeling inferior as a human being.

I expected this man to answer my question with a list of much-needed material things, such as oil lamps and medicines. How wrong I was! Note the joy he experienced on discovering that he can be the master of his own destiny. There was much laughter in the group as he reflected on what he had done, but there was an additional comic quality to the experience for me that he and others would not have seen. I, a smug Cambridge graduate, was being taught a profound truth by an uneducated villager: economics is not primarily about the principle of supply and

continued on next page

demand or giving monetary aid to relieve poverty. It is about empowering people to own their own human dignity. Education and structures must serve this principal purpose. The villager's words caused me to rethink my entire approach to economic and cultural change. Thinking about justice begins by listening to those who experience injustice.

Nonviolent Movements

Scripture and Nonviolence in the Philippines

While I was working in the Philippines in the 1980s, I came to hear of a remarkable faith-filled example of the power of dialogue in pursuit of justice. Arturo lived with his wife and four children on a large sugar plantation in a remote part of the country; he was paid a pittance for his work, and his family lived in extreme poverty. One day a Catholic priest gave Arturo a copy of the New Testament. When he opened it, Arturo noticed two of the Beatitudes: "Blessed are those who hunger and thirst for righteousness, for they will be filled. . . . Blessed are the peacemakers, for they will be called children of God" (Matt 5:6, 9). Arturo called some fellow workers together and read the text to them, asking what they thought it meant for them. Arturo listened, but finally he commented, "For me it means that we must work together for justice. That is what Jesus is asking of us. We are receiving unjust wages. What are we to do then?" Having prayed for some time with the group, Arturo then asked for responses. A friend said, "We must go to the manager and ask for justice!" They did, but were chased away by the manager and his gun. They prayed again, and Arturo repeated that it was God's will to go peacefully and ask for an increase in their wages. They did, but with the same violent response. Arturo tried alone, while the others prayed, but with the same results.

One day a piece of paper was thrown through the door of Arturo's hovel. It read, "Stop the agitation or we will kill you!" Arturo called his friends, and over several weeks they continued to pray together for strength. Arturo approached the manager yet again, but the vocal threats only intensified. The prayer group continued to meet, and Arturo said, "If we are to follow Christ and become like Christ, we must continue, but in a peaceful way." They all agreed. They could not submit to injustice. Later, masked men in a jeep drove past Arturo's small shelter and sprayed it with machine gun fire. Arturo and three of his family members were killed. Humanly speaking, this tragedy makes no sense. Faith-filled people, however, discover the transforming power of the cross and resurrection through prayerful dialogue: "No one has greater love than this, to lay down one's life for one's friends" (John 15:13).

South Africa's Truth and Reconciliation Commission

A remarkable example of a prophetic, paramodern joking ritual was South Africa's Truth and Reconciliation Commission, which followed the collapse of apartheid and was presided over by Archbishop Desmond Tutu. Under the slogan "revealing is healing," perpetrators were invited to confess to crimes committed under apartheid and apply for amnesty. In the liminal stage, tragic truths of abuse, murder, and torture surfaced, and the guilty were encouraged to admit their crimes and ask for forgiveness. The reaggregation stage was marked by the granting of amnesty, the symbol of the positive and uplifting resolution of immense personal and racial suffering.

People Power in the Philippines

The People Power Revolution against the Marcos regime in the Philippines illustrates what can happen when people embrace Gospel values that contradict accepted cultural standards. A reporter for *The New York Times*, reflecting on the February 1986 event, wrote: "It was an historic wonder to see: shabby knaves who murdered and cheated their countrymen of the precious vote were swept aside by people who rose up in an act of self-determination

continued on next page

inspired by the most basic human stuff—weeping, cheering, praying, singing and a sheer yearning for democracy."[33] I was in Manila
at the time and will not forget the scene in which over a million
people from all sections of society faced the possibility of death
from the guns of the dictator's soldiers, all the while praying the
rosary, singing hymns, sharing food, and laughing together. It was
a paradoxical three days—nonviolence confronting the weapons
of violence. The impossible can happen through the power of men
and women of all ages and statuses in society, if only they believe
that justice and dignity are their right by birth.

Theological Dialogue

Saint Augustine saw theology as reasoning or discourse about God
and faith. In the past this discourse was conducted only within and
between the different Christian churches. Of course, it still continues,
including discussions between the churches and non-Christian communities; but since the emergence of postmodernity it has increasingly
moved beyond church boundaries. Today in universities and elsewhere
studies of philosophy, literature, and the arts commonly evoke discussion
about the role of morality and religion in daily life. The film industry in
particular in recent times has become an arena in which such discourse
is progressively more popular, since movies at times rather dramatically
both mirror our cultural reality and help to shape it. Creation-centered
theology cannot ignore this reality. As Father Andrew Greeley writes:
"Catholicism has always believed in the sacramentality of creation. . . .
[The] pure, raw power of the film to capture the person who watches
it, both by its vividness and by the tremendous power of the camera to
concentrate and change perspectives, is a sacramental potential that is
hard for other art forms to match."[34] There needs to be a dialogic relationship between theology and the world of films. Films often explore
such themes as the human condition, the nature of reality, the ways
people should act; theology must also be concerned about these issues
and can be affirmed and challenged by the way films articulate them.[35]

Movies can be like parables when they question our comfortable
views of the world and the ways in which our theological thinking has
drifted from its prophetic role.[36] The questions can be: Are there signals
of transcendence in the stories of life portrayed on the large and small

screen with such intensity and professionalism? If so, what does the Gospel say that would enrich these signals? In what way can theology contribute to the world of films? There is a growing branch of theology that is using questions of this kind to foster dialogue with filmgoers in order to help them to see that, while many films are morally questionable, others reveal aspects of God's presence in contemporary culture.[37] Through a process of theological reflection on the themes of particular films, it is possible to deepen a people's understanding of the Gospel message. For example, Robert Jewett, a respected Pauline scholar, claims that some movies are able to "afford deeper access to the hidden heart of Paul's theology than mainstream theologians like myself have been able to penetrate."[38] One such example, he argues, is the ability of some contemporary films to provide more insights into St. Paul's emphasis on honor, shame, and grace than the writings of theologians; the latter are too concerned with individual guilt and not enough with the social implications of behavior so evident in Paul's epistles. Recently an ecumenical group screened ten classic comedies at the annual film festival in Los Angeles as a way to stimulate the dialogue between religion and the film world.

Summary

- A fundamental theme of this book is that Christ is the human face of God whose actions of justice, mercy, and compassion contradict the expectations of those who think only in terms of this world. Whenever we act according to the mind of Jesus Christ, we are uniting ourselves with the divine humor; we are seeing the world through Christ's eyes. Then with Christ we can gently laugh at our stupidities and those of humankind, always hoping that God will continue to be compassionate toward us.

- The most original insight of the Scriptures is that God speaks to us through nature, cultures, and history. Since there are significant positive movements in the emerging paramodern culture, such as the renewed emphasis on storytelling, supportive small groups, spirituality, myth and ritual, and multiculturalism, we can truly say that God is speaking to us in these movements and cultures. These glimmers of God's comforting comic presence can be uplifted and transformed by the gospel, however, only if we are first willing to listen in faith. Listening is the foundation of all authentic dialogue: "Be still, and know that I am God!" (Ps 46:10). Listening requires a willingness to let go of cherished securities that prevent us from discovering God's presence and pastorally responding in creative ways. It takes prophetic courage and openness to pray: "Speak, for your servant is listening" (1 Sam 3:10). Then we will discover little by little what it means to be laughing with God in this contemporary world.

Epilogue

I leave readers with a few stories to remind us of a central message of this book—that humor can be a way of revealing profoundly serious truths. The first story comes from the Hopi Indians of northeast Arizona in the United States. They believe that clowning is an essential quality of their identity, as their original ancestors were youthful male and female clowns. "Clowning," they say, "symbolizes the sacredness of humanity in the strict sense—that there is something sacred in being a finite and mortal being separated from god."[1] When Hopi retell this story of their founding identity they are describing the inherent defective gap between their daily lives and their image of spiritual excellence. To know that they are naturally fragile people is a source of consolation. They cannot be gods who often remain distant from their people.

The next two stories also assume that we humans are weak, but, unlike the Hopi experience, the God in these stories is never distant. Our God, creator of the heavens and the earth, calls us to be the stewards of all that has been created (Gen 1:28), but we often knowingly forget this task. Yet our God continues to love us, to take us by the hand as a forgiving parent (Isa 42:6). In fact God sends his Son to live among us by being born in poverty-stricken circumstances of an unknown Jewish woman (Luke 2:1-7). And so God's Son is able "to sympathize with our weaknesses . . . yet [be] without sin" (Heb 4:15). And it is this Son who rejoices to find one sheep that is silly enough to get lost (Luke 15:3-7). By human standards Jesus Christ, the Good Shepherd, is breaking sensible rules. Wise people in our world simply do not leave ninety-nine sheep to fend for themselves while they search for one brainless stray!

The final story is about a huge feast prepared by God who invites all the powerful elite, but they snub their host, offering rather weak excuses for not accepting the invitation (Luke 14:15-24). One has bought land that he must inspect and another has purchased oxen that need to be examined. Their love of material possessions hinders them from accepting the invitation. But God then acts as an unconventional host. Rejected by those who think they are the host's peers, this party organizer thumbs his nose at the accepted social conventions and energetically extends the invitation to the social outcasts of society—the powerless, voiceless, homeless, landless, crippled, and prostitutes: "For all who exalt themselves will be humbled, and those who humble themselves will be exalted" (Luke 14:11). God, the party host, says: "Rejoice with me" (Luke 15:6). And the guests and the host celebrate late into the night, laughing uproariously together.

Appendix:
Origins and Theories of Humor

The definition and explanations of humor in chapter 1 draw on the following views of the origins of humor. The different emphases in the theories illustrate why it is difficult to have a universally accepted definition of humor.

Incongruity

This theory owes much to the insights of the philosopher Immanuel Kant (1724–1804), who described humor as "an affection arising from a strained expectation being suddenly reduced to nothing."[1] The philosopher Arthur Schopenhauer has a similar view.[2] According to this hypothesis, we find something humorous because two contrary meanings are simultaneously combined. The unexpected meaning is suddenly substituted for the predictable one. When applied to divine humor, the contraries of God as creator and judge relating to sinful humankind are resolved through God's infinite mercy and love. This is summarized eloquently in the words of the psalmist: "For though the LORD is high, he regards the lowly" (Ps 138:6) and "If you, O LORD, should mark iniquities, Lord, who could stand? But there is forgiveness with you" (Ps 130:3-4).

Breaking Control

Humor, says philosopher Henri Bergson, undermines rigidity, pomposity, and arrogance. Comedy reminds us that human nature is limited and mortal. The self-important duchess who slips on a banana skin is shown to be subject, after all, to the laws of nature.[3] In brief, Bergson concludes, "rigidity is the comic, and laughter is its corrective."[4] In the case of Sarah, told by God that she was to have a child despite her advanced age, she just laughs in disbelief (Gen 18:12). Age prevents her from conceiving, but then we gently laugh at Sarah for not accepting the fact that God can break the law of aging. Her inflexible refusal to accept the possibility of God changing reality in such a dramatic way is a source of laughter to readers through the centuries.[5] Sigmund Freud also considered humor to be basically the breakdown of control: the joke or the humor is the relaxation of the conscious control in favor of the subconscious.[6]

Superiority

The theory that a sense of superiority is at the root of negative humor received significant support from the philosopher Thomas Hobbes (1588–1679) in *Leviathan* (first published in 1651): "The passion of laughter is nothing else but sudden glory arising from a sudden conception of some eminency in ourselves by comparison with the infirmity of others."[7] Henri Bergson also believed that in humor "we always find an avowed intention to humiliate and consequently to correct our neighbor."[8] Arthur Koestler, a philosopher well known for his writings on humor, noted that there is "a component of malice, debasement of the other fellow, and of aggressive-defensive self-assertion . . . in laughter—a tendency diametrically opposed to sympathy, helpfulness, and identification of the self with others."[9] In one assessment of New Zealand humor the authors concluded that humor there revealed undercurrents of misogyny, racism, and "those elements of bullying and violence that inform our folk-ways and underwrite our social life."[10] The feeling of superiority and aggression is poignantly evident in the mocking of Jesus by soldiers and others (Matt 27:29-30; Mark 15:29-32). Francis Buckley, a professor of law, has recently further refined this theory of humor's origin. He distinguishes two types of superiority, which he terms "positive" and "normative." In the former, laughter results from our feeling superior to the target of the joke, though we may or may not actually be so. In the latter, we laugh because we are actually superior to the object of the joke. When the target is weak, laughter can be cruel, but when it is powerful, the laughter can be revolutionary.[11]

Anxiety-Relief

According to Freud and Bergson, humor provides people with a socially acceptable chance to release nervous energy. I hear a knock at my living room window during the night. I quietly investigate as my fears of an intruder cause my stomach to churn. When a friend puts his head through the half-opened window I laugh with relief. For Freud, a joke releases the energy of the subconscious against the control of the conscious, but in ways that are socially acceptable. Without the opportunity to release nervous energy through laughter in this way we could become violent toward others. Glen Cavaliero, in his study of comedy in English literature, broadens this view.[12] Humor has its origin in the need we have to survive life's turmoil through the cultivation of enjoyment. Through humor we are able in a pleasurable way to grapple with the many frustrations and misfortunes that externally impede happiness as well as the vanities and sheer evil that human persons cause within themselves and society. Humor allows us to temporarily escape our normally anxious, reflective selves.

Notes

Introduction, pages xi–xviii

[1] J. Cheryl Exum and J. William Whedbee, "Isaac, Samson, and Saul: Reflections on the Comic and Tragic Visions," ed. J. Cheryl Exum, *Tragedy and Comedy in the Bible, Semeia*, no. 32 (1985): 6–7.

[2] Benedict XVI, Encyclical Letter, "God is Love" (*Deus Caritas Est*) *Special Supplement to the Pilot* (February 3, 2006): 6, 7.

[3] Joel S. Kaminsky suggests several reasons for the widespread tendency to underemphasize or completely disregard humor in the Scriptures: a general reverence for the text; a propensity for Christians to read the Old Testament from the perspective of the New Testament; a Jewish movement to avoid the literary playfulness of the text; and the fact that scholars have generally concentrated on source and form criticism, which have highlighted individual traditions rather than the final text and its literary structure. "Humor and the Theology of Hope: Isaac as a Humorous Figure," *Interpretation*, vol. 54, no. 4 (2000): 363.

[4] See Barry Sanders, *Sudden Glory: Laughter as Subversive History* (Boston: Beacon Press, 1995), 146.

[5] Walter Kasper, *An Introduction to Christian Faith* (London: Burns & Oates, 1980), 131–32.

[6] See Gerard W. Hughes, "The Enigma of the Smiling Crucifix," *The Tablet* (March 26, 2005): 4–5.

[7] Gerard Bessiere, "Humour-A Theological Attitude?," eds. Johann B. Metz and Jean-Pierre Jossua, *Fundamental Theology* (London: Concilium, 1974), 81.

[8] Blaise Pascal, cited by Chris Turner, *Planet Simpson* (London: Ebury Press, 2004), 65.

[9] See Katherine M. Hudson, "Transforming a Conservative Company: One Laugh at a Time," *Harvard Business Review* (July–August, 2001): 45–53.

[10] Soren Kierkegaard, *The Humor of Kierkegaard*, ed. Thomas C. Oden (Princeton: Princeton University Press, 2004), 32.

[11] Benedict XVI reported in *The Tablet* (August 19, 2006): 9.

[12] See Gerald A. Arbuckle, *Grieving for Change: A Spirituality for Refounding Gospel Communities* (London: Geoffrey Chapman, 1991), 61–107; *From Chaos to Mission: Refounding Religious Life Formation* (Collegeville, MN: Liturgical Press, 1995), 119–23.

[13] See Gerald A. Arbuckle, *Healthcare Ministry: Refounding the Mission in Tumultuous Times* (Collegeville, MN: Liturgical Press, 2000); *Violence, Society, and Change: A Cultural Approach* (Collegeville, MN: Liturgical Press, 2004).

Chapter 1, pages 1–18

[1] Laurence Olivier, cited by Shay Sayre and Cynthia King, *Entertainment and Society: Audiences, Trends, and Impacts* (Thousand Oaks, CA: Sage, 2003), 69.

[2] Conrad Hyers, *The Comic Vision and the Christian Faith: A Celebration of Life and Laughter* (New York: Pilgrim Press, 1981), 52.

[3] See the Appendix for a summary of the main views of the origins of humor.

[4] W.C. Fields quoted by F. Scott Spencer, "Those Riotous—Yet Righteous—Foremothers of Jesus: Exploring Matthew's Comic Genealogy," ed. Athalya Brenner, *Are We Amused? Humour About Women in the Biblical Worlds* (London: T&T Clark International, 2003), 9.

[5] See *The Economist* (August 3, 1996): 77.

[6] See Sayre and King, *Entertainment and Society*, 68–81.

[7] See Wen-Shu Lee, "Communication about Humor as Procedural Competence in Intercultural Encounters," eds. Larry Samovar and Richard Porter, *Intercultural Communication: A Reader*, 7th ed. (Belmont, CA: Wadsworth, 2000), 373–82.

[8] Keith Willey, *You Might as Well Laugh, Mate: Australian Humour in Hard Times* (Melbourne: Macmillan, 1984), 2.

[9] See Jonathan Este, "Throw another Sacred Cow on the Barbie," *Sydney Morning Herald* (December 30, 2000): 19.

[10] *The Economist* (December 20, 2003): 74.

[11] See Martin J. Buss, "Tragedy and Comedy in Hosea," ed. J. Cheryl Exum, *Tragedy and Comedy in the Bible*, *Semeia*, no. 32 (1985): 73–74.

[12] Peter Berger, *Redeeming Laughter: The Comic Dimension of Human Experience* (New York: Walter de Gruyter, 1997), 2.

[13] Ibid., 208; Berger's emphasis.

[14] See Paul E. McGhee, *Humor: Its Origin and Development* (San Francisco: W.H. Freeman, 1979), 6–7, 10.

[15] Berger, *Redeeming Laughter*, 27.

[16] See Northrop Frye, *The Great Code: The Bible and Literature* (London: Routledge and Kegan Paul, 1982), 169–71; J. Cheryl Exum and J. William Whedbee, "Isaac, Samson, and Saul: Reflections on the Comic and Tragic Visions," ed. J. Cheryl Exum, *Tragedy and Comedy in the Bible*, *Semeia*, no. 32 (1985): 8–9.

[17] See McGhee, *Humor*, 25–29.

[18] See Alfred R. Radcliffe-Brown, "On Joking Relationships," *Africa*, vol. 13 (1940): 195–210.

[19] These terms will be more fully explained in chapter 3.

[20] Henri Bergson, "Laughter: An Essay on the Meaning of the Comic," *Comedy*, ed. Wylie Sypher (Baltimore: Johns Hopkins University Press, 1980), 61.

[21] See Jakob Jonsson, *Humour, Irony in the New Testament* (Leiden: E.J. Brill, 1985), 181–82.

[22] See Raymond E. Brown, *The Death of the Messiah*, vol. 2 (New York: Doubleday, 1994), 1431.

[23] See Edwin M. Good, *Irony in the Old Testament* (London: SPCK, 1965), 29.

[24] See R. Alan Culpepper, "New Testament," *The Anchor Bible Dictionary*, vol. 3 (New York: Doubleday, 1992), 333.

[25] See Edward L. Greenstein, "Humor and Wit—Old Testament," *The Anchor Bible Dictionary*, vol. 3 (New York: Doubleday, 1992), 332.

[26] See Mahadev L. Apte, *Humor and Laughter: An Anthropological Approach* (Ithaca: Cornell University Press, 1985), 156–57.

[27] See Max Gluckman, *Custom and Conflict in Africa* (Oxford: Basil Blackwell, 1956), 109–36.

[28] William T. McLeod, ed., *The New Collins Dictionary* (Glasgow: Collins, 1987), 1155.

[29] See Greenstein, "Humor and Wit," 332.

[30] Mikhail M. Bakhtin, *The Dialogue Imagination: Four Essays*, trans. Michael Holquist and Caryl Emerson (Austin: University of Texas Press, 1981), 2.

[31] See William E. Mitchell, *Clowning as Critical Practice: Performance Humor in the South Pacific* (Pittsburgh: University of Pittsburgh Press, 1992), 10.

[32] See Xavier Leon-Dufour, *Dictionary of Biblical Theology* (London: Geoffrey Chapman, 1967), 57–58.

[33] See Richard Godfrey, *English Caricature: 1620 to the Present* (Haselemere: Victoria and Albert Museum, 1984), 10.

[34] Soren Kierkegaard, quoted by Wylie Sypher, *Comedy* (Baltimore: Johns Hopkins University Press, 1956), 196.

[35] See Simon Holdaway, "Blue Jokes: Humour in Police Work," eds. Chris Powell and George E. Paton, *Humour in Society: Resistance and Control* (Basingstoke: Macmillan, 1988), 106–22.

[36] Victor E. Frankl, *Man's Search for Meaning* (New York: Washington Square Press, 1963), 68.

[37] See F. Scott Spencer, "Those Riotous—yet Righteous—Foremothers of Jesus," 7–30.

[38] See Anton C. Zidjerveld, "Jokes and their Relations to Social Reality," *Social Research*, vol. 35 (1968): 286–311.

[39] See Jerome H. Neyrey, *Honor and Shame in the Gospel of Matthew* (Louisville: Westminster John Knox Press, 1998), 31.

[40] C.S. Lewis, *The Screwtape Letters* (New York: Macmillan, 1982), ix.

Chapter 2, pages 19–41

[1] Gerard Bessiere, "Humour—A Theological Attitude?," eds. Johann B. Metz and Jean-Pierre Jossua, *Fundamental Theology* (London: Concilium, 1974), 90.

[2] Wanda Nash, *Come, Let Us Play! Playfulness and Prayer* (London: Darton, Longman and Todd, 1999), xvii, xviii.

[3] See Bernhard W. Anderson, "Covenant," *The Oxford Companion to the Bible*, eds. Bruce M. Metzger and Michael D. Coogan (New York: Oxford University Press, 1993), 138–39.

[4] Karl Rahner quoted in *America* (October 31, 1970): 344.

[5] See Peter Berger, *A Rumour of Angels: Modern Society and the Rediscovery of the Supernatural* (Harmondsworth: Penguin Books, 1969), 89.

[6] See ibid., 90.

[7] Ibid.

[8] See Thomas C. Oden, ed., *The Humor of Kierkegaard: An Anthology* (Princeton: Princeton University Press, 2004), 25.

[9] See Paul Beauchamp, "Laughter," ed. Xavier Leon-Dufour, *Dictionary of Biblical Theology* (London: Geoffrey Chapman, 1967), 263.

[10] See John L. McKenzie, *Dictionary of the Bible* (London: Geoffrey Chapman, 1965), 494–95.

[11] I am grateful to John Drane for listing some of these examples. See his book, *The McDonaldization of the Church* (London: Darton, Longman and Todd, 2000), 122–23.

[12] See ibid., 123.

[13] See Joel S. Kaminsky, "Humor and the Theology of Hope: Isaac as a Humorous Figure," *Interpretation*, vol. 54, no. 4 (2000): 363–75.

[14] See Henri Cormier, *The Humor of Jesus* (New York: Alba House, 1977), 5.

[15] See Jakob Jonsson, "Irony and Humor," *The Oxford Companion to the Bible*, Metzger and Coogan, 325.

[16] See Walter Brueggemann, *The Message of the Psalms: A Theological Commentary* (Minneapolis: Augsburg, 1984), 36–38.

[17] See Arnold A. Anderson, *The New Century Bible Commentary: Psalms 73-150* (Grand Rapids: Eerdmans, 1981), 622–30.

[18] See Michael D. Coogan, "Chaos," *The Oxford Companion to the Bible*, Metzger and Coogan, 105.

[19] See Brueggemann, *The Message of the Psalms*, 79.

[20] See John J. Pilch, *The Cultural World of Jesus: Sunday by Sunday Cycle B* (Collegeville, MN: Liturgical Press, 1996), 31, 38.

[21] See Gerald A. Arbuckle, *Healthcare Ministry: Refounding the Mission in Tumultuous Times* (Collegeville, MN: Liturgical Press, 2000), 162–64.

[22] See Walter Brueggemann, *First and Second Samuel* (Atlanta: John Knox Press, 1990), 21.

[23] See William F. Maestri, *Mary: Model of Justice* (New York: Alba House, 1987), 5–16.

[24] Edwin M. Good, *Irony in the Old Testament* (London: S.P.C.K., 1965), 246.

[25] For a descriptive account of Paul's character see Jerome Murphy-O'Connor, *Paul: His Story* (Oxford: Oxford University Press, 2004), 110, 145, 165–66.

[26] See Jakob Jonsson, *Humour and Irony in the New Testament* (Leiden: E.J. Brill, 1985), 171–73.

[27] See Jerome Murphy-O'Connor, *Paul: His Story*, 166.

[28] See Brad H. Young, *The Parables: Jewish Tradition and Christian Interpretation* (Peabody, MA: Hendrickson, 1998), 7.

[29] See McKenzie, *Dictionary of the Bible*, 635–36.

[30] See Bruce J. Malina and Richard L. Rohrbaugh, *Social-Science Commentary on the Synoptic Gospels* (Minneapolis: Fortress Press, 1992), 347.

[31] McKenzie, *Dictionary of the Bible*, 766.

[32] See Arbuckle, *Earthing the Gospel*, 158–59.

[33] See George Soares-Prabhu, "The Unprejudiced Jesus and the Prejudiced Church," *The Way* (January 1987): 4–13.

[34] Conrad Hyers, *And God Created Laughter: The Bible as Divine Comedy* (Louisville: Westminster John Knox, 1987): 2.

Chapter 3, pages 42–55

[1] Mary Douglas, *Implicit Meanings: Essays in Anthropology* (London: Routledge and Kegan Paul, 1975), 96, 95, 101.

[2] Ibid., 90–114.

[3] This is an adaptation of definitions by Clifford Geertz, *The Interpretation of Cultures* (New York: Basic Books, 1973), 89, and Edgar H. Schein, *Organizational Culture and Leadership* (San Francisco: Jossey-Bass, 1985), 9.

[4] See Gerald A. Arbuckle, *Earthing the Gospel: An Inculturation Handbook for Pastoral Workers* (Maryknoll: Orbis Books, 1990), 26–43.

[5] Reported by Michael Idato, "Poms Bash Oz," *The Sunday Tasmanian* (November 16, 1997): 11.

[6] I am indebted to Adolfo Nicolas, SJ, for this definition.

[7] Rollo May, *The Cry for Myth* (New York: Delta, 1991), 15.

[8] See Gerald A. Arbuckle, "Mythology, Revitalization and the Refounding of Religious life," *Review for Religious*, 46, no. 1 (1987): 14–43.

[9] See May, *The Cry for Myth*, 91–107.

[10] See Robert Bocock, *Ritual in Industrial Society: A Sociological Analysis of Ritualism in Modern England* (London: George Allen & Unwin, 1974), 35.

[11] See Victor Turner, *The Ritual Process: Structure and Anti-Structure* (New York: Cornell University Press, 1966), 105–6.

[12] See ibid., 95.

[13] See Victor Turner, *Dramas, Fields and Metaphors: Symbolic Action in Human Society* (New York: Cornell University Press, 1974), 232.

[14] See Kenneth Maddock, *The Australian Aborigines: A Portrait of Their Society* (Harmondsworth: Penguin Books, 1974), 158–76.

[15] See Mary Douglas, *Purity and Danger: An Analysis of Concepts of Pollution and Taboo* (Harmondsworth: Penguin Books, 1966), 117.

[16] Karl Rahner, "Mardi Gras Tuesday: Christian Laughter and Crying," in *The Great Church Year: The Best of Karl Rahner's Homilies, Sermons, and Meditations*, ed. Albert Raffelt, trans. Harvey D. Egan (New York: Crossroad, 1995), 109.

[17] See Mikhail Bakhtin, *Rabelais and His World*, trans. Helene Iswolsky (Bloomington: Indiana University Press, 1984).

[18] See Roberto Damatta, *Carnivals, Rogues, and Heroes: An Interpretation of the Brazilian Dilemma*, trans. John Drury (Notre Dame: University of Notre Dame Press, 1991).

[19] Ibid., 130.

[20] See William E. Mitchell, ed., *Clowning as Critical Practice: Performance Humor in the South Pacific* (Pittsburgh: University of Pittsburgh Press, 1992), 38.

[21] See Andrew Stott, *Comedy* (London: Routledge, 2005), 40–61.

[22] See an excellent analysis by Conrad Hyers, *The Comic Vision and the Christian Faith: A Celebration of Life and Laughter* (New York: Pilgrim Press, 191), 64–65.

[23] See Angela Bennie, "He who Laughs Last," *Sydney Morning Herald* (June 21, 2003): 11.

[24] Douglas, *Purity and Danger*, 108.

[25] Anthony Burgess, quoted by Tony J. Watson, *In Search of Management: Culture, Chaos and Control in Managerial Work* (London: Routledge, 1994), 187.

[26] See John Docker, *Postmodernism and Popular Culture: A Cultural History* (Cambridge: Cambridge University Press, 1994), 217.

[27] See Konrad Lorenz, *On Aggression* (San Diego: Harcourt Brace, 1963), 275–99.

[28] Sigmund Freud comments: "In every epoch of history those who have had something to say but could not say it without peril have eagerly assumed a fool's cap. The audience at whom their forbidden speech was aimed tolerated it more easily if they could at the same time laugh and flatter themselves with the reflection that the unwelcome words were clearly nonsensical." *The Standard Edition of the Complete Psychological Works of Sigmund Freud*, vol. 4 (New York: Macmillan, 1953), 444.

[29] Peter Berger, *A Rumor of Angels: Modern Society and the Rediscovery of the Supernatural* (Harmondsworth: Penguin Books, 1969), 114.

Chapter 4, pages 56–69

[1] Karl Rahner, quoted in *America*, vol. 123, no. 13 (1970): 344.

[2] See Gerald A. Arbuckle, *Grieving for Change: A Spirituality for Refounding Gospel Communities* (London: Geoffrey Chapman, 1991), 61–85.

[3] See Walter Brueggemann, *Interpretation and Obedience: From Faithful Reading to Faithful Loving* (Minneapolis: Fortress Press, 1991), 317–18.

[4] See Arbuckle, *Grieving for Change*, 76–78. For commentaries see J. E. Hartley, *The Book of Job* (Grand Rapids: Eerdmans, 1988); J. G. Janzen, "Job" in *Interpretation:*

A Bible Commentary for Teaching and Preaching (Atlanta: John Knox Press, 1985); M. H. Pope, *Job* (New York: Doubleday, 1965).

[5] See William Whedbee, "The Comedy of Job," eds. Robert Polzin and David Robertson, *Studies in the Book of Job, Semeia,* no. 7 (1977): 1–44.

[6] Christopher Fry, quoted in ibid., 32.

[7] See David J. Clines, "The Book of Job," eds. Bruce M. Metzger and Michael D. Coogan, *The Oxford Companion to the Bible* (New York: Oxford University Press, 1993), 370.

[8] Exum and Whedbee, "Isaac, Samson, and Paul," 22–23.

[9] See Walter Brueggemann, *The Message of the Psalms* (Minneapolis: Augsburg, 1984), 59–60.

[10] See Elizabeth Kubler-Ross, *On Death and Dying* (New York: Macmillan, 1969).

[11] See Walter Brueggemann, "The Formfulness of Grief," *Interpretation,* 31, no. 3 (1977): 267–75.

[12] See Bernhard W. Anderson, *Creation Versus Chaos: The Reinterpretation of Mythical Symbolism in the Bible* (New York: Association Press, 1967), 132.

[13] See Gerald A. Arbuckle, *From Chaos to Mission: Refounding Religious Life Formation* (Collegeville, MN: Liturgical Press, 1996), 191–94.

[14] See Walter Brueggemann, *To Pluck Up, To Tear Down: Jeremiah 1–25* (Grand Rapids: Eerdmans, 1988), 12–19.

[15] Eric W. Heaton, *The Old Testament Prophets* (Harmondsworth: Penguin Books, 1961), 79.

[16] See Robert P. Carroll, *From Chaos to Covenant: Uses of Prophecy in the Book of Jeremiah* (London: SCM Press, 1981), 31–58; John of Taize, *The Pilgrim God: A Biblical Journey* (Washington, DC: The Pastoral Press, 1985), 95–113.

[17] See Bernhard Anderson, *Out of the Depths: The Psalms Speak for Us Today* (Philadelphia: Westminster Press, 1983), 76.

[18] Claus Westermann, *Elements of Old Testament Theology* (Atlanta: John Knox Press, 1982), 103.

Chapter 5, pages 70–90

[1] David Power, *Love without Calculation: A Reflection on Divine Kenosis* (New York: Crossroad, 2005), 61.

[2] Karl-Josef Kuschel, "The Destructive and Liberating Power of Laughter," *The Bright Side of Life, Concilium* (London: SCM Press, 2000), 119.

[3] See Wilfrid J. Harrington, "St Luke," ed. Reginald C. Fuller and others, *A New Catholic Commentary on Holy Scripture* (London: Nelson, 1969), 987–88; Eugene LaVerdiere, SSS, *The Annunciation to Mary* (Chicago: Liturgical Training Publications, 2004), 61–85.

[4] See Mark McVann's stimulating analyses: "One of the Prophets: Matthew's Testing Narrative as a Rite of Passage," *Biblical Theological Bulletin,* 23, no. 1 (1993): 14–20; and "Rituals of Status Transformation in Luke-Acts: the Case of Jesus the Prophet," ed. Jerome H. Neyrey, *The Social World of Luke-Acts: Models*

for Interpretation (Peabody, MA: Hendrickson, 1991), 333–60; Gerald A. Arbuckle, *From Chaos to Mission: Refounding Religious Life Formation* (Collegeville, MN: Liturgical Press, 1995), 121.

[5] McVann, "One of the Prophets," 18.

[6] Ibid., 19.

[7] See Bernhard W. Anderson, *Creation Versus Chaos: The Reinterpretation of Mythical Symbolism in the Bible* (New York: Association Press, 1967), 160–70.

[8] See Adrian Leske, "Matthew," ed. William R. Farmer, *The International Bible Commentary* (Collegeville, MN: Liturgical Press, 1998), 1284–85.

[9] See ibid., 1305.

[10] This analysis draws particularly on the following authors: Brad H. Young, *The Parables: Jewish Tradition and Christian Interpretation* (Peabody, MA: Hendrickson, 1998), 130–57; John R. Donahue, *The Gospel in Parable* (Philadelphia: Fortress Press, 1988), 151–62; Bruce J. Malina and Richard L. Rohrbaugh, *Social-Science Commentary on the Synoptic Gospels* (Minneapolis: Fortress Press, 1992), 371–72.

[11] See Gail R. O'Day, "The Gospel of John," eds. Leander E. Keck, *The New Interpreter's Bible*, vol. ix (Nashville: Abingdon Press, 1995), 721–24; Jean Vanier, *Drawn into the Mystery of Jesus through the Gospel of John* (London: Darton, Longman and Todd, 2004), 224–39.

[12] Conrad Hyers, *The Comic Vision and the Christian Faith* (New York: Pilgrim Press, 1981), 68.

[13] See I. H. Marshall, *The Gospel of Luke: A Commentary on the Greek Text* (Exeter: Paternoster Press, 1978), 66.

[14] See Gerald A. Arbuckle, *Grieving for Change: A Spirituality for Refounding Gospel Communities* (London: Geoffrey Chapman, 1991), 102–7.

[15] "Stabat Mater," *Lectionary* (London: Collins/Geoffrey Chapman, 1983), 1126.

[16] Hans Urs von Balthasar, *The von Balthasar Reader*, eds. M. Kehl and W. Loser (Edinburgh: T&T Clark, 1985), 324–25.

[17] See Gerald A. Arbuckle, *From Chaos to Mission: Refounding Religious Life Formation* (Collegeville, MN: Liturgical Press, 1995), 123.

[18] See Power, *Love without Calculation*, 5–8.

Chapter 6, pages 91–110

[1] Soren Kierkegaard, *Concluding Unscientific Postscript*, trans. D. F. Swenson and W. Lowrie (Princeton: Princeton University Press, 1941), 413.

[2] See Pontifical Council for Interreligious Dialogue, "Dialogue and Proclamation," *Origins* 21, no. 8 (1991): 126.

[3] For a fuller development of this material see chaps. 2, 5, 7, and 9 of my book *Violence, Society and the Church: A Cultural Approach* (Collegeville, MN: Liturgical Press, 2004).

[4] See Mary Douglas, *Purity and Danger: An Analysis of the Concepts of Pollution and Taboo* (London: Routledge and Kegan Paul, 1966), 54–72.

[5] See Mary Douglas, *Natural Symbols: Explorations in Cosmology* (London: Routledge and Kegan Paul, 1966), 65–81.

[6] See Mahadev L. Apte, *Humor and Laughter: An Anthropological Approach* (Ithaca: Cornell University Press, 1985), 161.

[7] See Arbuckle, *Violence, Society and the Church*, 101–51.

[8] See Harvey Cox, *The Seduction of the Spirit: The Use and Misuse of People's Religion* (New York: Simon and Schuster, 1973), 292–96.

[9] See David Cannadine, *In Churchill's Shadow* (London: Penguin Books, 2003), 205–23.

[10] Woody Allen, cited by ed. Mordecai Richler, *The Best of Modern Humour* (Harmondsworth: Penguin Books, 1984), xiv.

[11] William Shakespeare, *The History of Henry IV*, Part Two, Act 5, scene 5.

[12] See Steven Connor, *Postmodern Culture: An Introduction to Theories of the Contemporary* (Oxford: Basil Blackwell, 1989), 238.

[13] Andy Warhol quoted by Bernice Martin, *A Sociology of Contemporary Cultural Change* (Oxford: Basil Blackwell, 1981), 112.

[14] See David Lyon, *Jesus in Disneyland: Religion in Postmodern Times* (Cambridge: Polity, 2000), 18.

[15] Anthony Giddens, *Modernity and Self-Identity* (New York: Polity Press, 1991), 5.

[16] See Douglas Kellner, *Media Culture* (London: Routledge, 1995).

[17] Real name is Marshall Bruce Mathers III.

[18] See John Docker, *Postmodernism and Popular Culture: A Cultural History* (Cambridge: Cambridge University Press, 1994), 256.

[19] See Jorge J. E. Gracia, "The Secret of Seinfeld's Humor," ed. William Irwin, *Seinfeld and Philosophy: A Book about Everything and Nothing* (Chicago: Open Court, 2000), 148–59.

[20] See Steven Connor, *Postmodernist Culture: An Introduction to Theories of the Contemporary* (Oxford: Blackwell, 1997), 214.

[21] See Stuart Sim, *Fundamentalist World: The New Dark Age of Dogma* (London: Icon Books, 2004), 102–3; John R. Saul, *The Collapse of Globalism and the Reinvention of the World* (London: Penguin Books, 2005), 15–16.

[22] See Richard Kearney, *On Stories* (London: Routledge, 2002), 156.

[23] Jacques Derrida, "This Strange Institution called Literature," ed. D. Attridge, *Acts of Literature* (New York: Routledge, 1992), 109.

[24] See Andrew Stott, *Comedy* (New York: Routledge, 2005), 17–18.

[25] See Ervin Staub, *The Roots of Evil: The Origins of Genocide and Other Group Violence* (Cambridge: Cambridge University Press, 1989), 25.

[26] Alexander Solzhenitsyn quoted by Jonathan Glover, *Humanity: A Moral History of the Twentieth Century* (London: Jonathan Cape, 1999), 401.

[27] See Martin Esslin, *The Theatre of the Absurd* (Harmondsworth: Penguin Books, 1968).

[28] Eugene Ionesco (*La demystification par l'humour noir*) quoted in ibid., 187.

[29] See Samuel Beckett, *Waiting for Godot* (New York: Grove Press, 1954).

[30] See eds. Mark T. Conard and Aeon J. Skoble, *Woody Allen and Philosophy* (Chicago: Open Court, 2004).

[31] See Lou Ascione, "Dead Sharks and Dynamic Ham: The Philosophical Use of Humor in *Annie Hall*," ibid., 132–50.

[32] David Mirkin, cited by William Irwin and J. R. Lombardo, "The Simpsons and Allusion," ed. William Irwin, *The Simpsons and Philosophy* (Chicago: Open Court, 2001), 81.

[33] See ibid., 82.

[34] Extract quoted by Chris Turner, *Planet Simpson* (London: Ebury Press, 2004), 163.

[35] Quoted by ibid., vi.

[36] See Carl Matheson, "The Simpsons, Hyper-Irony, and the Meaning of Life," ibid., 108–25.

[37] Mark I. Pinsky, *The Gospel according to The Simpsons: The Spiritual Life of the World's Most Animated Family* (Louisville: Westminster John Knox Press, 2001), 152.

Chapter 7, pages 111–32

[1] Walter Kasper, *An Introduction to Christian Faith* (London: Burns & Oates, 1980), 131–32.

[2] Stephen Pattison, *A Critique of Pastoral Care* (London: SCM Press, 2000), 175.

[3] See Stephen B. Bevans, *Models of Contextual Theology* (Maryknoll: Orbis Books, 1992), 16–17.

[4] Decree on the Missionary Activity of the Church, 11.

[5] See Aylward Shorter, *Toward a Theology of Inculturation* (London: Geoffrey Chapman, 1988), 3–16; David J. Bosch, *Transforming Mission: Paradigm Shifts in Theology of Mission* (Maryknoll: Orbis Books, 1991), 452–57.

[6] Shorter, *Toward a Theology of Inculturation*, 78.

[7] See Pontifical Council for Interreligious Dialogue, "Dialogue and Proclamation," *Origins* 21, no. 8 (1991): 126.

[8] See Justin Taylor, "The Acts," ed. William R. Farmer, *The International Bible Commentary* (Collegeville, MN: Liturgical Press, 1998), 1535.

[9] Pope Gregory the Great, cited by A. J. Mason, *The Mission of St Augustine to England according the Original Documents, Being a Handbook for the Thirteenth Century* (Cambridge: Cambridge University Press, 1897), 89–90.

[10] See Gerald A. Arbuckle, *Earthing the Gospel: An Inculturation Handbook for Pastoral Workers* (London: Geoffrey Chapman, 1990), 10–20.

[11] See Joseph W. Bastien, "Humor and Satire," ed. Mircea Eliade, *The Encyclopedia of Religion*, vol. 6 (New York: Macmillan, 1987), 527.

[12] See Peter L. Berger, *Redeeming Laughter: The Comic Dimension of Human Experience* (New York: Walter de Gruyter, 1997), 15–37.

[13] Saint Basil, cited by Barry Sanders, *Sudden Glory: Laughter as Subversive History* (Boston: Beacon Press, 1995), 128.

[14] See ibid., 129.

[15] Saint Benedict of Nursia, cited in ibid., 135.

[16] See ibid., 129.

[17] See Thomas Aquinas, *Summa Theologica*, IIa, IIae, qu. CLXVIII, art. 2.

[18] See Marcel Metzger, *History of the Liturgy: The Major Stages* (Collegeville, MN: Liturgical Press, 1997), 72.

[19] Yves Congar, OP, "Christianity as Faith and as Culture," *East Asian Pastoral Review*, 18, no. 4 (1981): 310.

[20] Josef A. Jungmann, quoted by Geoffrey Wainwright in ed. Cheslyn Jones, *The Study of Liturgy* (London: SPCK, 1983), 37.

[21] See Maria J. Goldwasser, "Carnival," ed. Mircea Eliade, *The Encyclopedia of Religion*, vol. 3, 98.

[22] See Mikhail Bakhtin, *Rabelais and His World* (Bloomington: Indiana University Press, 1984).

[23] For an overview of the role of dancing in liturgies and its condemnation by ecclesiastical authorities see J. G. Davies, *Liturgical Dance: An Historical, Theological and Practical Handbook* (London: SCM Press, 1984), 19–80.

[24] See Harvey Cox, *The Feast of Fools: A Theological Essay on Festivity and Fantasy* (Cambridge: Harvard University Press, 1969), 3–6.

[25] Sanders, *Sudden Glory*, 146.

[26] See R. W. Southern, *Western Society and the Church in the Middle Ages* (Harmondsworth: Penguin Books, 1970), 300–358.

[27] Meister Eckhart, quoted by Wanda Nash, *Come Let Us Play!* (London: Darton, Longman and Todd, 1999), 79.

[28] See Cyprian Smith, *The Way of Paradox: Spiritual Life as Taught by Meister Eckhart* (London: Darton, Longman and Todd, 1987), 10.

[29] Julian of Norwich, quoted by Nash, *Come Let Us Play!*, 80.

[30] See Lauro Martines, *Scourge of Fire: Savonarola and Renaissance Italy* (London: Jonathan Cape, 2005).

[31] See Dante Alighieri, *Pugatorio*, XVI, 89.

[32] See Robin Kirkpatrick, *The Divine Comedy* (Cambridge: Cambridge University Press, 1987), 5. Dante decisively broke with the classical view that only humor from an intellectual elite was worth consideration. In his humor he united both the sublime and the ordinary, for that is what the Incarnation had achieved. See Erich Auerbach, *Mimesis: The Representation of Reality in Western Literature* (Princeton: Princeton University Press, 2003), 184–85.

[33] See Bastien, "Humor and Satire," 526.

[34] See Metzger, *History of the Liturgy*, 125.

[35] See Eamon Duffy, *The Stripping of the Altars: Traditional Religion in England 1400-1580* (New Haven: Yale University Press, 1992).

[36] See Geoffrey Wainwright, *Christian Initiation* (Richmond: John Knox Press, 1969), 37–38.

[37] See Harvey Cox, *The Feast of Fools: A Theological Essay on Festivity and Fantasy* (Cambridge: Harvard University Press, 1969), 5.

[38] See G. Voss, "Missionary Accommodation," *Missionary Academic Study*, no. 2 (New York: Society for the Propagation of the Faith, 1964), 17.

[39] See Justin Taylor, "Acts of the Apostles," 1532.

[40] "Instructio Vicariorum Apostolicorum ad Regna Synarum Tonchini et Cocinnae Proficiscentium" in *Collectanea Sacrae Congregationis de Propaganda Fide*, vol. 1 (Rome, 1907), 42.

[41] Ignatius of Loyola, quoted by Nash, *Come Let Us Play!*, 82.

[42] Mary Ward, cited by James R. Cain, "Cloister and the Apostolate of Religious Women," *Review for Religious* 27, no. 2 (1968): 663.

[43] See Cain, ibid., 659–71 and Robert McClory, *Faithful Dissenters: Stories of Men and Women who Loved and Changed the Church* (Maryknoll: Orbis Books, 2000), 54–77.

[44] See Cathleen Medwick, *Teresa of Avila: The Progress of a Soul* (New York: Alfred A. Knopf, 1999), 243, 246.

[45] Teresa of Avila, cited by James Martin, SJ, "The Most Infallible Sign: Recovering Joy, Humor and Laughter in the Spiritual Life," *America* (April 2, 2007), 16.

[46] See M. A. Screech, *Laughter at the Foot of the Cross* (London: Allen Lane, 1997), 176–85.

[47] Ibid., 9.

[48] See Leon-E. Halkin, *Erasmus: A Critical Biography* (Oxford: Blackwell, 1993), 21, 292.

[49] Screech, *Laughter at the Foot of the Cross*, 220.

[50] Victor Turner and Edith Turner, *Image and Pilgrimage in Christian Culture* (Oxford: Basil Blackwell, 1978), 32.

[51] Pattison, *A Critique of Pastoral Care*, 176.

[52] See Daniel L. Miglione, "Reappraising Barth's Theology," *Theology Today*, 43, no. 3 (1986): 309–14.

[53] Reinhold Niebuhr, *Discerning the Signs of the Times* (London: SCM Press, 1946), 99–100.

[54] See Cox, *The Feast of Fools*.

[55] Ibid., 157.

[56] Ibid., 10.

[57] Pius XII, Alocution, *Acta Apostolicae Sedis* 45 (December 6, 1953): 794.

[58] Pius XII cited by Louis Luzbetak, *The Church and Cultures* (Techny, IL: Divine Word, 1970), 343.

[59] Pius XII, Encyclical On the Promotion of Catholic Missions (Evangelii Praecones), ed. R. Hickey, *Modern Missionary Documents and Africa* (Dublin: Dominican Publications, 1982), 99.

[60] Vatican II, Pastoral Constitution on the Church in the Modern World (*Gaudium et Spes*), 1, in ed. Walter M. Abbott, SJ, *The Documents of Vatican II* (London: Geoffrey Chapman, 1966).

[61] See Vatican II, Constitution on the Sacred Liturgy (*Sacrosanctum Liturgicam*), 37.

[62] See Vatican II, Pastoral Constitution on the Church in the Modern World (*Gaudium et Spes*), 1–3.

[63] See Vatican II, Decree on the Missionary Activity of the Church (*Ad Gentes Divinitus*), 22.

[64] See Vatican II, Dogmatic Constitution on the Church (*Lumen Gentium*), 14–16.

[65] John XXIII, Opening Speech to the Council, in ed. Walter M. Abbott, SJ, *The Documents of Vatican II* (London: Geoffrey Chapman, 1966), 712–13.

[66] Paul VI, Apostolic Letter, "On Evangelisation" (*Evangelii Nuntiandi*) (Sydney: St Pauls Publications, 1982), 25.

[67] John Paul II, Apostolic Letter, "At the Beginning of the New Millennium" (*Novo Millennio Ineunte*) (Sydney: St Pauls Publications, 2001), 75.

[68] Benedict XVI, Encyclical, "God is Love" (*Deus Caritas Est*), *Special Supplement to The Pilot* (February 3, 2006), 3.

[69] See ibid., 6.

[70] See Gerald A. Arbuckle, *Refounding the Church: Dissent for Leadership* (Maryknoll: Orbis Books, 1993), 3–4.

[71] John L. Allen, "New Document Replaces 35 Years of Liturgy Work," *National Catholic Reporter* (May 25, 2001), 13.

[72] In a recent survey 31 percent of Americans see God as someone who is always wrathful and ever-watching. See *The Economist* (September 16, 2006), 44.

[73] Jerry Falwell, *Strength for the Journey* (New York: Simon & Schuster, 1987), 290.

[74] See Anatol Lieven, *An Anatomy of American Nationalism* (Oxford: Oxford University Press, 2004), 143–49.

[75] See comments by Grace Davie, *Religion in Britain since 1945* (Oxford: Blackwell, 1994), 68–69.

[76] World Council of Churches, "Mission and Evangelism: An Ecumenical Affirmation," *International Review of Mission* 71, no. 284 (1982): 438; see also Bosch, *Transforming Mission*, 452–55.

[77] See Ross Langmead, *The World Made Flesh: Towards an Incarnational Missiology* (Lanham: University Press of America, 2004), 15–58; Stephen B. Bevans and Roger P. Schroeder, *Constants in Context: A Theology of Mission for Today* (Maryknoll: Orbis Books, 2004), 348–95.

[78] *Faith in the City: The Report of the Archbishop of Canterbury's Commission on Urban Priority Areas* (London: Church Publishing House, 1985).

[79] See David F. Ford and Laurie Green, "Distilling the Wisdom," ed. Peter Sedgwick, *God in the City* (London: Mowbray, 1995), 16.

[80] Commission on Urban Life and Faith, *Faithful Cities: A Call for Celebration, Vision and Justice* (London: Church House Publishing, 2006), 8, 14–15, 49, 54–68.

[81] See Rowan Williams, ibid., v.

Chapter 8, pages 133–50

[1] David Lyon, *Jesus in Disneyland: Religion in Postmodern Times* (Cambridge: Polity, 2000), 144.

[2] John Paul II, Letter to Agostino Cardinal Casaroli, on Occasion of the Creation of the Pontifical Council for Culture, *Osservatore Romano* (English edition) (June 28, 1982), 7.

[3] Karl Rahner, *The Great Church Year: The Best of Karl Rahner's Homilies, Sermons and Meditations*, ed. Albert Raffelt (New York: Crossroad, 1993), 112.

[4] Ibid.

[5] John Paul II, Apostolic Letter, "At the Beginning of the New Millennium" (*Novo Millennio Ineunte*) (Sydney: St Pauls Publications, 2001), 53; original italics.

[6] See John Paul II, Encyclical Letter, "Mission of the Redeemer" (*Redemptoris Missio*) (Boston: St Paul Books & Media, 1990), pars. 69–72.

[7] World Council of Churches, *Guidelines on Dialogue with People of Living Faiths and Ideologies* (Geneva: WCC, 1979), 16.

[8] See Michael Barnes, *Theology and the Dialogue of Religions* (Cambridge: Cambridge University Press, 2002), 3–28, 133–56.

[9] See Stephen B. Bevans and Roger P. Schroeder, *Constants in Context: A Theology of Mission Today* (Maryknoll: Orbis Books, 2004), 348–95.

[10] See Pontifical Council for Interreligious Dialogue, "Dialogue and Proclamation," *Origins* 21, no. 8 (1991): 129.

[11] See Richard Kearney, *On Stories* (London: Routledge, 2002), 29–30.

[12] See Bruce Lescher, "Spiritual Direction: Stalking the Boundaries," ed. Robert Wicks, *Handbook of Spirituality for Ministers*, vol. 2 (New York: Paulist Press, 2000), 322–23.

[13] See Kearney, *On Stories*, 26.

[14] J.R.R. Tolkien, "On Fairy-Stories," *The Tolkien Reader* (Princeton, NJ: Princeton University Press, 1968), 88.

[15] See Robert Wuthnow, *Sharing the Journey: Support Groups and America's Quest for Community* (New York: Free Press, 1994), 289–314.

[16] See ibid., 3.

[17] See ibid., 365.

[18] See Gerald A. Arbuckle, *Refounding the Church: Dissent for Leadership* (Maryknoll: Orbis Books, 1993), 90–94.

[19] See Bernard Lee, *The Catholic Experience of Small Christian Communities* (New York: Paulist Press, 2000), 86–93.

[20] Karl Rahner, *The Shape of the Church to Come* (London: SPCK, 1972), 108.

[21] Jean Vanier, *Letter to My Brothers and Sisters in L'Arche* (Trosly: L'Arche, 1996), 12, 13, 29.

[22] William Johnston, *Mystical Theology* (London: HarperCollins, 1995), 134.

[23] Karl Rahner, *Theological Investigations*, no. 7, trans. David Bourke (New York: Herder and Herder, 1971), 15.

[24] See Dogmatic Constitution of the Church (*Lumen Gentium*), 40.

[25] Walter Burghardt, cited by Janet Ruffing, "Socially Engaged Contemplation," ed. Robert J. Wicks, *Handbook of Spirituality for Ministers*, vol. 2 (New York: Paulist Press, 2000), 422.

[26] See Thomas Keating, "Contemplative Prayer in the Christian Tradition," ed. Thomas Keating and others, *Finding Grace at the Center* (Still River: St. Bede Publications, 1978), 35–47.

[27] See Ernest E. Larkin, "Today's Contemplative Prayer Forms: Are they Contemplation?" *Review for Religious* 57, no. 1 (1998): 80–81.

[28] Ernest Larkin says that both forms of contemplation fit within the traditional pattern of *lectio divina*. The first three steps are active, namely, reading, meditation, prayer. The fourth step, contemplation in the strict sense, occurs when the soul is totally absorbed by the Spirit. The new forms of contemplative prayer can be listed between the third and fourth steps. They are called contemplative since they actively prepare the person for infused contemplation. See ibid., 81–82.

[29] See John Main, *Moment of Christ: The Path of Meditation* (London: Darton, Longman, and Todd, 1984).

[30] See M. Basil Pennington, "Centering Prayer—Prayer of Quiet," in ed. Thomas Keating, *Finding Grace at the Center*, 3–21, 63.

[31] See Secretariat U.S.A. Bishops' Committee on the Liturgy, *Christian Initiation of Adults: A Commentary* (Washington, DC: National Conference of Catholic Bishops, 1985); Johannes Wagner, ed., *Adult Baptism and the Catechumenate* (New York: Paulist Press, 1967).

[32] Mary Douglas, *Purity and Danger: An Analysis of Concepts of Pollution and Taboo* (Harmondsworth: Penguin Books, 1966), 117.

[33] Francis Xavier Clines, *The New York Times* (March 2, 1986), 1E.

[34] Andrew Greeley, *God in Popular Culture* (Chicago: Thomas More, 1988), 250.

[35] See Clive Marsh, "Film and Theologies of Culture," eds. Clive Marsh and Gaye Ortiz, *Explorations in Theology and Film* (Oxford: Blackwell, 1977), 27.

[36] See David J. Graham, "The Uses of Film in Theology," in ibid., 39–40.

[37] See for example: Mark I. Pinsky, *The Gospel according to The Simpsons* (Louisville: Westminster John Knox Press, 2001); Robert Jewett, *Saint Paul at the Movies: The Apostle's Dialogue with American Culture* (Louisville: Westminster John Knox Press, 1993); Clive Marsh and Gaye Ortiz, eds., *Explorations in Theology and Film: Movies and Meaning* (Oxford: Blackwell, 1997).

[38] Robert Jewett, *Saint Paul Returns to the Movies: Triumph over Shame* (Grand Rapids: Eerdmans, 1999), 20; Robert K. Johnston, *Reel Spirituality: Theology and Film in Dialogue* (Grand Rapids: Baker, 2000), 79–80.

Epilogue, pages 151–52

[1] John Loftin, *Religion and Hopi Life in the Twentieth Century* (Bloomington: Indiana University Press, 1991), 112.

Appendix, pages 153–55

[1] Immanuel Kant, *Critique of Judgment*, trans. J. C. Meredith (Oxford: Oxford University Press, 1952), 199.

[2] See Arthur Schopenhauer, *The World as Will and Representation*, vol. 2 (New York: Dover, 1966), 91.

[3] See Henri Bergson, "Laughter," in *Comedy*, ed. Wylie Sypher (Baltimore: Johns Hopkins University Press, 1956), 61–190.

[4] Ibid., 79.

[5] See explanation by Spencer, "Those Riotous—Yet Righteous—Foremothers of Jesus," 12.

[6] See Sigmund Freud, *Jokes and Their Relation to the Unconscious*, trans. John Strachedy (New York: W.W. Norton, 1983), 144–58.

[7] Thomas Hobbes, quoted by Arthur Koestler, *The Act of Creation* (London: Pan Books, 1970), 54.

[8] Henri Bergson, quoted in ibid.

[9] Arthur Koestler, *Insight and Outlook: An Inquiry into the Common Foundations of Science, Art and Social Ethics* (New York: Macmillan, 1949), 56.

[10] See John Barnett and Lesley Kaiser, *The Penguin Book of New Zealand Jokes* (Auckland: Penguin Books, 1996), 12–13.

[11] See Francis H. Buckley, *The Morality of Laughter* (Ann Arbor: University of Michigan Press, 2003), 191–200.

[12] See Glen Cavaliero, *The Alchemy of Laughter: Comedy in English Fiction* (Houndmills: Palgrave, 2000), 238–45.

Bibliography

Abbott, Walter M. *The Documents of Vatican II*. London: Geoffrey Chapman, 1966.

Alighieri, Dante. *The Divine Comedy*. Edited by Robin Kirkpatrick. Cambridge: Cambridge University Press, 1987.

Anderson, Bernhard W. *Creation Versus Chaos: The Reinterpretation of Mythical Symbolism in the Bible*. New York: Association Press, 1967.

———. *Out of the Depths: The Psalms Speak for Us Today*. Philadelphia: Westminster Press, 1983.

———. "Covenant." In *The Oxford Companion to the Bible*, edited by Bruce M. Metzger and Michael D. Coogan. New York: Oxford University Press, 1993.

Apte, Mahadev L. *Humor and Laughter: An Anthropological Approach*. Ithaca: Cornell University Press, 1985.

Arbuckle, Gerald A. "Mythology, Revitalization and the Refounding of Religious Life." *Review for Religious* 46, no. 1 (1987).

———. *Earthing the Gospel: An Inculturation Handbook for Pastoral Workers*. Maryknoll: Orbis Books, 1990.

———. *Grieving for Change: A Spirituality for Refounding Gospel Communities*. London: Geoffrey Chapman, 1991.

———. *From Chaos to Mission: Refounding Religious Life Formation*. Collegeville, MN: Liturgical Press, 1995.

———. *Healthcare Ministry: Refounding the Mission in Tumultuous Times*. Collegeville, MN: Liturgical Press, 2000.

———. *Violence, Society and the Church: A Cultural Approach*. Collegeville, MN: Liturgical Press, 2004.

Arnold, A. Anderson. *The New Century Bible Commentary: Psalms 73-150*. Grand Rapids: Eerdmans, 1981.

Auerbach, Erich. *Mimesis: The Representation of Reality in Western Literature*. Princeton: Princeton University Press, 2003.

Bakhtin, Mikhail M. *The Dialogue Imagination: Four Essays*. Translated by Michael Holquist and Caryl Emerson. Austin: University of Texas Press, 1981.

———. *Rabelais and His World*. Translated by Helene Iswolsky. Bloomington: Indiana University Press, 1984.

Barnes, Michael. *Theology and the Dialogue of Religions*. Cambridge: Cambridge University Press, 2002.

Bastien, Joseph W. "Humor and Satire." In *The Encyclopedia of Religion*, edited by Mircea Eliade. Vol. 6. New York: Macmillan, 1987.

Beckett, Samuel. *Waiting for Godot*. New York: Grove Press, 1954.

Benedict XVI. *God is Love (Deus Caritas Est)*. Encyclical Letter. *Special Supplement to The Pilot*, February 3, 2006.

Berger, Peter A. *Rumour of Angels: Modern Society and the Rediscovery of the Supernatural*. Harmondsworth: Penguin Books, 1969.

———. *Redeeming Laughter: The Comic Dimension of Human Experience*. New York: Walter de Gruyter, 1997.

Bergson, Henri. "Laughter: An Essay on the Meaning of the Comic." In *Comedy*, edited by Wylie Sypher, 61–190. Baltimore: Johns Hopkins University Press, 1980.

Bessiere, Gerard. "Humour—A Theological Attitude?" *Concilium: Fundamental Theology* 5, no. 10. Edited by Johann Baptist Metz and Jean-Pierre Jossua (1974): 81.

Bevans, Stephen B. *Models of Contextual Theology*. Maryknoll: Orbis Books, 1992.

Bevans, Stephen B., and Roger P. Schroeder. *Constants in Context: A Theology of Mission for Today*. Maryknoll: Orbis Books, 2004.

Billig, Michael. *Laughter and Ridicule: Towards a Social Critique of Humour*. London: SAGE Publications, 2005.

Bocock, Robert. *Ritual in Industrial Society: A Sociological Analysis of Ritualism in Modern England*. London: George Allen & Unwin, 1974.

Bosch, David J. *Transforming Mission: Paradigm Shifts in Theology of Mission*. Maryknoll: Orbis Books, 1991.

Brown, Raymond E. *The Death of the Messiah*. Vol. 2. New York: Doubleday, 1994.

———. *An Introduction to the New Testament*. New York: Doubleday, 1997.

Brueggemann, Walter. *The Message of the Psalms: A Theological Commentary*. Minneapolis: Augsburg, 1984.

———. *First and Second Samuel*. Atlanta: John Knox Press, 1987.

———. *To Pluck Up, To Tear Down: Jeremiah 1-25*. Grand Rapids: Eerdmans, 1988.

———. *Interpretation and Obedience: From Faithful Reading to Faithful Loving*. Minneapolis: Fortress Press, 1991.

Buckley, Francis H. *The Morality of Laughter*. Ann Arbor: University of Michigan Press, 2003.

Buss, Martin J. "Tragedy and Comedy in Hosea." *Semeia: Tragedy and Comedy in the Bible*, edited by J. Cheryl Exum, 32 (1985).

Cain, James. "Cloister and the Apostolate of Religious Women." *Review for Religious* 27, no. 2 (1968).

Cannadine, David. *In Churchill's Shadow*. London: Penguin Books, 2003.

Carroll, Robert P. *From Chaos to Covenant: Uses of Prophecy in the Book of Jeremiah*. London: SCM Press, 1981.

Cavaliero, Glen. *The Alchemy of Laughter: Comedy in English Fiction*. Houndmills: Palgrave, 2000.

Commission on Urban Life and Faith. *Faithful Cities: A Call for Celebration, Vision and Justice*. London: Church House Publishing, 2006.

Conard, Mark T., and Aeon J. Skoble, eds. *Woody Allen and Philosophy*. Chicago: Open Court, 2004.

Connor, Steven. *Postmodern Culture: An Introduction to Theories of the Contemporary*. Oxford: Basil Blackwell, 1989.

Cormier, Henri. *The Humor of Jesus*. New York: Alba House, 1977.

Cox, Harvey. *The Feast of Fools: A Theological Essay on Festivity and Fantasy*. Cambridge: Harvard University Press, 1969.

———. *The Seduction of the Spirit: The Use and Misuse of People's Religion*. New York: Simon and Schuster, 1973.

Culpepper, R. Alan. "New Testament." In *The Anchor Bible Dictionary*. Vol. 3. New York: Doubleday, 1992.

Damatta, Roberto. *Carnivals, Rogues, and Heroes: An Interpretation of the Brazilian Dilemma*. Edited by John Drury. Notre Dame: University of Notre Dame Press, 1991.

Davie, Grace. *Religion in Britain since 1945*. Oxford: Blackwell, 1994.

Davies, J. G. *Liturgical Dance: An Historical, Theological and Practical Handbook*. London: SCM Press, 1984.

Derrida, Jacques. "This Strange Institution called Literature." In *Acts of Literature*, edited by D. Attridge. New York: Routledge, 1992.

Docker, John. *Postmodernism and Popular Culture: A Cultural History*. Cambridge: Cambridge University Press, 1994.

Donahue, John R. *The Gospel Parable*. Philadelphia: Fortress Press, 1988.

Douglas, Mary. *Purity and Danger: An Analysis of Concepts of Pollution and Taboo*. Harmondsworth: Penguin Books, 1966.

———. *Natural Symbols: Explorations in Cosmology*. London: Routledge and Kegan Paul, 1966.

———. *Implicit Meanings: Essays in Anthropology*. London: Routledge and Kegan Paul, 1975.

Drane, John. *The McDonaldization of the Church*. London: Darton, Longman, and Todd, 2000.

Dundes, Alan. *Cracking Jokes: Studies of Sick Humor Cycles and Stereotypes*. Berkeley: Ten Speed Press, 1987.

Ehrenreich, Barbara. *Dancing in the Streets: A History of Collective Joy*. London: Granta Books, 2007.

Esslin, Martin. *The Theatre of the Absurd*. Harmondsworth: Penguin, 1968.

Exum, J. Cheryl, and J. William Whedbee, "Isaac, Samson, and Saul: Reflections on the Comic and Tragic Vision." *Semeia: Tragedy and Comedy in the Bible*. Edited by J. Cheryl Exum, 32 (1985).

Frankl, Victor E. *Man's Search for Meaning*. New York: Washington Square Press, 1963.

Freud, Sigmund. *Jokes and Their Relation to the Unconscious*. Translated by John Strachedy. New York: W.W. Norton, 1983.

Frye, Northrop. *The Great Code: The Bible and Literature*. London: Routledge and Kegan Paul, 1982.

Geertz, Clifford. *The Interpretation of Cultures*. New York: Basic Books, 1973.

Gluckman, Max. *Custom and Conflict in Africa*. Oxford: Basil Blackwell, 1956.

Godfrey, Richard. *English Caricature: 1620 to the Present*. Haslemere: Victoria and Albert Museum, 1984.

Good, Edwin M. *Irony in the Old Testament*. London: S.P.C.K., 1965.

Gracia, Jorge J. E. "The Secret of Seinfeld's Humor." In *Seinfeld and Philosophy: A Book about Everything and Nothing*, edited by William Irwin. Chicago: Open Court, 2000.

Greenstein, Edward L. "Humor and Wit—Old Testament," *The Anchor Bible Dictionary*. Vol. 3. New York: Doubleday, 1992.

Halkin, Leon-E. *Erasmus: A Critical Biography*. Oxford: Blackwell, 1993.

Hardcastle, Gary L., and George A. Reisch. *Monty Python and Philosophy*. Chicago: Open Court, 2006.

Hartley, J. E. *The Book of Job*. Grand Rapids: Eerdmans, 1988.

Heaton, Eric W. *The Old Testament Prophets*. Harmondsworth: Penguin Books, 1961.

Holdaway, Simon. "Blue Jokes: Humour in Police Work." In *Humour in Society: Resistance and Control*, edited by Chris Powell and George E. Paton. Basingstoke: Macmillan, 1988.

Hudson, Katherine M. "Transforming a Conservative Company: One Laugh at a Time." *Harvard Business Review* (July–August, 2001).

Hughes, Gerard W. "The Enigma of the Smiling Crucifix." *The Tablet* (March 26, 2005).

Hyers, Conrad. *The Comic Vision and the Christian Faith: A Celebration of Life and Laughter*. New York: Pilgrim Press, 1981.

———. *And God Created Laughter: The Bible as Divine Comedy*. Louisville: Westminster John Knox, 1987.

Irwin, William, and others, eds. *The Simpsons and Philosophy*. Chicago: Open Court, 2001.

Jacobson, Howard. *Seriously Funny: From the Ridiculous to the Sublime*. Harmondsworth: Viking, 1997.

Jewett, Robert. *Saint Paul Returns to the Movies: Triumph over Shame*. Grand Rapids: Eerdmans, 1999.

John Paul II. Letter to Agostino Cardinal Casaroli, on Occasion of the Creation of the Pontifical Council for Culture. *Osservatore Romano* (English edition). June 28, 1982.

———. *Mission of the Redeemer (Redemptoris Missio)*. Encyclical Letter. Boston: St. Paul Books & Media, 1990.

———. *At the Beginning of the New Millennium (Novo Millennio Ineunte)*. Apostolic Letter. Sydney: St Pauls Publications, 2001.

Jonsson, Jakob. *Humour, Irony in the New Testament*. Leiden: E.J. Brill, 1985.

Kaminsky, Joel S. "Humor and the Theology of Hope: Isaac as a Humorous Figure." *Interpretation* 54, no. 4 (2000).

Kant, Immanuel. *Critique of Judgement*. Translated by J. C. Meredith. Oxford: Oxford University Press, 1952.

Kasper, Walter. *An Introduction to Christian Faith*. London: Burns & Oates, 1980.

Kearney, Richard. *On Stories*. London: Routledge, 2002.

Kierkegaard, Soren. *Concluding Unscientific Postscript*. Translated by D. F. Swenson and W. Lowrie. Princeton: Princeton University Press, 1941.

———. *The Humor of Kierkegaard*. Edited by Thomas C. Oden. Princeton: Princeton University Press, 2004.

Koestler, Arthur. *Insight and Outlook: An Inquiry into the Common Foundations of Science, Art and Social Ethics*. New York: Macmillan, 1949.

———. *The Act of Creation*. London: Pan Books, 1970.

Kreitzer, Larry J. *Pauline Images in Fiction and Film*. Sheffield: Sheffield Academic Press, 1999.

Kubler-Ross, Elizabeth. *On Death and Dying*. New York: Macmillan, 1969.

Kuschel, Karl-Josef. *Laughter: A Theological Reflection*. London: SCM Press, 1994.

Langmead, Ross. *The Word Made Flesh: Towards an Incarnational Missiology*. Lanham: University Press of America, 2004.

Larkin, Ernest E. "Today's Contemplative Prayer Forms." *Review for Religious* 57, no. 1 (1998).

LaVerdiere, Eugene. *The Annunciation to Mary*. Chicago: Liturgical Training Publications, 2004.

Lee, Bernard. *The Catholic Experience of Small Christian Communities*. New York: Paulist Press, 2000.

Lee, Wen-Shu. "Communication about Humor as Procedural Competence in Intercultural Encounters." In *Intercultural Communication: A Reader*, edited by Larry Samovar and Richard Porter. 7th ed. Belmont, CA: Wadsworth, 2000.

Leon-Dufour, Xavier, ed. *Dictionary of Biblical Theology*. London: Geoffrey Chapman, 1967.

Lescher, Bruce. "Spiritual Direction: Stalking the Boundaries." In *Handbook of Spirituality for Ministers*, edited by Robert Wicks. Vol. 2. New York: Paulist Press, 2000.

Leske, Adrian. "Matthew." In *The International Bible Commentary*, edited by William R. Farmer. Collegeville, MN: Liturgical Press, 1998.

Levi-Strauss, Claude. *Structural Anthropology*. New York: Penguin, 1968.

Lewis, C. S. *The Screwtape Letters*. New York: Macmillan, 1982.

Lorenz, Konrad. *On Aggression*. San Diego: Harcourt Brace, 1963.

Lyon, David. *Jesus in Disneyland: Religion in Postmodern Times*. Cambridge: Polity, 2000.

Maestri, William F. *Mary: Model of Justice*. New York: Alba House, 1987.

Main, John. *Moment of Christ: The Path of Meditation*. London: Darton, Longman and Todd, 1984.

Marsh, Clive, and Gaye Ortiz, eds. *Explorations in Theology and Film: Movies and Meaning*. Oxford: Blackwell, 1997.

Marshall, I. H. *The Gospel of Luke: A Commentary on the Greek Text*. Exeter: Paternoster Press, 1978.

Martin, Rod A. *The Psychology of Humor: An Integrative Approach*. Burlington: Elsevier Academic Press, 2007.

Martines, Lauro. *Scourge of Fire: Savonarola and Renaissance Italy*. London: Jonathan Cape, 2005.

May, Rollo. *The Cry of Myth*. New York: Delta, 1991.

McGhee, Paul E. *Humor: Its Origin and Development*. San Francisco: W.H. Freeman, 1979.

McKenzie, John L. *Dictionary of the Bible*. London: Geoffrey Chapman, 1965.

McLeod, William T., ed. *The New Collins Dictionary*. Glasgow: Collins, 1987.

McVann, Mark. "Rituals of Status Transformation in Luke-Acts: the Case of Jesus the Prophet." In *The Social World of Luke-Acts: Models for Interpretation*, edited by Jerome H. Neyrey. Peabody: Hendrickson, 1991.

————. "One of the Prophets: Matthew's testing Narrative as a Rite of Passage." *Biblical Theological Bulletin* 23, no. 1 (1993).

Medwick, Cathleen. *Teresa of Avila: The Progress of a Soul*. New York: Alfred A. Knopf, 1999.

Metzger, Marcel. *History of the Liturgy: The Major Stages*. Collegeville, MN: Liturgical Press, 1997.

Miglione, Daniel L. "Reappraising Barth's Theology," *Theology Today* 43, no. 3 (1986).

Mitchell, William E. *Clowning as Critical Practice: Performance Humor in the South Pacific*. Pittsburgh: University of Pittsburg Press, 1992.

Murphy, Francesca A. *The Comedy of Revelation*. Edinburgh: T&T Clark, 2000.

Murphy-O'Connor, Jerome. *Paul: His History*. Oxford: Oxford University Press, 2004.

Nash, Walter. *The Language of Humour: Style and Technique in Comic Discourse*. London: Longman, 1985.

Nash, Wanda. *Come, Let Us Play! Playfulness and Prayer*. London: Darton, Longman, and Todd, 1999.

Neyrey, Jerome H. *Honor and Shame in the Gospel of Matthew*. Louisville: Westminster John Knox Press, 1998.

Niebuhr, Reinhold. *Discerning the Signs of the Times*. London: SCM Press, 1946.

O'Day, Gail R. "The Gospel of John." In *The New Interpreter's Bible*, edited by Leander E. Keck and others. Vol. ix. Nashville: Abingdon Press, 1995.

Palmer, Jerry. *Taking Humour Seriously*. London: Routledge, 1984.

Pattison, Stephen. *A Critique of Pastoral Care*. London: SCM Press, 2000.

Paul VI. *On Evangelisation (Evangelii Nuntiandi)*. Apostolic Letter. Sydney: St Pauls Publications, 1982.

Pilch, John J. *The Cultural World of Jesus: Sunday by Sunday Cycle B*. Collegeville, MN: Liturgical Press, 1996.

Pinsky, Mark I. *The Gospel according to The Simpsons: The Spiritual Life of the World's Most Animated Family*. Louisville: Westminster John Knox Press, 2001.

Pius XII. *On the Promotion of Catholic Missions (Evangelii Praecones)*. Encyclical. In *Modern Missionary Documents and Africa*, edited by R. Hickey. Dublin: Dominican Publications, 1982.

Powell, Chris, and George E. Paton, eds. *Humour in Society: Resistance and Control*. London: Macmillan, 1988.

Power, David. *Love without Calculation: A Reflection on Divine Kenosis*. New York: Crossroad, 2005.

Radcliffe-Brown, Alfred R. "On Joking Relationships." *Africa* 13 (1940).

Rahner, Karl. *The Shape of the Church to Come*. London: SPCK, 1972.

———. *The Great Church Year: The Best of Karl Rahner's Homilies, Sermons and Meditations*. Edited by Albert Raffelt. New York: Crossroad, 1995.

Report of the Archbishop of Canterbury's Commission on Urban Priority Areas. *Faith in the City: A Call for Action by Church and Nation*. London: Church Publishing House, 1985.

Sanders, Barry. *Sudden Glory: Laughter as Subversive History*. Boston: Beacon Press, 1995.

Saul, John R. *The Collapse of Globalism and the Reinvention of the World*. London: Penguin Books, 2005.

Sayre, Shay, and Cynthia King. *Entertainment and Society: Audiences, Trends, and Impacts*. Thousand Oaks: Sage, 2003.

Schopenhauer, Arthur. *The World as Will and Representation*. Vol. 2. New York: Dover, 1966.

Screech, A. A. *Laughter at the Foot of the Cross*. London: Allen Lane, 1997.

Sedgwick, Peter. *God in the City*. London: Mowbray, 1995.

Shorter, Aylward. *Toward a Theology of Inculturation*. London: Geoffrey Chapman, 1988.

Sim, Stuart. *Fundamentalist World: The New Dark Age of Dogma*. London: Icon Books, 2004.

Smith, Cyprian. *The Way of Paradox: Spiritual Life as Taught by Meister Eckhart*. London: Darton, Longman, and Todd, 1987.

Southern, R. W. *Western Society and the Church in the Middle Ages*. Harmonds-worth: Penguin Books, 1970.

Spencer, F. Scott. "Those Riotous—Yet Righteous—Foremothers of Jesus: ex-ploring Matthew's Comic Genealogy." In *Are We Amused? Humour About Women in the Biblical Worlds*, edited by Athalya Brenner. London: T&T Clark International, 2003.

Stivers, Richard. *The Culture of Cynicism: American Morality in Decline*. Oxford: Basil Blackwell, 1994.

Stott, Andrew. *Comedy*. London: Routledge, 2005.

Tolkien, J.R.R. *The Tolkien Reader*. Princeton: Princeton University Press, 1968.

Turner, Chris. *Planet Simpson*. London: Ebury Press, 2004.

Turner, Victor. *The Ritual Process: Structure and Anti-Structure*. New York: Cornell University Press, 1966.

———. *Dramas, Fields and Metaphors: Symbolic Action in Human Society*. New York: Cornell University Press, 1974.

———. *From Ritual to Theatre: The Human Seriousness of Play*. New York: Per-forming Arts Journal Publications, 1982.

Turner, Victor, and Edith Turner. *Image and Pilgrimage in Christian Culture*. Ox-ford: Basil Blackwell, 1978.

Vanier, Jean. *Letter to My Brothers and Sisters in L'Arche*. Trosly: L'Arche, 1996.

———. *Drawn into the Mystery of Jesus through the Gospel of John*. London: Darton, Longman, and Todd, 2004.

Von Balthasar, Hans, M. Kehl, and W. Loser, eds. *The Von Balthasar Reader*. Ed-inburgh: T&T Clark, 1985.

Westermann, Claus. *Elements of Old Testament Theology*. Atlanta: John Knox Press, 1982.

Whedbee, William. "The Comedy of Job." *Semeia: Studies in the Book of Job*. Edited by Robert Polzin and David Robertson, 7 (1977).

Willey, Keith. *You Might as Well Laugh, Mate: Australian Humour in Hard Times*. Melbourne: Macmillan, 1984.

World Council of Churches. *Guidelines on Dialogue with People of Living Faiths and Ideologies*. Geneva: WCC, 1979.

Wuthnow, Robert. *Sharing the Journey: Support Groups and America's Quest for Community*. New York: Free Press, 1994.

Young, Brad H. *The Parables: Jewish Tradition and Christian Interpretation*. Pea-body: Hendrickson, 1998.

Zidjerveld, Anton C. "Jokes and their Relations to Social Reality." *Social Research* 35 (1968).

General Index

Index of Scripture